Dr Sebi Bible

25 Books in 1

*The Complete Guide to Discover Dr Sebi's Magical Wisdom
and Achieve a Radiant Lifelong Health*

Natalia Brown

Table of Contents

Introduction

Considering the side effects associated with modern medical treatments, many of us are seeking lasting, natural solutions to combat the risks of chronic illnesses. Throughout his life, Dr. Sebi dedicated himself to exploring how medicinal herbs, plants, and organic foods impact our mental and physical health. He suggested that specific herbs and foods could potentially prevent or even treat symptoms of diseases typically deemed incurable, such as chronic kidney disease, diabetes, anxiety, STDs, and more. Dr. Sebi authored several books on these cures, indicating the breadth of his research, which is too extensive to grasp fully in a single reading. To address this, I have compiled this comprehensive guide to his methods and recommendations. This collection includes basic guidelines, a list of recommended foods, chapters on curing various diseases, and a plethora of recipes to incorporate into your daily diet to boost health and immunity. The guide is organized into 25 distinct mini-books, each detailing the contents of its chapters.

Book 1: Dr. Sebi Nutritional Guide

Principles of Alkaline Nutrition

The principles of alkaline nutrition, as advocated by Dr. Sebi, focus on the fundamental concept that maintaining a slightly alkaline pH within the body is key to good health. According to Dr. Sebi, the ideal pH level of the body should range from 7.35 to 7.45, which is slightly alkaline. The modern diet, however, often tends to lean towards acidity due to a high consumption of processed foods, meat, dairy, and sugars. This shift towards an acidic environment can potentially lead to various health issues including chronic diseases like diabetes and hypertension.

Dr. Sebi classified foods that support an alkaline environment as "electric." These are foods that naturally increase the body's electrical conductivity and are typically non-hybrid, naturally grown, and free from chemical treatments. Such foods mainly include certain fruits, vegetables, nuts, and ancient grains that are unmodified and native to their environments.

The diet primarily advocates for a plant-based approach, focusing on whole, raw plants which are less likely to create acid during the digestive process. This includes a variety of leafy greens, fruits, nuts, seeds, and legumes, with an emphasis on those that are indigenous and naturally alkaline-forming. The belief is that these foods help maintain the body's alkalinity and thus promote better health and vitality by preventing the accumulation of toxins and acidity in the body.

Benefits of an Alkaline Diet

Adopting an alkaline diet, as recommended by Dr. Sebi, is believed to offer a multitude of health benefits. These benefits arise primarily from the diet's focus on natural, plant-based foods and the exclusion of acid-forming foods. Here are some of the key benefits attributed to maintaining an alkaline environment within the body:

1. Enhanced Detoxification: An alkaline diet promotes the elimination of toxins and excess acids from the body. This is due to the increased intake of antioxidants and fiber from fruits and vegetables, which help cleanse the body at a cellular level.

2. Improved Digestive Health: By reducing acid-forming foods like dairy and processed grains, and increasing the consumption of vegetables and fruits, the alkaline diet can help alleviate common digestive issues such as bloating, indigestion, and constipation. The dietary fiber in these plant-based foods aids in regular bowel movements and the maintenance of a healthy gut flora.

3. Increased Energy Levels: Alkaline foods can contribute to increased energy levels. This effect is partly due to the minimization of the energy spent on digesting heavy, acid-forming foods, which often leave individuals feeling sluggish. The high nutrient density of alkaline foods provides the body with vitamins and minerals that are vital for cellular health and energy.

4. Improved Bone Health: Some studies suggest that an alkaline diet can help reduce bone turnover, which might protect against osteoporosis. The theory is that an acidic environment in the body causes it to leach minerals from the bones to maintain a balanced pH, whereas an alkaline environment reduces this mineral loss.

5. Disease Prevention: Following an alkaline diet may lower the risk of chronic diseases such as hypertension, arthritis, and diabetes. This preventive aspect is thought to stem from the anti-inflammatory properties of many alkaline foods, which help reduce inflammation—a known trigger for various chronic conditions.

6. Better Skin Health: An alkaline diet can also improve skin health by hydrating the body and providing essential nutrients that support skin repair and maintenance. Foods high in vitamins A, C, and E, which are abundant in an alkaline diet, are particularly good for maintaining healthy, radiant skin.

Overall, while the evidence supporting some of these benefits is still emerging, many people who follow the alkaline diet report feeling more energetic and healthier overall. It's important to approach such dietary changes with a balanced perspective, ideally under the guidance of a healthcare provider, to ensure all nutritional needs are met.

Key Foods and Their Properties

In Dr. Sebi's nutritional approach, key foods are selected based on their alkalinity, nutritional content, and minimal starch content. These foods are considered to be "electric," meaning they naturally energize the body. Here are some of the key foods and their properties that are emphasized in Dr. Sebi's diet:

1. Leafy Greens: Vegetables like kale, dandelion greens, and watercress are highly alkaline and rich in minerals such as iron, calcium, potassium, and magnesium. They are also high in vitamins, including K, C, E, and many of the B vitamins, which play vital roles in maintaining cellular health and energy levels.

2. Fruits: Sebi's diet recommends low-sugar fruits such as apples, berries, melons, and grapes, which are less likely to cause blood sugar spikes. These fruits are rich in dietary fiber, antioxidants, and vitamins, which help in detoxifying the body and boosting immune function.

3. Nuts and Seeds: Almonds, hemp seeds, and Brazil nuts are included for their high levels of essential fatty acids, protein, and other nutrients that support heart health and reduce inflammation. They are also a good source of selenium, which is a powerful antioxidant.

4. Grains: While many grains are excluded in a typical alkaline diet, Dr. Sebi approved certain ancient grains like quinoa and amaranth. These grains are gluten-free, high in protein, and full of lysine, an essential amino acid that helps with tissue growth and repair.

5. Herbs and Spices: Herbs like basil, oregano, and cilantro, and spices such as cayenne pepper and ginger, are important for their health-promoting properties. They are not only powerful antioxidants but also have anti-inflammatory and antibacterial benefits that support overall health.

6. Seamoss and Bladderwrack: These sea vegetables are staples in Dr. Sebi's diet for their high mineral content, especially iodine, which is crucial for thyroid function. They are also rich in soluble fiber, which can aid digestion and promote a feeling of fullness.

7. Natural Oils: Olive oil and coconut oil are recommended for their healthy fat content and beneficial effects on heart health. These oils are used in moderation to add flavor and aid in the absorption of fat-soluble vitamins.

Each of these foods is chosen to help maintain the alkaline balance in the body while providing essential nutrients that promote health and well-being. Dr. Sebi's dietary guidelines emphasize eating whole, unprocessed foods to maximize the benefits derived from their natural properties.

Basic Meal Plan

Creating a basic meal plan following Dr. Sebi's nutritional guidelines involves incorporating a variety of the key alkaline foods discussed earlier. The goal is to ensure that meals are balanced, nourishing, and maintain the body's alkaline state. Here is an example of a simple, one-day meal plan based on Dr. Sebi's principles:

Breakfast

- Kamut Porridge: Made with kamut grain (an ancient wheat variety approved by Dr. Sebi), cooked in spring water and topped with agave syrup and fresh berries like strawberries or blueberries.
- Herbal Tea: Choose from burdock root, dandelion, or elderberry teas, all of which have detoxifying properties.

Mid-Morning Snack

- Walnut and Date Snack: A handful of raw walnuts and a few dates offer a good mix of protein, healthy fats, and a natural sweet taste.

Lunch

- Wild Rice and Vegetable Bowl: Cooked wild rice served with steamed vegetables such as butternut squash, zucchini, and a mix of leafy greens like kale or spinach. Dress the bowl with a squeeze of key lime juice and a drizzle of cold-pressed olive oil.
- Seamoss Drink: A beverage made from seamoss gel mixed with spring water and lime juice, known for its mineral-rich properties and ability to promote digestion.

Afternoon Snack

- Spiced Chickpea Salad: Chickpeas tossed with cucumber, tomatoes, cilantro, and a dressing of olive oil, lime juice, and a pinch of sea salt and cayenne pepper.

Dinner

- Vegetable Stew: A hearty stew made with approved vegetables like bell peppers, onions, and mushrooms, simmered in a tomato base with herbs and spices. Serve with a small portion of quinoa.

- Herbal Tea: A cup of herbal tea such as raspberry leaf or ginger to aid digestion and relax the body before bed.

Evening Snack

- Baked Apple: An apple cored and filled with a mixture of crushed almonds, cinnamon, and a drizzle of agave, then baked until tender.

This meal plan is designed to be hydrating, nutrient-dense, and alkalizing, aligning with Dr. Sebi's recommendations for a diet that promotes health and energy. The inclusion of various herbs and spices not only enhances flavor but also supports the body's natural detoxification processes. Each meal includes components that are easy to digest, ensuring that the body maintains its focus on healing and maintaining an alkaline state.

Tips for Getting Started

Starting on Dr. Sebi's alkaline diet can be a significant change, so it's important to approach this transition with a clear understanding and solid preparation. First, educate yourself thoroughly about the principles of the diet. Understanding why certain foods are recommended and others are excluded will help you make informed choices and stay motivated.

Once you're ready to begin, start by clearing your kitchen of non-compatible foods. This includes processed items, dairy, non-approved grains, and any foods that are considered acidic according to Dr. Sebi's guidelines. Removing these items from your home reduces temptation and makes room for healthier options.

Next, stock up on Dr. Sebi-approved foods. Invest in quality fruits, vegetables, nuts, seeds, and grains that are central to the diet. Having these items on hand will make it easier to prepare meals that fit the diet's requirements.

It's also helpful to plan your meals in advance. This can prevent situations where you're unsure of what to eat, leading to potential dietary missteps. Meal planning helps maintain a balanced diet and ensures that you're including a variety of nutrients in your diet each day.

Finally, remember that any dietary change can be challenging at first, especially one as specific as Dr. Sebi's alkaline diet. Be patient with yourself as you adapt to this new way of eating. Over time, it will become more natural and an integral part of your daily routine.

Alkaline water benefits

Alkaline water, a fundamental element of Dr. Sebi's Nutritional Guide, is lauded for its numerous health benefits, particularly its role in supporting an alkaline diet. This type of water has a higher pH level compared to regular drinking water, which helps neutralize acid in the bloodstream, thereby improving overall health.

One of the key benefits of alkaline water is its superior hydration capabilities. It is believed to be more readily absorbed by the body's cells than regular water, enhancing hydration. This improved hydration is crucial for the body's detoxification processes, aiding in the efficient flushing out of acidic wastes and toxins.

Additionally, drinking alkaline water regularly can help maintain the body's pH balance by neutralizing excess acids found in the bloodstream. This is particularly vital given the modern diet's propensity for acidic foods, including processed meats, grains, and sugars.

Alkaline water is also valued for its antioxidant properties. It contains negative oxidation-reduction potential (ORP), which means it can act as a potent antioxidant, scavenging for harmful free radicals and preventing them from causing cellular damage. The antioxidant effects of alkaline water are believed to contribute to improved cellular health and longevity.

Moreover, the consumption of alkaline water is often associated with various systemic benefits, including better digestive health, more effective immune response, and increased energy levels. These improvements stem from the water's ability to help the body more effectively manage its acidic waste products and support overall metabolic processes.

Thus, incorporating alkaline water into one's diet is seen as a beneficial step in adhering to Dr. Sebi's nutritional guidelines, aiming to promote an alkaline environment within the body that supports health and prevents disease.

Transitioning Tips from a Standard to an Alkaline Diet

Transitioning from a standard diet to an alkaline diet, as recommended in Dr. Sebi's Nutritional Guide, involves making significant changes to your eating habits. This shift can seem daunting at first, but with a strategic approach, it can be smoothly managed. Here are some practical tips for effectively transitioning to an alkaline diet:

Gradual Changes

Instead of making an abrupt shift, it's often more effective to introduce changes gradually. Start by incorporating more alkaline foods into your diet, such as fresh fruits, vegetables, nuts, and seeds, while simultaneously reducing the intake of acidic foods like meat, dairy, and processed foods. This gradual approach helps your body adjust without overwhelming it.

Understand Alkaline Foods

Spend some time learning about which foods are considered alkaline and which are acidic. Dr. Sebi's diet specifically emphasizes natural, plant-based foods that are minimally processed. Familiarizing yourself with the food list from Dr. Sebi's guide can help you make informed choices when shopping or dining out.

Meal Planning

Plan your meals ahead of time to avoid the temptation of falling back on your old dietary habits. Meal planning not only helps in sticking to the diet but also ensures that you have a variety of nutrients in your diet. Prepare a weekly menu and shop accordingly. This can include alkaline staples like amaranth, wild rice, quinoa, and fresh, organic fruits and vegetables.

Hydration

Drinking plenty of alkaline water or herbal teas is crucial in an alkaline diet. Proper hydration aids in digestion, helps flush out toxins, and keeps the body's systems functioning optimally. It's especially important as your body adjusts to the new diet and begins to detoxify.

Find Recipes You Enjoy

One of the joys of adopting a new diet is discovering new recipes. Look for alkaline recipes that excite your palate. The internet, especially health-focused cooking blogs, and cookbooks dedicated to alkaline diets can be great resources. Enjoying what you eat will make it easier to stick to the diet change.

Listen to Your Body

Pay attention to how your body responds to the new diet. Some people may experience detox symptoms such as headaches or fatigue initially. These are often temporary and should diminish as your body adjusts. However, if you continue to feel unwell, consider consulting with a healthcare provider or a nutritionist familiar with alkaline diets.

Community Support

Transitioning to a new diet can be challenging, but you don't have to do it alone. Seek out communities, either online or locally, who are also following Dr. Sebi's alkaline diet. Sharing experiences, challenges, and successes with like-minded individuals can provide encouragement and new ideas.

Focus on Overall Well-being

Finally, remember that transitioning to an alkaline diet is not just about food—it's a holistic approach to improving your overall well-being. Incorporate other healthful practices such as regular exercise, stress management, and adequate sleep to fully benefit from your new lifestyle.

Managing Cravings and Withdrawal Symptoms

Transitioning to Dr. Sebi's alkaline diet often brings challenges, including managing cravings and withdrawal symptoms that come with reducing or eliminating processed foods, sugars, and other acid-forming foods. Here's how to handle these changes effectively.

Understanding that cravings are a natural response when you change your diet is crucial. These cravings are your body reacting to the absence of familiar foods, particularly if you previously consumed large amounts of sugar, caffeine, or processed items. Knowing that these cravings are just a temporary part of the adjustment process can help you stay committed to your new diet.

To manage cravings effectively, consider substituting with healthy alternatives that comply with the alkaline diet. For example, if you're craving something sweet, opt for alkaline-friendly fruits like berries or apples. If you're missing crunchy snacks, try raw nuts or seeds. These replacements not only satisfy your cravings but also help maintain the body's alkaline balance.

Staying hydrated is another key strategy. Dehydration can often present itself as hunger or cravings. Drinking plenty of alkaline water or herbal teas can help mitigate this, making it easier to distinguish between actual hunger and dehydration. Ensuring adequate hydration also supports overall digestion and helps flush out toxins, which can reduce cravings over time.

As your body adjusts to the new diet, you may experience withdrawal symptoms such as headaches, fatigue, or irritability. These symptoms are normal and usually temporary. Support your body through this transition by getting adequate sleep, practicing stress-reducing techniques like meditation or yoga, and ensuring you eat regularly to stabilize blood sugar levels.

Finally, it's important to be patient with yourself during this transition. Dietary changes can be demanding on both a physical and emotional level. Allow yourself time to adapt, and remember that occasional setbacks are part of the journey towards a healthier lifestyle. With persistence and the right strategies, you can effectively manage cravings and withdrawal symptoms, making your transition to an alkaline diet a successful one.

Book 2: Dr. Sebi Healing Treatments

Dr. Sebi's Healing Philosophy

Dr. Sebi's healing philosophy centers on the idea that the body can heal itself if provided with the right natural ingredients, particularly those that encourage an alkaline environment. He believed that diseases are chiefly caused by the accumulation of mucus and toxins, which disrupt the body's natural pH balance. According to Dr. Sebi, these accumulations stem from consuming acidic and unnatural foods.

At the heart of Dr. Sebi's approach is the theory that mucus is the fundamental cause of disease. He suggested that mucus and inflammation in various organs and systems lead to diseases—mucus in the lungs might lead to respiratory diseases, in the pancreas could result in diabetes, and in the joints might cause arthritis. By eliminating mucus and reducing acidity, one can restore the body's natural health.

Dr. Sebi promoted an alkaline, plant-based diet as a cornerstone of health. This diet excludes meat, dairy, and processed foods while emphasizing natural, mineral-rich foods that maintain the alkalinity of the blood and prevent diseases. The diet includes vegetables, fruits, nuts, seeds, and certain grains that are believed to possess cleansing properties and are less likely to cause mucus build-up.

Detoxification is another key aspect of his philosophy. Dr. Sebi advocated for cellular cleansing through detoxification to purge the cells of toxins and rejuvenate their health. He recommended herbal supplements and a significant intake of water as part of the detox process, aiming to eliminate toxins accrued from poor dietary choices, pollution, and other environmental factors.

Moreover, Dr. Sebi valued the healing power of herbs and natural botanicals. He formulated various herbal compounds tailored to different ailments, designed to address the root causes of diseases at a cellular level. These herbal remedies aimed to reduce body acidity and promote healing by enhancing cellular nutrition and oxygenation.

Dr. Sebi's holistic view of health also extended to mental and emotional well-being. He stressed the importance of spiritual health and a positive mindset as essential components of overall well-being. Practices like meditation, spending time in nature, and mindfulness were recommended to complement the physical health regimen, suggesting a comprehensive lifestyle change that goes beyond diet.

Overall, Dr. Sebi's healing philosophy is a call to return to a more natural, less processed way of living, positing that such a lifestyle can rejuvenate the body's inherent ability to heal and maintain optimal health.

Common Treatments and Their Uses

Dr. Sebi's approach to healing incorporated a variety of natural treatments, each tailored to address specific health issues by detoxifying the body and restoring its natural alkaline state. These treatments were based on the use of specific diets, herbal supplements, and lifestyle adjustments that aligned with his holistic philosophy. Here's a closer look at some of the common treatments Dr. Sebi recommended and their intended uses:

Alkaline Diet: Central to Dr. Sebi's methodology was the alkaline diet, which he prescribed to cleanse the body of acidity that contributes to disease. This diet emphasizes the consumption of whole, raw foods such as fruits, vegetables, nuts, and seeds—all selected from his approved list. The diet is intended to reduce inflammation, cleanse the digestive tract, and revitalize the body's essential functions.

Herbal Teas and Supplements: Dr. Sebi formulated a range of herbal teas and supplements, each designed to target specific ailments or support general health. These included herbal compounds for cleansing the liver, improving kidney function, and boosting the immune system. Herbs like burdock root, sarsaparilla, and elderberry were frequently used in these preparations, recognized for their detoxifying and restorative properties.

Fasting and Cleansing Protocols: Dr. Sebi recommended periodic fasting as a method to allow the body to heal and rejuvenate. During fasting periods, the consumption of solid foods is reduced or eliminated, while herbal teas and plenty of alkaline water are consumed to aid in the detoxification process. These fasting protocols were designed to purge the body of toxins accumulated from poor dietary habits and environmental exposures.

Mucus Removal: A cornerstone of Dr. Sebi's treatments was the removal of mucus from the body, which he believed was the root cause of many diseases. He developed specific dietary recommendations and herbal treatments that focus on dissolving and expelling mucus from the body, particularly from the lungs, lymphatic system, and digestive tract.

Cellular Nourishment: Dr. Sebi emphasized the importance of cellular health in preventing and treating disease. His treatments often included supplements that are rich in minerals like iron, calcium, and potassium, which are essential for cellular processes. He believed that nourishing the cells with mineral-rich foods and supplements would restore their vitality and enhance the body's natural healing abilities.

External Applications: In addition to oral supplements and diets, Dr. Sebi also recommended topical applications of certain herbal products for skin issues and external infections. These included natural salves and ointments made from herbs known for their healing and antiseptic properties.

Case Studies and Results

Dr. Sebi's healing treatments have been associated with numerous anecdotal reports and case studies detailing significant improvements in health, particularly among individuals suffering from chronic illnesses. These reports often emphasize recovery achieved through strict adherence to his alkaline diet and the use of herbal supplements that focus on detoxification and mucus elimination.

One notable case involved a patient with type 2 diabetes who experienced dramatic changes after following Dr. Sebi's regimen. By adhering to the alkaline diet and integrating specific herbal supplements to support pancreas health and reduce blood sugar levels, the patient reportedly saw a significant reduction in their reliance on insulin. Over several months, this individual not only improved their diabetic condition but also reported enhanced overall well-being and energy levels.

Respiratory health improvements are also frequently mentioned among those following Dr. Sebi's methods. For example, a person suffering from chronic asthma, who had been reliant on steroid inhalers, embarked on a treatment plan consisting of mucus-removing herbs and a shift to an alkaline diet. Over time, this individual reported fewer asthma attacks and a reduced need for their previous medication regimen. The improvement was attributed to the reduction of mucus in the lungs, which Dr. Sebi believed was a primary irritant and blockage that contributed to asthma symptoms.

In addition to specific disease outcomes, many adherents of Dr. Sebi's teachings report a general increase in vitality and health. These improvements are often described in terms of better digestive health, clearer skin, enhanced mental clarity, and increased energy. Such holistic benefits are seen as evidence of the body's improved ability to detoxify and nourish itself when supported by the right diet and herbal treatments.

Though these case studies are primarily anecdotal and lack the rigour of controlled clinical trials, they provide compelling narratives that have helped to popularize Dr. Sebi's holistic approach to health and wellness. His followers often celebrate these stories as proof of the potential that natural remedies and dietary changes have to fundamentally alter and improve one's health.

Criticisms and Considerations

Dr. Sebi's healing treatments, while embraced by many for their perceived benefits, have also faced criticisms and considerations from various quarters, including medical professionals and dietitians. These criticisms are important to consider for anyone thinking about adopting his methods.

Lack of Scientific Evidence

One of the primary criticisms of Dr. Sebi's approach is the lack of rigorous scientific evidence to support his claims. While there are numerous anecdotal accounts of improvement in health conditions from individuals following his diet and treatment plans, these results have not been substantiated through controlled scientific studies. The medical community generally requires such evidence to validate the efficacy of health treatments, and without it, Dr. Sebi's methods remain controversial.

Extreme Dietary Restrictions

Dr. Sebi's diet is notably strict, eliminating all animal products, wheat, and processed foods, among other things. Such restrictive eating can lead to nutritional deficiencies if not carefully managed. Dietitians often caution that eliminating entire food groups can deprive the body of essential nutrients like protein, calcium, and vitamin B12, which are crucial for overall health.

Safety of Herbal Supplements

The safety of the herbal supplements recommended by Dr. Sebi has also been a point of contention. Since dietary supplements are not regulated with the same rigor as pharmaceuticals in many countries, there is concern about the consistency and purity of herbal products. Potential interactions between herbal treatments and conventional medications are another concern, particularly for those with underlying health conditions or those taking other medications.

Financial and Accessibility Issues

Following Dr. Sebi's treatment protocol can also be financially burdensome and logistically challenging for some. The diet requires a significant amount of fresh, organic produce and specialized supplements, which can be more expensive and less accessible than conventional foods. This could potentially limit the availability of Dr. Sebi's treatments to a broader audience, particularly in areas where such resources are scarce.

The Promises of Cure

Dr. Sebi claimed to cure all diseases with his treatments, a statement that has been widely criticized as misleading and potentially harmful. Promising a cure for conditions like HIV/AIDS and cancer can lead to patients foregoing conventional medical treatments in favor of pursuing his alternative therapies exclusively, which may delay receiving proven medical interventions.

Considerations for Adoption

For those considering Dr. Sebi's methods, it is crucial to approach them with a critical eye and ideally, in consultation with healthcare providers. Balancing skepticism with openness is important, as is considering one's unique health needs and conditions. Adapting elements of his diet—such as increasing the intake of fruits and vegetables and reducing processed foods—can be beneficial without necessarily adhering to all his protocols.

Integrating Treatments into Daily Life

Integrating Dr. Sebi's treatments into daily life requires a holistic commitment to lifestyle changes that foster the body's natural healing abilities. This integration is grounded in adapting to an alkaline diet, regular use of herbal supplements, and incorporating detoxification routines, all aimed at maintaining the body's natural balance and health.

The process begins with the diet, which is the cornerstone of Dr. Sebi's philosophy. Transitioning to an alkaline diet involves gradually eliminating acidic foods and incorporating alkaline alternatives. For example, dairy milk can be replaced with almond or hemp milk, white rice with quinoa or wild rice, and increasing the intake of fresh fruits and vegetables. Planning meals ahead of time can help in ensuring that each meal adheres to the principles of alkalinity, making it easier to stick to the diet consistently.

Herbal supplements are another crucial component of Dr. Sebi's treatments. These are intended to cleanse and nourish the body at a cellular level. Integrating these into daily life means understanding what each supplement is used for and the best time to take them to maximize their benefits. For instance, some herbal teas are best consumed in the morning to energize the body and support digestion, while others might be taken at night for their calming effects. It's important to source high-quality, pure herbal products to ensure their efficacy and safety.

Detoxification and cleansing are periodic practices that enhance the diet's effectiveness and support overall bodily health. This might involve implementing short fasting periods, using specific detoxifying herbs, or dedicating certain days to consume only raw or liquid foods. Such practices help to regularly purge the body of toxins and maintain a state of health that prevents disease accumulation.

For those looking to adopt Dr. Sebi's treatments, it's also crucial to make these practices a consistent part of life. This means making conscious choices every day, from selecting the right foods and supplements to setting aside time for relaxation and meditation, which can also aid in detoxification and stress reduction.

Successfully integrating Dr. Sebi's treatments into one's daily routine requires commitment and mindfulness. It involves more than just dietary changes; it's about adopting a lifestyle that values natural, holistic approaches to health. With careful planning and dedication, these practices can become a natural part of daily life, leading to improved health and wellbeing.

Combining Treatments for Synergistic Effects

Dr. Sebi's approach to healing emphasized the importance of combining various treatments to achieve synergistic effects, enhancing the overall efficacy of his methods. This strategy involves the careful coordination of diet, herbal supplements, and lifestyle practices to maximize health benefits. Here's how combining treatments can work synergistically within the framework of Dr. Sebi's healing treatments:

Diet and Herbal Supplements: The core of Dr. Sebi's method is an alkaline diet, which works to reduce acidity in the body, thereby creating an environment less conducive to disease. When this diet is combined with specific herbal supplements, the body can achieve optimal levels of detoxification and nourishment. For example, while the diet provides essential minerals and vitamins, herbal supplements can target specific health issues, such as boosting liver function or improving digestion, thereby complementing the diet effectively.

Fasting and Detoxification: Fasting is a practice recommended by Dr. Sebi to facilitate deep bodily cleansing and healing. When fasting is combined with the alkaline diet and specific herbal teas or supplements, the body is supported in eliminating toxins more efficiently. This process not only clears the digestive tract but also enhances cellular rejuvenation, leading to improved overall vitality.

Lifestyle Modifications: Dr. Sebi also advocated for changes in lifestyle that support the physical treatments. Regular physical activity, adequate sleep, and stress management are all essential components that work in conjunction with the diet and herbal supplements. For instance, engaging in moderate exercise while following the alkaline diet helps improve circulation and oxygenation of the body, which enhances the detoxification process facilitated by the herbs.

Holistic Practices: Integrating holistic practices such as meditation and spending time in nature also plays a crucial role in supporting Dr. Sebi's treatments. These practices help reduce stress and improve mental well-being, which are vital for maintaining the immune system and supporting the body's natural healing abilities. When combined with dietary and herbal treatments, these practices can lead to a more balanced and healthy life.

Safety and Precautions in Natural Healing

While natural healing treatments like those proposed by Dr. Sebi offer numerous benefits, it's crucial to approach them with an understanding of potential risks and necessary precautions. Ensuring safety while engaging in Dr. Sebi's methodologies involves several important steps.

Firstly, anyone considering Dr. Sebi's treatments, especially those involving significant dietary changes and herbal supplements, should consult with a healthcare provider. This step is particularly important for individuals with chronic health conditions or those on prescription medications, as natural supplements can sometimes interact with drugs in unpredictable ways.

The market for herbal supplements is not as tightly regulated as that for pharmaceuticals. This lack of regulation can lead to inconsistencies in the quality and purity of products. When following Dr. Sebi's treatments, it's crucial to source supplements from reputable suppliers that guarantee the authenticity and safety of their products. This minimizes the risk of contamination and ensures that the products are effective.

Additionally, Dr. Sebi's diet is very restrictive and excludes many foods that are traditionally considered nutritious, such as certain grains, dairy, and animal proteins. Those who follow this diet need to be particularly mindful to avoid nutritional deficiencies. Ensuring a well-planned diet that provides all essential nutrients is crucial. This may involve consulting with a nutritionist who can help tailor the diet to meet all individual health needs, ensuring that the body receives adequate vitamins, minerals, and other nutrients essential for health and well-being.

Finally, while the benefits of natural healing and an alkaline diet are touted by many of its adherents, it's important for individuals to monitor their own health responses closely and adjust their treatments as necessary. The effectiveness of such treatments can vary widely among individuals, and what works for one person may not work for another. Regular monitoring and adjustments ensure that the chosen health regimen remains beneficial and safe over time.

Lifestyle Factors that Complement Healing Treatments

Adopting Dr. Sebi's healing treatments goes beyond just dietary changes and herbal supplements; it also encompasses a broader spectrum of lifestyle adjustments that complement and enhance the effectiveness of his natural remedies. These lifestyle factors are integral to the holistic approach Dr. Sebi advocated for achieving optimal health.

Physical Activity: Regular exercise is a cornerstone of a healthy lifestyle that supports any healing regimen. Dr. Sebi emphasized the importance of gentle, yet effective physical activities such as walking, yoga, and stretching. These forms of exercise enhance circulation, aid in the detoxification process, and help maintain muscle tone without overly taxing the body.

Adequate Rest and Sleep: Quality sleep is crucial for healing and restoration. Dr. Sebi stressed the importance of getting sufficient, restful sleep as a part of the healing process. Sleep supports the body's regenerative processes, helps regulate hormone levels, and strengthens the immune system, all of which are essential for overcoming illness and maintaining health.

Hydration: Drinking plenty of fluids, particularly pure spring water and herbal teas, was another lifestyle factor that Dr. Sebi highlighted. Proper hydration helps flush toxins from the body, aids in digestion and nutrient absorption, and maintains cellular health. Dr. Sebi often recommended alkaline water to further support the body's pH balance.

Stress Management: Dr. Sebi recognized that emotional and mental health impacts physical health. He advocated for practices that reduce stress such as meditation, deep breathing exercises, and spending time in nature. Managing stress effectively can reduce inflammation, enhance immune function, and promote a positive outlook—factors that all contribute to healing.

Natural Environment: Dr. Sebi believed that being in a clean, natural environment could significantly enhance healing. Fresh air and sunlight are vital, providing vitamin D and improving mood and energy levels. Whenever possible, he encouraged spending time outdoors to reconnect with nature, which has its own therapeutic effects.

Community and Social Support: Maintaining a supportive network of family and friends can provide emotional support and motivation. Dr. Sebi often talked about the healing power of being surrounded by people who encourage and support your healing journey. Social interactions can improve mental health and reduce feelings of isolation, which is especially important during periods of healing.

Book 3: Dr. Sebi Herb Encyclopedia

Most Important Herbs According to Dr. Sebi

Dr. Sebi's approach to natural healing prominently featured the use of specific herbs that he deemed crucial for detoxification and nourishment of the body. These herbs were selected for their potent properties and alignment with his alkaline diet principles.

Burdock root was one of Dr. Sebi's favorites due to its blood purifying and anti-inflammatory properties. Rich in antioxidants such as phenolic acids, quercetin, and luteolin, burdock root helps cleanse the blood, improve skin health, and aid in liver detoxification, removing heavy metals from the body.

Sea moss, another key herb recommended by Dr. Sebi, is valued for its high mineral content, especially iodine, essential for thyroid function. It provides 92 of the 102 essential minerals found in the human body, soothes mucous membranes, and aids in digestion.

Sarsaparilla is known for its ability to cleanse the blood and treat skin conditions. It contains compounds that mimic the effects of natural steroids, which are beneficial in treating conditions like psoriasis, arthritis, and eczema. Dr. Sebi valued sarsaparilla for its ability to increase the bioavailability of other herbs and improve hormonal balance.

Elderberry was often highlighted by Dr. Sebi for its immune-boosting properties. Rich in vitamins and antioxidants, it is particularly effective in fighting colds and flu and promotes skin health and has anti-inflammatory benefits.

Bladderwrack, a type of seaweed, is another source of iodine and has traditionally been used for thyroid issues. It's also rich in alginic acid, which can act as a laxative to help remove toxins from the bowels.

Dandelion is used both as a food and medicine and is a powerful detoxifier. Dr. Sebi recommended dandelion for its liver cleansing abilities and its natural diuretic properties, which help the kidneys flush out excess toxins and salt.

Nettle is included in his protocols for its rich content of vitamins A, C, K, and several B vitamins, as well as minerals like iron, calcium, magnesium, and potassium. It supports the kidneys and urinary tract and has notable anti-inflammatory properties.

These herbs collectively represent the foundation of Dr. Sebi's herbal medicine cabinet, each chosen for its specific health benefits and ability to support the body's natural detoxification processes, enhance nutrient absorption, and maintain an alkaline state conducive to good health.

Specific Healing Properties of Herbs

Dr. Sebi's approach to healing strongly emphasized the intrinsic power of herbs to address specific health issues and promote overall wellness. Each herb in his protocol was selected for its unique properties and its ability to work synergistically within the body to restore balance and health.

Burdock root is highly valued for its detoxifying properties. It aids in removing heavy metals and toxins from the bloodstream, essential for cleansing the liver. Moreover, its anti-inflammatory properties can soothe and heal various skin issues such as eczema, psoriasis, and acne, making it a staple in natural skin care regimens.

Sea moss is celebrated for its dense mineral content, providing a broad spectrum of nutrients essential for bodily functions. Rich in iodine, it supports thyroid health, and its mucilaginous consistency helps nourish the skin, improve digestion, and boost immunity.

Sarsaparilla is known for its vitality-boosting and blood-purifying effects. It contains compounds that bind with toxins to facilitate their removal from the body. Additionally, its anti-inflammatory and antioxidant properties help in treating skin conditions and improving joint health.

Elderberry is predominantly recognized for its immune-enhancing capabilities. It is a rich source of vitamins that aid in combating colds and flu. The high antioxidant content also helps reduce inflammation and supports respiratory health, making it beneficial for conditions like bronchitis and sinus infections.

Bladderwrack, a type of seaweed, naturally contains iodine, crucial for thyroid function. It also features fucoidan, a complex carbohydrate with anti-inflammatory properties, helping to reduce the risk of chronic diseases such as arthritis, heart disease, and diabetes.

Dandelion is renowned for its liver-supporting and detoxifying effects. It acts as a diuretic, facilitating the removal of toxins from the kidneys and urinary tract. Rich in antioxidants and vitamins, dandelion supports overall detoxification and aids in digestive health.

Nettle offers a wide array of health benefits, including supporting joint health, providing allergy relief, and reducing inflammatory responses. It is highly nutritious, serving as a natural source of vitamins and minerals essential for maintaining bone health and overall vitality.

Together, these herbs form the cornerstone of Dr. Sebi's herbal medicine philosophy, each chosen not just for their individual healing abilities but also for their potential to enhance one another's effects. This holistic treatment strategy underscores Dr. Sebi's belief that natural, plant-based treatments can effectively restore and rejuvenate the body.

How to Use Herbs Effectively

Using herbs effectively is crucial for harnessing their therapeutic properties, a principle central to Dr. Sebi's approach to healing. To make the most of the herbs recommended by Dr. Sebi, understanding the correct usage, preparation, and dosage is essential.

Firstly, it's important to understand the specific purpose of each herb. Dr. Sebi's herbal encyclopedia includes a variety of plants, each with unique healing properties. For instance, some herbs might be used for their detoxifying effects on the liver, while others may be chosen for their ability to boost the immune system or reduce inflammation. By understanding what each herb does, you can target specific health issues more effectively.

Proper preparation of herbs is key to maximizing their effectiveness. Dr. Sebi often recommended making teas or infusions as a way to extract the healing compounds of herbs. For example, simmering burdock root or elderberry can release their beneficial compounds into the water, creating a potent herbal tea. Some herbs might also be used in their raw form, added to smoothies or salads, depending on their nature and intended use.

Correct dosing is another critical aspect of using herbs effectively. Each herb has a recommended dosage range that optimizes its benefits while minimizing potential side effects. Dr. Sebi provided guidelines on how much of each herb should be consumed, whether in the form of teas, capsules, or powders. Following these guidelines ensures that you are using a safe and effective amount.

Additionally, the timing of when you take certain herbs can enhance their benefits. Some herbs are best taken on an empty stomach to aid in detoxification, while others might be more effective if taken with meals to aid digestion or to leverage their blood-sugar regulating properties.

Consistency is also crucial when using herbal remedies. Many herbs need to be taken regularly over a period to achieve the desired effects. Building a routine around your herbal treatment allows the body to gradually incorporate and maximize the healing potential of the herbs.

Finally, combining herbs can often lead to synergistic effects, where the combined impact is greater than the sum of using each herb individually. Dr. Sebi recommended certain herbal combinations that work together to enhance each other's effects, such as combining anti-inflammatory herbs with those that support circulation for comprehensive benefits.

Understanding these aspects of herbal usage — from the specific purposes of each herb, through to their preparation, dosing, and combination — is integral to effectively implementing Dr. Sebi's healing treatments. By following these guidelines, individuals can safely and effectively utilize herbs to support their health and well-being.

Herb Combinations for Specific Treatments

Dr. Sebi emphasized the importance of combining herbs to enhance their effectiveness in treating specific health issues. This synergistic approach helps to maximize the therapeutic benefits of each herb while broadening the scope of conditions that can be addressed. Here are some examples of herb combinations recommended by Dr. Sebi for specific treatments:

Detoxification and Liver Health: For detoxifying the body and supporting liver function, Dr. Sebi often combined burdock root with dandelion root. Burdock root is known for its blood purifying properties, while dandelion root enhances liver detoxification and helps in bile production. Together, these herbs work to cleanse the liver and improve overall detoxification processes in the body.

Immune System Support: To boost the immune system, particularly during cold and flu season, Dr. Sebi recommended a combination of elderberry and sea moss. Elderberry is rich in antioxidants and vitamins that help fight viruses, while sea moss provides a wealth of minerals that support overall cell health and immunity. This combination not only helps to prevent illness but also aids in faster recovery.

Respiratory Health: For improving respiratory health, particularly for those dealing with conditions like asthma or bronchitis, Dr. Sebi suggested combining mullein with eucalyptus. Mullein is beneficial for its soothing effects on the bronchial tubes and its ability to reduce mucus production. Eucalyptus helps to open the airways, providing relief from congestion and making breathing easier.

Digestive Support: For aiding digestion and alleviating issues such as bloating and indigestion, a combination of peppermint and ginger was recommended. Peppermint soothes the stomach lining and relaxes the gastrointestinal tract, while ginger aids in digestion and helps to reduce inflammation. Together, they provide comprehensive support for the digestive system.

Joint and Muscle Pain: For relieving joint and muscle pain, particularly in cases of arthritis or sports injuries, Dr. Sebi advised using a combination of sarsaparilla and nettle. Sarsaparilla contains compounds that may mimic the natural steroids in the body, helping to reduce inflammation. Nettle is known for its rich mineral content and anti-inflammatory properties, making it effective in reducing pain and supporting joint health.

Skin Health: To improve skin health and treat conditions such as eczema or acne, a combination of yellow dock and burdock root can be effective. Yellow dock helps to clear toxins that lead to skin issues, while burdock root's anti-inflammatory properties help to calm skin irritation and promote healing.

These combinations illustrate Dr. Sebi's holistic approach to healing, where herbs are used not only for their individual benefits but also for their combined effects to treat specific health issues more effectively. When using these combinations, it's important to consider the proper ratios and dosages to ensure optimal results and safety.

Responsible Harvesting and Storage of Herbs

Responsible harvesting and storage of herbs are crucial aspects of maintaining their potency and effectiveness, principles that were integral to Dr. Sebi's approach to natural healing. Here's how to ensure that herbs are harvested and stored correctly to preserve their medicinal properties:

Responsible Harvesting

The process of harvesting herbs is not just about taking what you need from plants; it's also about doing so in a way that does not harm the environment or deplete resources. Dr. Sebi advocated for sustainable harvesting practices which include:

- Timing: Herbs should be harvested at the right time of their growth cycle to ensure they contain the maximum amount of active compounds. For example, many herbs are best harvested just before they start to flower, as this is when their energy is most concentrated in the leaves.

- Method: When harvesting, it's important to use clean, sharp tools to make precise cuts. This helps to preserve the integrity of the plant and prevents damage that could lead to disease. Additionally, only parts of the plant that are needed should be taken, leaving enough so that the plant can continue to grow healthily.

- Respect for Nature: Harvesting should be done with respect for nature, taking only what is needed and leaving the environment as undisturbed as possible. This means avoiding over-harvesting and ensuring that enough plants are left to reproduce.

Proper Storage

Once harvested, proper storage is essential to maintain the quality and efficacy of herbs. Dr. Sebi highlighted several key considerations for storing herbs:

- Drying: Many herbs need to be dried to extend their shelf life and concentrate their flavors and medicinal properties. Herbs should be dried quickly after harvesting to prevent mold and decay. The drying process should be done in a cool, dark, and dry place with good air circulation.

- Containers: Once dried, herbs should be stored in airtight containers to protect them from moisture and light. Glass jars with tight-fitting lids are ideal as they do not impart any flavors and prevent air from entering.

- Labeling: Proper labeling is crucial to ensure that herbs are used correctly. Labels should include the name of the herb, the date of harvest, and any specific preparation instructions. This is particularly important for ensuring that the herbs are used within their optimal time frame.

- Environment: The storage area should be cool, dark, and dry. Temperature fluctuations and exposure to light can degrade the quality of herbs over time, so it's important to store them in an environment that maintains their potency.

Rare Herbs and Their Unique Benefits

 Dr. Sebi's approach to herbal medicine often included lesser-known, rare herbs that possess unique healing properties. These herbs were valued for their specific benefits and roles in traditional and holistic health practices. Understanding the unique benefits of these rare herbs can offer additional tools for those seeking natural health solutions.

Cascara Sagrada: Often used in small doses, Cascara Sagrada is known for its effectiveness as a natural laxative. It helps to stimulate peristalsis and facilitates easier bowel movements. Aside from its primary role in relieving constipation, it also helps to cleanse the colon and can aid in detoxification processes.

Blue Vervain: This herb is praised for its calming effects on the nervous system. Blue Vervain is used to alleviate symptoms of stress and anxiety, promoting a sense of calm. Additionally, it serves as a powerful liver detoxifier and is believed to help with hormonal balance, making it particularly beneficial for those suffering from mood swings associated with hormonal shifts.

Irish Moss: While commonly grouped with sea moss, Irish Moss stands out due to its high nutrient content, particularly its ability to provide mucilage that soothes the digestive system. It's rich in iodine and antioxidants, supporting thyroid function and improving skin health. Its carrageenan content makes it a useful remedy for respiratory ailments, as it acts as an expectorant.

Soursop Leaf: Known for its potent anti-inflammatory and analgesic properties, Soursop Leaf is used in traditional medicine to treat a range of conditions from arthritis to headaches and even to aid in cancer prevention. It contains a unique composition of antioxidants that help to fight free radicals and improve cellular health.

Guaco: This herb is celebrated for its ability to loosen mucus and improve respiratory function. Guaco is often used in treatments for bronchitis and other respiratory infections due to its expectorant properties. Additionally, it has anti-inflammatory and antimicrobial benefits, enhancing its effectiveness in treating cold and flu symptoms.

Contribo: Rare and powerful, Contribo has a long history in traditional medicine for its use in digestive disorders and detoxification. It is known for its strong bitter properties that can stimulate digestive juices, enhancing digestion and absorption of nutrients.

These rare herbs, each with unique healing properties, were carefully chosen by Dr. Sebi for their specific benefits and roles in supporting health. Incorporating these herbs into a holistic health regimen, as Dr. Sebi advocated, provides a broad spectrum of natural remedies that can address a wide range of health issues effectively and naturally.

Herbal Preparations and Dosages

Proper preparation and dosing of herbs are critical to maximizing their healing potential, a principle strongly emphasized in Dr. Sebi's teachings. Here's how Dr. Sebi recommended preparing and dosing various herbs to ensure their effectiveness:

Preparation Methods:

1. Teas and Infusions: Many of Dr. Sebi's herbs are best consumed as teas or infusions. For leaves and flowers, a typical preparation involves steeping about one to two teaspoons of the dried herb in a cup of boiling water for 10-15 minutes. For roots and barks, which are tougher, the preparation may require simmering the herb in water for 15-30 minutes to extract the active compounds effectively.

2. Tinctures: Some herbs are also prepared as tinctures to concentrate their medicinal properties. This involves soaking the herb in a solution of water and alcohol for several weeks, shaking the mixture regularly. The final product is strained and used in much smaller doses than teas, typically measured in drops, which can be added to water or tea.

3. Capsules: Dr. Sebi also recommended using powdered herbs encapsulated in vegan capsules for ease of consumption and precise dosing. This method is particularly useful for bitter herbs or those that require precise dosages.

4. Topical Applications: Certain herbs are used externally in the form of poultices, salves, or oils. These are typically applied directly to the skin for conditions like rashes, burns, or joint pain. The preparation involves either simmering the herb in oil or mixing the powdered herb with a base like beeswax to create a salve.

Dosages:

Determining the right dosage of an herb depends on several factors, including the individual's age, weight, and overall health condition. Dr. Sebi provided general guidelines but also emphasized the importance of listening to the body's responses and adjusting dosages accordingly.

1. Teas and Infusions: A general recommendation for herbal teas is one cup, two to three times a day. However, for stronger medicinal herbs, Dr. Sebi often suggested starting with smaller amounts to see how the body reacts.

2. Tinctures: Due to their concentration, tinctures are typically dosed in drops, ranging from 5 to 20 drops per use, depending on the herb's potency and the desired effect.

3. Capsules: Dosages for capsules can vary, but a common recommendation is one to two capsules taken one to two times daily, again depending on the herb and the specific health issue being addressed.

4. Topical Applications: For external applications, the herb is typically applied to the affected area as needed. The frequency and amount can depend on the severity of the condition and the preparation used.

Dr. Sebi stressed the importance of consistency and patience when using herbal treatments. Natural remedies often require time to show benefits, and their effectiveness is enhanced by regular and proper usage. Additionally, Dr. Sebi advised consultation with a healthcare provider knowledgeable in herbal medicine to help guide appropriate dosages and applications, especially when used in conjunction with other treatments.

Growing Your Own Herbs at Home

Growing your own herbs at home is a rewarding way to engage with Dr. Sebi's principles, ensuring you have access to the freshest and most potent medicinal plants. Cultivating your own herbs allows you to control the environment they grow in, making sure they're organic and free from harmful chemicals.

When starting your home herb garden, first choose herbs that align with your health needs and are also suitable for the growing conditions available to you. Common herbs that Dr. Sebi recommended, such as basil, parsley, cilantro, and mint, are relatively easy to grow and can be used both medicinally and in cooking.

Whether you set up your garden indoors or outdoors will depend on your space and climate. Indoor gardens need pots with good drainage placed in spots that receive at least six hours of sunlight daily. For an outdoor garden, select an area that gets sufficient sunlight and prepare the soil by enriching it with organic matter to ensure it is fertile and drains well.

You can start your herbs from seeds or seedlings, with seedlings offering a quicker start, especially for slower-growing varieties. Make sure to space your plants according to recommended guidelines to prevent overcrowding, which can stunt growth and increase susceptibility to disease.

Regular watering is key to a healthy herb garden, but it's crucial to avoid overwatering, as herbs generally prefer well-drained soil. The amount of water needed will vary with the weather conditions and the type of soil, with herbs like basil and cilantro needing more water, while rosemary, thyme, and lavender thrive in drier conditions. Ensuring good air circulation around the plants will help prevent fungal diseases.

Harvest your herbs regularly to encourage new growth and prolong the plants' vitality. Use sharp scissors or pruning shears to cut the herbs gently, ideally in the morning when their essential oils are most concentrated and before the heat of the day sets in.

Natural pest control is important to keep your herbs healthy without resorting to chemical pesticides. Encourage beneficial insects, use neem oil, or create a homemade spray from water and mild soap to deal with pests organically.

If you find yourself with more herbs than you can use immediately after harvesting, you can dry them for long-term storage. Tie the herbs into small bundles and hang them upside down in a dry, warm place out of direct sunlight. Once dried, store them in airtight containers in a cool, dark place to maintain their medicinal properties.

Book 4: Dr. Sebi Alkaline & Anti-Inflammatory Diet

Definition of Alkaline and Anti-Inflammatory Diets

Dr. Sebi's dietary approach centers around the principles of alkaline and anti-inflammatory diets, which are designed to promote optimal health by minimizing acidity and inflammation in the body. Understanding these principles can help explain why such diets are beneficial and how they function to maintain health and prevent disease.

Definition of Alkaline Diet

The alkaline diet is based on the concept that the foods you eat can affect the pH balance of your body. The pH scale, which ranges from 0 to 14, determines how acidic or alkaline a substance is. A pH less than 7 is considered acidic, a pH of 7 is neutral, and a pH greater than 7 is alkaline. The human body naturally maintains a slightly alkaline pH of about 7.4. According to Dr. Sebi, consuming foods that further promote alkalinity can help maintain this balance, enhancing health and protecting against diseases.

The alkaline diet emphasizes consuming a high proportion of fresh vegetables, fruits, nuts, and seeds, all of which have an alkalizing effect on the body. Foods that are highly acidic, such as processed foods, sugar, dairy, and meat, are minimized or eliminated because they can lower the body's pH and contribute to a more acidic environment.

Principles of the Alkaline Diet

1. Enhance Detoxification: Alkaline foods support the body's natural detoxification processes by helping to cleanse the blood and organs. This can lead to the elimination of toxins from the body, which might otherwise contribute to various health issues.

2. Improve Energy and Vitality: By reducing the load on the body's acid-detoxifying mechanisms (such as the kidneys and liver), the alkaline diet can help increase energy levels and overall vitality.

3. Prevention of Diseases: Maintaining an alkaline environment in the body is believed to reduce the risk of chronic diseases such as hypertension, diabetes, arthritis, and low bone density.

Definition of Anti-Inflammatory Diet

An anti-inflammatory diet involves eating foods that reduce the inflammatory response within the body. Chronic inflammation is linked to numerous health conditions, including heart diseases, cancers, and autoimmune diseases. Dr. Sebi's approach emphasizes foods that naturally combat inflammation while avoiding those that can trigger or exacerbate it.

Principles of the Anti-Inflammatory Diet

1. Focus on Whole Foods: The diet promotes whole, nutrient-dense foods that are rich in antioxidants — substances that can reduce oxidative stress and lower inflammation.

2. Elimination of Pro-Inflammatory Foods: This diet reduces the intake of foods known to cause inflammation, such as trans fats, high-fructose corn syrup, and refined carbs.

3. Inclusion of Omega-3 Fatty Acids: Including foods high in omega-3 fatty acids (such as certain seeds and nuts) which are known for their anti-inflammatory properties.

By combining the alkaline and anti-inflammatory diets, Dr. Sebi created a holistic dietary approach that not only prevents acidity and inflammation but also boosts overall health, supports immune function, and enhances the body's natural healing abilities. This dietary strategy is at the core of his teachings, reflecting his belief in the power of natural, plant-based nutrition to maintain health and treat disease.

Foods to Favor and Avoid

Dr. Sebi's alkaline and anti-inflammatory diet emphasizes a plant-based menu, focusing on foods that maintain the body's pH balance while offering high nutrient and antioxidant content. Here's an overview of the foods recommended by Dr. Sebi, as well as those to avoid.

Foods to Favor

The diet strongly supports the consumption of fresh, raw fruits and vegetables, particularly those that are low in sugar and high in essential minerals. Leafy greens such as kale, spinach, and arugula are staples due to their high nutrient density. Other vegetables like avocados, bell peppers, cucumbers, zucchini, and squash are encouraged for their health benefits and alkalinity. Fruits are also a crucial part of the diet, with apples, berries, melons, and grapes being favored for their antioxidants and low glycemic impact.

Nuts and seeds such as almonds, Brazil nuts, sesame seeds, hemp seeds, and flaxseeds are included for their healthy fats, proteins, and alkaline properties. These are essential for maintaining cellular health and providing sustained energy.

Dr. Sebi permits the consumption of certain grains that are traditionally considered alkaline. Quinoa, amaranth, and wild rice are approved grains, valued for their nutrient content and gluten-free status.

Herbs and spices play a significant role in this diet, not just for flavor enhancement but also for their health properties. Basil, parsley, thyme, oregano, and particularly turmeric are highlighted for their therapeutic benefits, including turmeric's strong anti-inflammatory qualities.

Selected legumes such as chickpeas and lentils are permitted and are valued for their protein and compatibility with an alkaline diet.

Natural oils like olive oil and coconut oil are recommended for cooking and dressing foods. These oils are chosen for their health benefits and minimal impact on the body's pH levels.

Foods to Avoid

Dr. Sebi's diet restricts the consumption of any foods that may increase acidity or inflammation in the body. This includes all meat and animal products, dairy, processed foods, and artificial additives. Traditional grains such as wheat and corn, along with their derivatives, are also avoided due to their potential to disrupt the alkaline balance.

Sugars and artificial sweeteners are particularly discouraged as they can cause spikes in blood sugar and contribute to systemic inflammation. Instead, natural sweeteners like agave and date sugar are sometimes used sparingly.

Sample Daily Menus

Creating daily menus that adhere to Dr. Sebi's alkaline and anti-inflammatory diet can help individuals experience the full benefits of his holistic approach to health. Here is a sample of daily menus that incorporate Dr. Sebi's guidelines, providing balanced, nutritious meals throughout the day.

Sample Daily Menu 1

Breakfast: Start your day with a smoothie made from alkaline-friendly fruits such as apples, blueberries, and a handful of kale or spinach. Add some hemp seeds for extra protein and a tablespoon of sea moss gel for its rich mineral content.

Mid-Morning Snack: Enjoy a small bowl of homemade guacamole with sliced cucumbers and bell peppers for dipping.

Lunch: Prepare a quinoa salad with chopped kale, cherry tomatoes, cucumbers, and avocados. Dress the salad with a simple lemon juice and olive oil dressing and top with crushed almonds.

Afternoon Snack: Have a handful of Brazil nuts and a few dates for a quick, energizing snack.

Dinner: Make a hearty vegetable stew with butternut squash, zucchini, onions, and garbanzo beans. Season with turmeric, ginger, and garlic for their anti-inflammatory properties. Serve this over a small portion of wild rice.

Evening Tea: Wind down with a cup of herbal tea made from ginger and elderberry to boost immunity and promote relaxation before bed.

Sample Daily Menu 2

Breakfast: Prepare a bowl of amaranth porridge sweetened with agave syrup and topped with slices of fresh fruit like strawberries and kiwi.

Mid-Morning Snack: Snack on a few pieces of dried sea moss and a small serving of walnuts to keep energy levels up.

Lunch: Assemble a refreshing salad with spinach, arugula, sliced oranges, and red onion. Add a sprinkle of hemp seeds and dress with a lime and olive oil vinaigrette.

Afternoon Snack: Savor a smoothie made from coconut water, frozen mango chunks, and a tablespoon of flaxseed powder.

Dinner: Cook a stir-fry with a variety of allowed vegetables such as bell peppers, broccoli, and mushrooms. Use coconut oil for frying and serve this with quinoa for a complete meal.

Evening Tea: Enjoy a cup of chamomile tea to aid digestion and help you settle down for the night.

These sample menus are designed to provide a balanced intake of nutrients while adhering to Dr. Sebi's alkaline and anti-inflammatory principles. Each meal incorporates a variety of foods that support alkalinity and reduce inflammation, ensuring that you can enjoy a diverse and flavorful diet while maintaining your health goals.

Long-Term Health Impacts

Adopting Dr. Sebi's alkaline and anti-inflammatory diet can have profound long-term health impacts, especially since it emphasizes enhancing overall health by promoting an alkaline environment within the body and reducing inflammation. Over time, adhering to this diet may lead to significant health benefits across various bodily systems.

By focusing on natural, minimally processed foods and eliminating acidic and inflammatory foods, Dr. Sebi's diet supports the body's natural detoxification processes. This reduced toxin accumulation is crucial for mitigating chronic diseases and slowing aging processes. The diet also promotes digestive health through its high fiber content from fruits, vegetables, and grains, which helps maintain regular bowel movements and a healthy gut microbiota, essential for preventing digestive disorders.

Chronic inflammation is linked to numerous diseases, including heart disease, diabetes, and Alzheimer's. The anti-inflammatory nature of Dr. Sebi's diet—rich in antioxidants and devoid of processed foods—can significantly lower systemic inflammation and associated disease risks. Cardiovascular health benefits as well, as the diet's plant-based focus reduces intake of unhealthy fats and promotes heart-healthy nutrients, improving cholesterol levels and reducing the risk of heart disease.

The immune system also benefits from the vitamins, minerals, and antioxidants in the diet, which bolster the body's defense against infections and may improve its ability to prevent cancer. Additionally, the diet's low glycemic index helps in maintaining stable blood sugar levels, which is beneficial for diabetes prevention and management.

Joint and bone health see improvements from the diet's anti-inflammatory properties and rich mineral content, vital for maintaining bone density and alleviating arthritis symptoms. Skin health is enhanced by the high intake of vitamins and minerals, which can help reduce signs of aging and prevent skin conditions like eczema and acne.

Weight management is another advantage of Dr. Sebi's diet. The focus on whole, nutrient-dense foods and the exclusion of high-calorie processed foods naturally leads to weight loss and helps maintain a healthy weight, reducing the risk of obesity-related diseases such as diabetes and certain cancers.

Diet Adaptations for Different Needs

Adapting Dr. Sebi's alkaline and anti-inflammatory diet to suit individual needs and conditions is crucial for ensuring its effectiveness and sustainability. Everyone has unique health profiles, dietary restrictions, and nutritional requirements that may necessitate modifications to any dietary regimen. Here's a closer look at how Dr. Sebi's diet can be tailored to meet diverse health goals and personal needs.

For Athletes and Physically Active Individuals: Those who engage in high levels of physical activity may require more calories and protein to support their energy needs and muscle recovery. Although Dr. Sebi's diet primarily emphasizes plant-based foods, athletes might need to increase their intake of protein-rich plants such as hemp seeds, chickpeas, and quinoa. Including calorie-dense foods like avocados, nuts, and coconut products can also help meet the higher energy demands typical of active lifestyles.

For Weight Management: Individuals aiming to lose weight can benefit from the diet's naturally low-calorie, high-fiber content. Emphasizing a variety of vegetables and fruits can increase satiety and reduce overall calorie intake. However, it's important to ensure a balanced intake of nutrients, and adding moderate portions of seeds and nuts can provide essential fats and proteins.

For Older Adults: As metabolism slows with age, older adults may require fewer calories but need more of certain nutrients, such as calcium, vitamin D, and B vitamins, to maintain bone health and vitality. Adapting the diet to include nutrient-rich foods like amaranth, almonds, and wild rice that are high in these nutrients is beneficial. Additionally, adapting food textures and preparation methods may be necessary to accommodate any difficulties with chewing or digestion.

For Those with Chronic Conditions: Individuals managing chronic diseases like diabetes or heart disease may need specific dietary adjustments. Dr. Sebi's diet, which naturally excludes processed sugars and unhealthy fats, generally aligns well with the needs of these conditions. However, those with diabetes should continuously monitor their blood sugar levels, as the intake of fruits and other carbohydrates needs to be managed carefully.

For Pregnancy and Lactation: Pregnant and breastfeeding women have increased nutritional needs to support fetal growth and milk production. While Dr. Sebi's diet is nutrient-rich, extra attention may be needed to ensure adequate intake of iron, calcium, and omega-3 fatty acids, which are crucial during these stages. Supplements and fortified foods might be necessary to meet these heightened nutritional requirements.

For Children and Adolescents: Growing children and teenagers have high energy and nutrient needs to support their development. The diet is rich in vital nutrients, but it's important to ensure that young individuals receive sufficient calories and proteins. Including a variety of grains, legumes, and seeds can help provide these essential nutrients.

Tailoring Dr. Sebi's alkaline and anti-inflammatory diet according to individual health profiles, age, activity levels, and physiological conditions can help maximize its health benefits while ensuring nutritional adequacy. Personalizing the diet in this way allows it to be more effective and sustainable over the long term, catering to the unique needs of each individual.

Effects of an Alkaline Diet on Skin Health

Dr. Sebi's alkaline diet, emphasizing the consumption of plant-based, mineral-rich foods, profoundly impacts skin health by fostering an internal environment that promotes clarity and resilience. Here's how the alkaline diet enhances skin health through various mechanisms.

The alkaline diet's focus on detoxification plays a crucial role in skin appearance. By supporting enhanced kidney and liver function, the diet aids in the effective elimination of toxins and waste products from the body. Since the skin is also a major detox organ, improved detoxification results in fewer breakouts, reduced dullness, and a clearer complexion.

Hydration is another key aspect of the alkaline diet that benefits the skin. Alkaline-rich foods, particularly fruits and vegetables, are high in water content, helping to hydrate the body and the skin. Adequate hydration is essential for maintaining skin elasticity and suppleness, preventing dryness, and reducing the visibility of wrinkles and fine lines.

Furthermore, the diet is rich in antioxidants, which are abundant in various fruits and vegetables like berries, leafy greens, and carrots. Antioxidants help combat oxidative stress and damage caused by free radicals, which can lead to premature aging and skin deterioration. By increasing the body's antioxidant defenses, the alkaline diet shields the skin from environmental aggressors such as pollution and UV radiation, promoting a healthier and more youthful appearance.

In addition to these benefits, the anti-inflammatory properties of the alkaline diet can alleviate skin conditions such as eczema, psoriasis, and acne. These conditions are often exacerbated by systemic inflammation, which the diet helps to soothe, leading to reduced redness and irritation and an improvement in overall skin condition.

Anti-Inflammatory Herbs and Spices

Dr. Sebi's alkaline and anti-inflammatory diet prominently features a variety of herbs and spices that are effective in reducing inflammation throughout the body. These natural elements are essential to the diet, harnessing potent anti-inflammatory properties to help manage chronic inflammation and bolster overall health.

Turmeric is a cornerstone of anti-inflammatory herbs, highly regarded for its active compound, curcumin. Curcumin has been extensively researched and proven to significantly reduce inflammation at the molecular level. It works by inhibiting key enzymes and cytokines involved in the inflammatory process, offering relief from various conditions associated with inflammation, such as arthritis and other chronic pains. To maximize absorption, turmeric is often paired with black pepper, which contains piperine, a substance that enhances curcumin's bioavailability.

Ginger, much like turmeric, is renowned for its powerful anti-inflammatory effects. It contains compounds called gingerols and shogaols, which help soothe inflammation, particularly in the digestive system, and reduce nausea. Ginger is also effective in relieving pain and swelling associated with inflammatory conditions.

Basil is not just a flavorful addition to meals; it also has significant health benefits, thanks to its anti-inflammatory properties. It contains eugenol, a natural chemical that acts similarly to over-the-counter anti-inflammatory medications by blocking enzymes in the body that cause swelling.

Alkaline Diet and Athletic Performance

Dr. Sebi's alkaline diet, known for promoting an alkaline environment within the body, offers significant benefits for athletic performance. This diet is particularly beneficial for athletes and those engaged in regular physical activities as it enhances physical performance, improves recovery times, and supports overall athletic health.

The alkaline diet helps reduce bodily acidity, which can significantly impact muscle efficiency and endurance. Lower acidity levels in the body help decrease muscle soreness and fatigue, allowing athletes to sustain higher performance levels for longer periods. This is especially important in endurance sports where prolonged muscle functionality is essential.

Additionally, the alkaline diet is rich in minerals such as potassium and magnesium, which are crucial for muscle function and recovery. These minerals aid in muscle contraction and relaxation, help prevent cramps, and facilitate quicker recovery after intense workouts. The high level of antioxidants found in the alkaline diet also contributes to reduced oxidative stress during physical exertion, protecting the body from free radicals and speeding up recovery.

Enhanced hydration is another key benefit of the alkaline diet, as it encourages the consumption of high water-content foods and alkaline water. Proper hydration is essential for optimal blood flow, which ensures that nutrients and oxygen are efficiently delivered to the muscles, and metabolic wastes are removed promptly. This not only improves athletic performance but also enhances overall health.

Furthermore, by reducing inflammation, the alkaline diet helps to mitigate chronic inflammation, which can lead to overuse injuries in athletes. Chronic inflammation can impede recovery and degrade athletic performance over time. By incorporating anti-inflammatory foods, athletes can maintain stronger, healthier bodies that are less prone to injuries and capable of quicker recovery.

Overall, Dr. Sebi's alkaline diet supports athletes by providing a rich source of nutrients that optimize muscle function, improve hydration, reduce inflammation, and aid in faster recovery. By adhering to this diet, athletes can hope to achieve not only enhanced performance but also a greater overall state of health.

Book 5: Dr. Sebi Remedies Book

Remedies for Cold and Flu

Dr. Sebi's approach to treating common ailments such as colds and flu emphasizes natural remedies that align with his overall philosophy of using plant-based, mineral-rich foods and herbs to support the body's healing processes. These remedies focus on boosting the immune system, reducing inflammation, and alleviating symptoms to help the body recover more quickly from illness.

Elderberry is a key recommendation from Dr. Sebi for fighting the cold and flu. Rich in vitamins and antioxidants, elderberry syrup or tea can boost the immune system, reduce inflammation, and shorten the duration of symptoms. The antiviral properties of elderberries make them particularly effective in combating respiratory viruses, making it an excellent remedy during the flu season.

Sea moss is another potent remedy due to its high content of essential minerals and vitamins that support immune function. It also helps soothe mucous membranes, which can become irritated during a cold. Adding sea moss gel to smoothies or consuming it directly can help reduce congestion and maintain hydration, which is crucial during recovery from respiratory illnesses.

Ginger is renowned for its powerful anti-inflammatory and antioxidant properties, making it an excellent choice for alleviating cold and flu symptoms. Drinking ginger tea can help relieve a sore throat, reduce nausea, and decrease inflammation. It also induces sweating and warming effects, providing comfort when feeling chilled.

Garlic, with its strong natural antibiotic and immune-boosting properties, is effective in combating cold and flu viruses. Consuming raw garlic or taking garlic supplements can help fight off infections. For those who find raw garlic too potent, lightly cooking it or taking it in capsule form can be alternative ways to benefit from its properties.

Mullein is often recommended by Dr. Sebi for its ability to clear the lungs and expel mucus, making it particularly beneficial for those suffering from bronchial congestion and persistent coughs associated with the flu.

Linden flower tea is favored for its antipyretic (fever-reducing) properties and is soothing for headaches, muscle aches, and nasal congestion that often accompany the flu.

Utilizing these natural remedies at the onset of cold or flu symptoms can significantly alleviate discomfort and accelerate recovery. Dr. Sebi stressed the importance of supporting the body's natural defenses with holistic treatments, not only to combat illnesses but also to enhance overall health and vitality.

Natural Skin Care Treatments

Dr. Sebi's approach to natural skin care emphasizes the use of herbal treatments and holistic practices that nurture and heal the skin using purely natural ingredients. These ingredients are chosen for their abilities to cleanse, nourish, and rejuvenate the skin, promoting a healthy complexion and addressing common skin issues effectively.

One of the cornerstone ingredients in Dr. Sebi's skin care regimen is sea moss, celebrated for its high mineral content including sulfur, which possesses antimicrobial and anti-inflammatory properties. Applying sea moss gel topically as a face mask can deeply hydrate and soothe the skin, helping to reduce acne and eczema. Its natural minerals and vitamins also aid in nourishing the skin, enhancing its elasticity and natural barrier.

Burdock root is another key component, known primarily for its blood-purifying effects. Using burdock root can have a significant impact on skin health, as it helps detoxify the blood and clear up common skin problems like acne and eczema from the inside out. Burdock root tea is popular for its internal benefits, while topical applications in the form of creams or lotions can directly alleviate skin irritations and enhance skin appearance.

Aloe vera is also integral to Dr. Sebi's natural skin care treatments due to its soothing, moisturizing, and healing properties. The gel from the aloe vera plant is particularly effective when used fresh. It can be applied directly to the skin to soothe burns, hydrate dry skin, and speed up the healing of cuts and minor wounds. Aloe vera is also an excellent treatment for reducing inflammation associated with acne and other skin irritations.

Incorporating these natural elements into daily skin care routines can transform skin health over time, reflecting Dr. Sebi's holistic approach to wellness that extends beyond mere appearance to encompass overall bodily health. By treating the skin with natural, plant-based products, individuals can achieve not only a healthier complexion but also a more vibrant, rejuvenated overall appearance.

Digestive Health Remedies

Dr. Sebi's approach to enhancing digestive health centers around using natural remedies to cleanse, repair, and optimize the digestive system. His recommendations include a variety of herbs and foods that help maintain a healthy gut, improve digestion, and alleviate common gastrointestinal issues. Here's an overview of some effective digestive health remedies from Dr. Sebi's teachings:

Sea Moss: Sea moss is highly regarded in Dr. Sebi's protocol for its soothing properties, particularly for the mucous membranes throughout the body, including those in the digestive tract. Rich in minerals and vitamins, sea moss helps to nourish the gut lining, promote healthy gut bacteria, and ensure smooth digestion. It can be consumed in gel form or added to smoothies and other dishes as a nutritive thickener.

Burdock Root: Known for its blood-cleansing properties, burdock root also aids digestion by stimulating bile production and enhancing the liver's ability to process toxins. Consuming burdock root tea or incorporating it into your diet can help alleviate bloating and improve the overall function of the digestive system.

Sarsaparilla: This root is often used in Dr. Sebi's remedies for its ability to bind to endotoxins in the gut and remove them from the body. This detoxifying effect can reduce gastrointestinal inflammation and support a healthy gut flora balance, making it effective in managing conditions like irritable bowel syndrome (IBS) and other inflammatory bowel diseases.

Aloe Vera: Aloe vera is renowned for its soothing and healing properties, especially for the lining of the digestive tract. Drinking aloe vera juice can help heal ulcers, reduce acidity, and soothe the gastrointestinal tract. It's particularly beneficial for those suffering from acid reflux or gastroesophageal reflux disease (GERD).

Ginger: Ginger is a powerful remedy for various digestive issues. It helps reduce nausea, promotes motility in the gastrointestinal tract, and has strong anti-inflammatory properties that can alleviate stomach pain. Ginger tea is a simple and effective way to harness these benefits, especially useful during indigestion or to calm stomach upset.

Stress Management Strategies

Dr. Sebi's approach to health encompasses not only physical well-being but also mental and emotional balance. He advocated for specific strategies to manage stress, recognizing its profound impact on overall health. Here's how Dr. Sebi suggested addressing stress through natural remedies and lifestyle adjustments:

Herbal Teas: Dr. Sebi often recommended herbal teas as a calming remedy to help soothe the mind and body. Herbs like chamomile, lavender, and lemon balm are known for their relaxing properties. Drinking these teas can help reduce anxiety and promote better sleep, which are crucial for effective stress management.

Deep Breathing Exercises: Deep breathing is a simple yet powerful technique to reduce stress. Dr. Sebi emphasized the importance of breathing deeply to increase oxygen intake and stimulate the parasympathetic nervous system, which helps calm the body and mind. Regular practice can help alleviate stress symptoms and enhance overall vitality.

Meditation and Mindfulness: Meditation was another cornerstone of Dr. Sebi's stress management strategy. He encouraged practices that foster mindfulness, which involves being fully present and engaged in the moment without judgment. Meditation can help manage stress by improving focus, reducing anxiety, and enhancing emotional resilience.

Dietary Adjustments: According to Dr. Sebi, an alkaline diet rich in whole, plant-based foods can significantly influence stress levels. Foods high in magnesium, such as leafy greens, nuts, and seeds, are particularly beneficial as magnesium helps regulate cortisol levels, which are often elevated during stress.

Physical Activity: Regular physical activity is essential for stress reduction. Dr. Sebi recommended gentle, restorative exercises such as walking, yoga, or tai chi to help relieve stress. These activities not only improve physical health but also boost endorphins, the body's natural mood elevators.

Connecting with Nature: Spending time in natural settings was a key aspect of Dr. Sebi's lifestyle recommendations for stress management. Being outdoors and engaging with nature can help decrease stress hormone levels and improve feelings of happiness and well-being.

Preparation and Dosing of Remedies

Dr. Sebi's approach to natural healing emphasized not only the choice of remedies but also the proper preparation and dosing to ensure their effectiveness. Understanding how to prepare and dose these remedies correctly is crucial for maximizing their healing potential. Here's an overview of Dr. Sebi's guidelines for the preparation and dosing of his recommended remedies:

Preparation Methods

1. Herbal Teas: Many of Dr. Sebi's remedies involve the use of herbal teas, which require careful preparation to preserve the therapeutic properties of the herbs. To make a tea, boil water and pour it over the herb, allowing it to steep covered for 10 to 15 minutes. This method helps extract the active compounds effectively while retaining the volatile oils and essences that are beneficial for health.

2. Tinctures: Dr. Sebi also recommended tinctures for their potency and ease of absorption. Tinctures are prepared by soaking herbs in a solution of alcohol and water for several weeks to extract the active compounds. The mixture should be shaken daily to ensure effective extraction and then strained to produce a concentrated liquid that can be dosed in small amounts.

3. Capsules and Powders: For herbs that are best consumed in higher concentrations or for those who prefer not to taste the herb, capsules and powders are recommended. These should be prepared by finely grinding the dried herbs and filling capsules or storing the powder in airtight containers protected from light and moisture.

Dosing Recommendations

The effectiveness of herbal remedies depends significantly on proper dosing, which varies based on the individual's age, health condition, and the specific remedy.

1. Teas: Generally, it is advised to drink 1-2 cups of herbal tea daily, depending on the strength of the herb and the desired therapeutic effect. Some potent herbs may require smaller doses, while others may be taken more frequently.

2. Tinctures: Tinctures are more concentrated and therefore typically dosed in drops. The usual dosage can range from 5 to 30 drops, taken 1-3 times per day. The exact number of drops should be tailored based on the herb's potency and the individual's response to the treatment.

3. Capsules and Powders: Dosages for capsules and powders should be provided based on the concentration of the herb and its recommended intake level. Generally, taking one or two capsules 1-2 times per day with water is sufficient for most herbs. Powders can be mixed into water, smoothies, or other liquids.

Natural Pain Relief Solutions

Dr. Sebi's approach to natural pain relief emphasizes using plant-based treatments and holistic methods that address the root causes of pain, focusing on reducing inflammation, detoxifying the body, and enhancing overall health. His remedies are designed to help alleviate pain by restoring the body's natural balance and promoting healing.

Key to Dr. Sebi's pain relief strategy are anti-inflammatory herbs such as turmeric and ginger. Turmeric contains curcumin, a potent anti-inflammatory compound that helps reduce inflammation throughout the body, particularly beneficial for conditions like arthritis and muscle strains. Ginger, similarly, is effective in easing inflammation and also supports digestive health, which can be linked to systemic inflammation. These herbs can be incorporated into daily routines as teas, supplements, or even added to meals, offering a natural way to manage and alleviate pain.

Dr. Sebi strongly advocated for an alkaline diet to combat the acidity he believed contributed to inflammation and pain. By increasing the intake of alkaline foods such as leafy greens, cucumbers, avocados, and consuming alkaline water, the body's pH levels are maintained, potentially reducing inflammation and the pain it causes.

Sea moss was another crucial element in Dr. Sebi's natural pain relief arsenal due to its rich mineral content. Packed with potassium and calcium, sea moss supports bone strength and circulation, which are essential for reducing pain, particularly in the joints and muscles.

For topical pain relief, Dr. Sebi recommended using natural remedies like aloe vera, which soothes skin irritations and burns due to its cooling and anti-inflammatory properties. Other herbs like comfrey and arnica can be used in poultices or creams applied directly to affected areas to reduce swelling and alleviate pain effectively.

Additionally, Dr. Sebi suggested regular mineral baths using substances like Epsom salt, which is rich in magnesium. These baths help to detoxify the body and relax muscles, providing both therapeutic and pain-relieving benefits. The magnesium in Epsom salt is particularly effective for relaxing tense areas and improving overall muscle function.

Enhancing Immune Function with Herbs

Dr. Sebi's holistic approach to health emphasizes the use of natural herbs to enhance immune function, recognizing that a strong immune system is crucial for preventing illness and maintaining overall health. Among the variety of herbs he recommended, elderberry stands out due to its significant immune-boosting properties.

Elderberry is highly regarded for its rich content of antioxidants and vitamins that help fight infections, especially useful during cold and flu seasons. The bioflavonoids and other proteins in elderberry juice destroy the ability of cold and flu viruses to infect a cell. People who use elderberry often notice faster recovery times and reduced symptoms.

Another important herb in Dr. Sebi's immune-enhancing repertoire is sea moss. Packed with essential minerals and vitamins, sea moss supports overall immune function and helps maintain mucous membrane health, which is vital for protecting the body from infections. Sea moss is a source of potassium chloride, which helps to reduce inflammation and phlegm in the mucous membranes, making it beneficial for respiratory health.

Dr. Sebi also recommended the use of echinacea, a powerful herb known for its immune-boosting effects. Echinacea increases the body's natural defense by producing more white blood cells, which combat pathogens. This herb is particularly effective in fighting infections and speeding up recovery from illness.

In addition to these herbs, Dr. Sebi suggested incorporating garlic into the diet for its potent antimicrobial and immune-enhancing properties. Garlic contains allicin, a compound that has been shown to boost the disease-fighting response of some types of white blood cells in the body when they encounter viruses, such as those that cause the common cold or flu.

Herbal Remedies for Seasonal Allergies

Dr. Sebi's approach to treating seasonal allergies emphasizes the use of natural herbal remedies that support immune function and reduce inflammatory responses. His holistic strategy involves herbs that cleanse the body, particularly the blood and mucous membranes, which play a crucial role in managing allergic reactions.

One of the primary herbs Dr. Sebi recommended for allergies is nettle. Nettle is highly valued for its natural antihistamine properties, which come from its ability to block the body's production of histamine, the chemical responsible for many allergy symptoms such as runny nose, watery eyes, and itching. Drinking nettle tea daily during allergy season can help mitigate these symptoms and strengthen the immune system.

Burdock root is another key herb in Dr. Sebi's arsenal for fighting allergies. Known for its potent blood-cleansing properties, burdock root works by helping to remove toxins from the bloodstream, including allergens that trigger histamine reactions. This cleansing action can lead to a reduction in the severity of allergic responses. Burdock root can be consumed in several ways, such as in teas or as a cooked vegetable, making it a versatile addition to an allergy-fighting regimen.

Dr. Sebi also highlighted the importance of maintaining a clean internal environment to help alleviate allergies. His dietary recommendations, such as avoiding mucus-forming foods like dairy and processed grains, complement the use of herbal remedies by minimizing the body's mucous production and inflammation, common issues during allergy seasons.

Book 6: Dr. Sebi Herpes Cure

Overview of Herpes and Its Impact on the Body

Dr. Sebi's approach to understanding and treating herpes involves a holistic perspective on the virus and its effects on the body. Herpes simplex virus (HSV) manifests in two primary forms: HSV-1, which typically causes oral herpes, and HSV-2, which usually results in genital herpes, although both types can affect either area of the body.

Herpes simplex virus is highly contagious and is transmitted through direct contact with infected body fluids or lesions. The virus is characterized by episodes of active outbreaks, which include blisters and sores on the affected areas. Between outbreaks, the virus lies dormant in the nerve cells, which can make it challenging to treat.

The most immediate and noticeable impact of herpes is the outbreak of painful sores and blisters. These outbreaks can cause significant discomfort and emotional distress. However, the impact of herpes goes beyond these visible symptoms. On a systemic level, recurrent outbreaks can signal an underlying imbalance in the immune system. The virus can cause persistent inflammation and may weaken the immune system, making the body more susceptible to other infections and diseases.

Beyond the physical symptoms, herpes often carries a significant psychological burden due to the stigma associated with the condition. This can lead to feelings of shame, anxiety, and depression, affecting an individual's overall quality of life and emotional well-being.

Dr. Sebi advocated for addressing herpes by strengthening the body's immune system and using natural remedies to reduce the frequency and severity of outbreaks. His holistic approach emphasized the importance of a healthy diet, herbal supplements, and lifestyle changes to support the body's natural healing processes and manage the effects of the virus.

Dr. Sebi's Specific Treatment for Herpes

Dr. Sebi's specific treatment for herpes emphasized using natural, holistic methods to strengthen the body's immune system and combat the herpes simplex virus. He believed that enhancing the body's natural healing capabilities and adopting a diet that promotes alkalinity could significantly reduce the severity and frequency of herpes outbreaks.

Central to Dr. Sebi's approach was adherence to a strictly alkaline diet. This diet involves consuming large amounts of raw and whole foods such as fruits, vegetables, nuts, and seeds that are approved on Dr. Sebi's nutritional guide. He taught that reducing the body's acidity could help create an environment less conducive to viral replication, thereby suppressing the activity of the virus. Foods particularly helpful for those with herpes include sea moss, which is rich in essential minerals that boost immune function, and burdock root, known for its powerful blood purifying properties which help eliminate toxins and support overall immune health.

Additionally, Dr. Sebi recommended specific herbal supplements known for their antiviral and immune-boosting properties. These included elderberry, which has been shown to help fight viruses and improve immune response, and echinacea, which can enhance the body's natural immune function and reduce inflammation, potentially decreasing the severity of symptoms during outbreaks.

Dr. Sebi also stressed the importance of adequate hydration and detoxification. Drinking plenty of natural spring water and consuming herbal teas designed to cleanse the liver and kidneys can help flush out toxins and support the body's natural defenses.

Overall, Dr. Sebi's treatment for herpes aimed not just at managing symptoms but at fundamentally improving the body's alkaline state and immune function to naturally suppress the virus over time.

Treatment Planning and Phases

Dr. Sebi's approach to treating herpes was structured around a comprehensive plan that involved several phases, each designed to detoxify the body, rebuild the immune system, and directly combat the herpes simplex virus. Here's an outline of the treatment planning and phases according to Dr. Sebi's methodology:

Phase 1: Detoxification

The initial phase of the treatment focuses on detoxifying the body, which is crucial for removing toxins and impurities that can impair immune function. Dr. Sebi recommended a strict dietary regimen that eliminates all acid-forming foods and incorporates alkaline foods that cleanse and nourish the body. Herbal detox teas and supplements such as burdock root, dandelion, and sarsaparilla are used to enhance the cleansing process, specifically targeting the liver, kidneys, and blood.

Phase 2: Nutritional Replenishment

After detoxification, the second phase involves replenishing the body with essential nutrients to restore immune health. This phase continues the use of an alkaline diet rich in vitamins, minerals, and antioxidants found in whole foods like fruits, vegetables, and whole grains. Key supplements like sea moss, which is high in minerals necessary for cellular functions, and bladderwrack, another source of essential nutrients, are emphasized. This phase aims to strengthen the body's natural defenses against viral infections.

Phase 3: Antiviral Treatments

The third phase introduces more specific antiviral herbs that Dr. Sebi identified as effective against the herpes simplex virus. Herbs such as elderberry, which has proven antiviral properties against herpes simplex, and garlic, known for its broad-spectrum antimicrobial and immune-boosting qualities, are incorporated. This phase focuses on directly suppressing the virus's ability to replicate and reducing the frequency and severity of outbreaks.

Phase 4: Maintenance and Prevention

The final phase is about maintaining the health improvements achieved and preventing future outbreaks. This involves continuing with a balanced alkaline diet, regular intake of supportive herbs, and adherence to lifestyle practices that support overall health and stress management. Regular monitoring and adjustments are recommended to ensure the body remains in optimal health and capable of managing the herpes virus long-term.

Preventing Herpes with An Alkaline Diet

Dr. Sebi advocated strongly for the use of an alkaline diet as a means to prevent and manage herpes outbreaks. According to his philosophy, maintaining a high level of bodily alkalinity reduces the environment in which the herpes virus can thrive. Here's how an alkaline diet can play a crucial role in preventing herpes, according to Dr. Sebi's teachings:

The cornerstone of Dr. Sebi's approach is the belief that excessive acidity within the body creates an ideal environment for viruses like herpes simplex to replicate and manifest as symptoms. By adjusting the diet to increase alkalinity, the body's natural resistance to viruses is enhanced, making it less hospitable for the virus to survive and proliferate.

An alkaline diet focuses on consuming natural plant-based foods that are low in acidity and high in minerals. Foods such as leafy greens, ripe fruits, and certain grains like quinoa and amaranth are staples of the alkaline diet. These foods help balance the body's pH levels, boost the immune system, and provide essential nutrients that promote overall health.

Dr. Sebi recommended eliminating all forms of processed and artificial foods, dairy products, meats, and sugars, which can increase acidity and inflammation in the body. Instead, his dietary guidelines emphasize natural, whole foods that support cellular health and detoxification.

Herbs also play a significant role in the alkaline diet for preventing herpes. Herbs like burdock root, which cleanses the blood, and sea moss, which is rich in iodine and other minerals, are suggested to improve immune function and reduce the likelihood of outbreaks.

Hydration is another crucial factor in maintaining alkalinity in the body. Dr. Sebi advised drinking plenty of spring water and consuming hydrating foods to help flush toxins from the body and support overall cellular function.

Testimonials and Case Studies

Dr. Sebi's holistic approach to treating herpes has garnered a variety of testimonials and case studies from individuals who have followed his methods. These personal accounts often emphasize significant improvements in managing and reducing herpes symptoms, with some suggesting a dramatic reduction in the frequency and severity of outbreaks.

Many individuals who adopted Dr. Sebi's alkaline diet and herbal treatments report not only fewer and less severe outbreaks but also an overall increase in energy and well-being. For example, some have shared that transitioning to an alkaline diet helped them feel more energized and less prone to the fatigue and malaise that can accompany herpes outbreaks. Others note improvements in skin health and a reduction in other symptoms related to inflammation.

Additionally, some case studies highlight the role of specific herbs and dietary changes in managing the virus. People often cite the use of sea moss for its high mineral content and immune-boosting properties, elderberry for its antiviral effects, and burdock root for its ability to detoxify the blood as key components in their recovery and management of herpes.

These testimonials and case studies contribute to a body of anecdotal evidence supporting Dr. Sebi's claim that a holistic, natural approach can significantly impact the management of herpes. While individual results vary, and such testimonials do not equate to scientific proof, they provide compelling narratives about the potential benefits of following Dr. Sebi's dietary guidelines and herbal treatments for those suffering from herpes.

Supporting Immune Health to Combat Herpes

Dr. Sebi's approach to combating herpes centers heavily on supporting and boosting the immune system. A strong immune system is crucial for fighting off the herpes simplex virus and managing outbreaks effectively. According to Dr. Sebi, reinforcing the body's natural defenses through diet, supplements, and lifestyle adjustments can significantly help in managing herpes. Here's how he proposed to support immune health to combat herpes:

Alkaline Diet: At the core of Dr. Sebi's recommendations is the alkaline diet, which is designed to increase the body's alkalinity. The herpes virus thrives in acidic conditions, and by promoting alkalinity through diet, it becomes harder for the virus to survive and replicate. The diet includes a heavy emphasis on raw vegetables, fruits, nuts, and legumes that are high in essential nutrients and have alkalizing effects.

Herbal Supplements: Dr. Sebi suggested using specific herbs that have immune-boosting properties. Herbs such as elderberry, which is known for its antiviral and immune-enhancing capabilities, and burdock root, which purifies the blood and improves lymphatic function, are staples in his protocol. Other recommended herbs include sea moss for its high mineral content that nourishes the body and boosts immune function, and sarsaparilla, known for its ability to increase bioavailability of other herbs and cleanse the blood.

Adequate Hydration: Keeping the body well-hydrated is essential for immune health. Dr. Sebi emphasized the importance of drinking plenty of spring water to help flush toxins from the body and support cellular functions, which is vital for a strong immune system.

Stress Management: Stress is a known trigger for herpes outbreaks and can weaken the immune system. Dr. Sebi recommended practices such as meditation, deep breathing exercises, and spending time in nature to reduce stress levels. Managing stress effectively not only helps in preventing outbreaks but also aids in maintaining overall immune resilience.

Sufficient Rest: Adequate sleep is essential for immune health. Dr. Sebi advised ensuring regular, restful sleep as a critical component of the regimen to combat herpes. Sleep is when the body repairs itself, and compromising on sleep can weaken the immune system, making the body more susceptible to outbreaks.

Lifestyle Adjustments for Managing Herpes

Dr. Sebi's approach to managing herpes emphasizes the importance of overall lifestyle adjustments aimed at enhancing the body's natural ability to combat the herpes virus and minimize outbreaks. These modifications are critical for supporting immune function and overall well-being.

Stress is a significant trigger for herpes outbreaks, as it weakens the immune system, making it harder for the body to fight off the virus. Dr. Sebi recommended incorporating practices such as meditation, yoga, and deep breathing exercises into daily routines to help maintain a calm and balanced mental state, thereby reducing the likelihood of stress-induced outbreaks.

Ensuring sufficient and quality sleep is another critical factor in managing herpes. Sleep is a time of healing and restoration for the body, including the immune system. Dr. Sebi advised maintaining a regular sleep schedule and creating a restful sleeping environment to promote deep, restorative sleep.

Regular physical activity boosts overall health and immune function, which is vital for fighting the herpes virus. Dr. Sebi encouraged engaging in moderate exercises such as walking, swimming, or cycling, which help reduce stress and improve physical health without overly exhausting the body.

Moderate sun exposure is encouraged for its vitamin D boosting effects, essential for immune health. However, Dr. Sebi also warned against excessive sun exposure, which can trigger herpes outbreaks, particularly oral herpes around the lips. Using a natural, chemical-free sunscreen and monitoring time spent in direct sunlight can help manage this risk.

Certain irritants can trigger herpes outbreaks, including harsh chemicals found in soaps, body care products, and laundry detergents. Dr. Sebi recommended using natural and mild products to avoid such triggers. Additionally, for genital herpes, wearing loose, breathable clothing and avoiding tight garments can help prevent irritation that may lead to outbreaks.

Engaging in holistic practices such as acupuncture or reflexology was also suggested by Dr. Sebi to help balance the body's energy systems and improve overall well-being, which can be beneficial in managing herpes.

Stress and Its Role in Herpes Outbreaks

Dr. Sebi emphasized the significant role stress plays in triggering herpes outbreaks and its overall impact on the body's ability to manage the herpes simplex virus. According to his teachings, stress weakens the immune system, which is crucial for controlling the virus's activity and managing the frequency and severity of outbreaks.

Stress triggers the body's fight or flight response, which causes various physiological changes, including the release of stress hormones like cortisol. Elevated cortisol levels can suppress immune function, making the body more susceptible to infections, including the reactivation of dormant viruses like herpes simplex.

Dr. Sebi believed that managing stress is a critical component of any treatment plan for herpes. He advocated for adopting a holistic approach to stress management, which includes:

1. Dietary Choices: Following an alkaline diet to help maintain balance in the body and reduce the acidity that can worsen the body's stress response.

2. Herbal Remedies: Utilizing calming herbs such as chamomile, lavender, and valerian, which can help reduce stress and promote relaxation.

3. Meditation and Mindfulness: Engaging in practices that foster mental clarity and relaxation, such as meditation and mindfulness exercises, to help mitigate the effects of stress.

4. Physical Activity: Incorporating regular exercise, which can help lower stress levels and improve overall physical health. Activities such as yoga and tai chi are especially beneficial as they also focus on breath control and mental discipline.

5. Adequate Rest: Ensuring sufficient sleep each night, which is essential for the immune system to repair and regenerate, helping to keep the body strong and better able to fend off viral activity.

6. Natural Environments: Spending time in nature to help reduce stress levels and promote a sense of well-being. Studies show that natural settings have a calming effect and can help reduce cortisol levels.

Book 7: Dr. Sebi Kidney Health

Importance of Kidney Health

Dr. Sebi placed a significant emphasis on kidney health, viewing the kidneys as crucial organs in maintaining the body's overall wellness and balance. He highlighted that healthy kidneys perform essential tasks including filtering blood, removing toxins, and balancing bodily fluids and electrolytes.

The kidneys are responsible for filtering waste products from the blood and excreting them through urine. This detoxification process is critical because it protects the body from toxicity and prevents a buildup of waste that can lead to various health issues. Dr. Sebi stressed that impaired kidney function could lead to the accumulation of toxins in the body, which can cause numerous problems, ranging from minor ailments to severe diseases.

Additionally, kidneys help regulate blood pressure by controlling the volume of blood (by adjusting the volume of water excreted) and the amount of artery-constricting salts in the body. This regulation is vital for preventing hypertension, which is a risk factor for kidney disease and other cardiovascular conditions.

Kidneys also play a key role in bone health by producing an active form of vitamin D that promotes calcium absorption and bone growth. Without proper kidney function, the body may suffer from weakened bones, increasing the risk of fractures and osteoporosis.

Furthermore, the kidneys produce important hormones that aid in the production of red blood cells, which carry oxygen throughout the body. These hormones are crucial in maintaining adequate energy levels and overall vitality.

Understanding the critical functions of the kidneys, Dr. Sebi advocated for a diet rich in natural, plant-based foods that support kidney health. He recommended avoiding excessive protein, salt, and other substances that can strain the kidneys. Instead, he promoted the consumption of fruits and vegetables that are high in antioxidants and natural diuretics which help cleanse and protect the kidneys.

Diets and Herbs for Kidney Support

Dr. Sebi emphasized the importance of dietary choices and herbal remedies in supporting kidney health. He advocated for a plant-based alkaline diet along with specific herbs that aid in cleansing and nourishing the kidneys, helping to enhance their function and prevent damage. Here's an overview of the diets and herbs recommended by Dr. Sebi for kidney support:

Alkaline Diet for Kidney Health:

Dr. Sebi recommended an alkaline diet to help reduce the strain on the kidneys by minimizing the production of acidic waste in the body. This diet includes:

- Fruits: Such as apples, bananas, dates, and grapes, which are gentle on the kidneys and help in cleansing.

- Vegetables: Including cucumbers, bell peppers, avocados, and kale, which are high in antioxidants and essential nutrients that support kidney function.

- Grains: Small amounts of alkaline grains like quinoa, rye, and wild rice can be beneficial.

- Nuts and Seeds: Moderate amounts of almonds and Brazil nuts are recommended for their nutrient content, particularly magnesium, which is beneficial for kidney health.

Herbal Remedies:

Dr. Sebi prescribed specific herbs known for their renal benefits, which help in detoxifying and healing the kidneys:

- Burdock Root: Known for its blood purifying properties, it helps to cleanse the kidneys, remove waste, and increase urine flow.

- Dandelion Root: Acts as a diuretic, helping to eliminate toxic build-up in the kidneys and improving filtration functions.
- Parsley: Another diuretic herb that helps cleanse the kidneys and bladder, parsley is rich in vitamins and minerals, supporting overall kidney health.

- Nettle: Historically used for kidney and urinary tract infections, nettle helps flush harmful bacteria from the urinary tract.

Hydration:

Dr. Sebi also stressed the importance of adequate hydration. Drinking sufficient natural spring water helps to flush toxins from the kidneys, maintain a healthy blood volume, and keep electrolytes in balance.

Lifestyle Changes:

In addition to diet and herbs, Dr. Sebi advised reducing exposure to toxins and chemicals that can harm the kidneys, such as pharmaceuticals, non-organic foods, and environmental pollutants. Regular physical activity and avoiding excessive protein intake were also part of his recommendations to maintain optimal kidney health.

Specific Treatment Plans for Kidney Diseases

Dr. Sebi's approach to treating kidney diseases involved specific treatment plans that centered around a holistic dietary and herbal regimen aimed at cleansing, repairing, and optimizing kidney function. These plans are designed to reduce the burden on the kidneys, allowing them to heal and function more efficiently. Here's a detailed look at Dr. Sebi's specific treatment plans for kidney diseases:

Alkaline Diet: Central to Dr. Sebi's treatment for kidney diseases is adhering to a strictly alkaline diet. This diet helps reduce acidity in the body, which is crucial because high acidity can further stress the kidneys, exacerbate inflammation, and contribute to the accumulation of waste products. The diet includes:

- High intake of fresh vegetables and fruits that help cleanse the kidneys and provide essential nutrients and antioxidants.

- Inclusion of natural diuretics like cucumber and watermelon, which help increase urine output and facilitate the removal of toxins.

- Limited consumption of proteins, particularly animal proteins, as excessive protein can strain the kidneys.

Herbal Remedies: Dr. Sebi recommended specific herbs known for their kidney-supportive properties:

- Burdock Root: This herb is celebrated for its ability to detoxify the blood, helping to relieve the kidneys of some of their filtering responsibilities.

- Dandelion Root: Acts as a natural diuretic, supporting the kidneys in eliminating waste and excess water, and helping to manage blood pressure levels.

- Uva Ursi: Known for its antiseptic and astringent properties, Uva Ursi is used to treat urinary tract infections, which are common in individuals suffering from chronic kidney conditions.

- Nettle: Besides being a natural diuretic, nettle helps in supporting blood flow and nutrient uptake, which is vital for kidney health.

Hydration: Proper hydration is fundamental in Dr. Sebi's treatment plans for kidney diseases. Consuming adequate amounts of natural spring water is essential to help the kidneys flush out sodium and toxins from the body.

Stress Management and Exercise: Stress reduction techniques such as yoga and meditation are recommended to reduce physical stress, which can impact kidney health. Light to moderate exercise helps maintain circulation and overall health without overtaxing the kidneys.

Avoidance of Toxins: Dr. Sebi stressed the importance of reducing exposure to toxins that can worsen kidney health. This includes avoiding certain medications, chemicals, and environmental pollutants as much as possible.

Kidney Disease Prevention

Dr. Sebi placed a strong emphasis on preventing kidney disease through natural and holistic methods, focusing on diet, herbal treatments, and lifestyle adjustments to support kidney health and prevent the onset of disease. Here's an overview of his approach to kidney disease prevention:

Central to preventing kidney disease, according to Dr. Sebi, is maintaining an alkaline diet. This diet minimizes the intake of acidic foods that can burden the kidneys and promotes the consumption of foods that help regulate the body's pH levels. Foods recommended in this diet include fresh vegetables like cucumbers, bell peppers, and leafy greens which are high in antioxidants and help reduce inflammation. Fruits such as berries, apples, and bananas provide essential vitamins and minerals while supporting detoxification processes. Nuts and seeds, particularly almonds and hemp seeds, offer beneficial fats and protein content that are easy on the kidneys.

Adequate hydration is vital for kidney health. Dr. Sebi advocated for the consumption of plenty of spring water to help flush toxins from the kidneys, aiding in their proper functioning and preventing build-up that can lead to disease.

Dr. Sebi recommended several herbs known for supporting kidney health, including dandelion root, which acts as a natural diuretic to help the kidneys flush out excess toxins and salt. Nettle is rich in nutrients that support overall kidney function and health, making it another key component of his preventative strategy.

Daily Kidney Health Maintenance Tips

Dr. Sebi emphasized the importance of daily practices to maintain kidney health, focusing on diet, hydration, and natural remedies. Here's a detailed look at his recommendations:

Maintaining an alkaline diet is crucial for kidney health. Dr. Sebi advised eating a diet rich in fruits, vegetables, and whole foods that help reduce acidity in the body and promote kidney function. Specific foods such as watermelon, cucumbers, and leafy greens are particularly beneficial because they are hydrating and help flush toxins from the kidneys.

Hydration is another key aspect of kidney health. Dr. Sebi stressed the importance of drinking adequate amounts of natural spring water throughout the day to help the kidneys filter waste from the blood and excrete toxins through urine effectively. This constant hydration supports the kidneys in their critical functions and helps prevent the buildup of substances that could lead to kidney stones or other complications.

Incorporating herbal remedies known for supporting kidney health was also a significant part of Dr. Sebi's approach. Herbs like dandelion root and nettle are excellent for their diuretic properties, helping to eliminate excess water and toxins, thus relieving the kidneys from overwork. These herbs can be taken as teas or supplements.

Reducing intake of salts and animal proteins can also aid in maintaining kidney health by reducing the workload on these organs, thus preventing potential stress and damage. Dr. Sebi recommended minimizing the consumption of these substances to help keep the kidneys functioning smoothly.

Regular detoxification through fasting or consuming detoxifying foods and herbs helps keep the kidneys clean and efficient. This practice can be particularly beneficial for clearing out any accumulations that might impair kidney function over time.

Natural Diuretics and Their Role in Kidney Health

Dr. Sebi recognized the importance of natural diuretics in promoting kidney health. Natural diuretics help the body eliminate excess fluid and salts through urine, which is crucial for maintaining the balance of body fluids and preventing conditions that stress the kidneys, such as high blood pressure and edema.

Natural diuretics support the kidneys' primary function of filtering and eliminating waste from the blood. By increasing urine production, these substances help clear the kidneys of excess sodium and water, reducing the burden on these vital organs and helping them to function more efficiently.

Reducing blood pressure is another key benefit of natural diuretics. Accumulation of excess fluid in the body can lead to increased blood pressure, which is a major risk factor for kidney disease. By helping to remove this excess fluid, natural diuretics alleviate pressure on blood vessels and the kidneys, thus supporting overall cardiovascular and renal health.

Dr. Sebi often highlighted several plants and herbs as effective natural diuretics, including:

- Dandelion: Both the leaf and root of dandelion are used for their diuretic properties. They help increase urine production and decrease swelling, which can relieve pressure on the kidneys.

- Parsley: Known to act as a mild diuretic, parsley helps to flush out excess fluid from the body, preventing the buildup of toxins and supporting kidney health.

- Hibiscus: The flowers of the hibiscus plant are used in teas and are known for their diuretic effects as well as their ability to help lower blood pressure levels.

- Cucumber: High in water content and naturally diuretic, cucumbers help hydrate and cleanse the kidneys.

- Watermelon: This fruit is not only rich in water but also in nutrients that support detoxification and urine production, aiding kidney function.

Impact of Hydration on Kidney Function

Dr. Sebi stressed the critical role of hydration in maintaining kidney health and overall bodily functions. Proper hydration is essential because the kidneys rely on a sufficient flow of fluids to flush out waste products and toxins through the urine. Without adequate water intake, kidney function can become impaired, leading to a buildup of toxins in the body that can cause various health issues.

Water is the primary medium through which the kidneys filter waste from the blood. Adequate hydration ensures that the kidneys can produce enough urine to remove these wastes effectively. Insufficient water intake reduces urine output, which may cause waste products to accumulate in the body, potentially leading to kidney stones and other renal complications.

Staying well-hydrated is key to preventing the formation of kidney stones. Kidney stones form when certain minerals and salts in the urine concentrate and solidify. Adequate hydration dilutes these substances in the urine, making stone formation less likely.

Furthermore, hydration is crucial for regulating blood volume and blood pressure. The kidneys play a fundamental role in managing blood pressure by controlling the volume of blood, which is influenced by the body's hydration levels. Proper hydration helps maintain normal blood volume and pressure, reducing strain on the kidneys and supporting their healthy function.

Dr. Sebi advocated drinking plenty of natural spring water throughout the day to support kidney function. He recommended avoiding dehydrating beverages such as those containing caffeine and alcohol, which can increase the kidneys' workload. Instead, he suggested herbal teas and natural fruit juices in moderation to supplement water intake, ensuring that the kidneys are well-supported in their critical roles in detoxification and maintaining homeostasis in the body.

Detoxification and Kidney Cleansing

Dr. Sebi emphasized the importance of detoxification and kidney cleansing as fundamental aspects of maintaining kidney health and overall vitality. He believed that regular cleansing of the kidneys helps remove accumulated toxins and waste products, which is essential for preventing disease and ensuring that the kidneys function efficiently. Here's an exploration of Dr. Sebi's approach to detoxification and kidney cleansing:

Herbal Cleansing: Dr. Sebi recommended specific herbs that are known for their kidney-cleansing properties. These herbs include:

- Dandelion Root: Acts as a natural diuretic, stimulating the kidneys to eliminate toxins through urine. It helps to cleanse the blood and has a beneficial effect on both kidney function and digestion.

- Burdock Root: Known for its blood purifying properties, burdock root is also effective in promoting increased urine flow, helping to flush out kidney stones and other toxins from the kidneys.

- Parsley: A powerful diuretic, parsley helps increase urine production and flush out toxins. Its high antioxidant content also supports kidney health by combating oxidative stress.

- Uva Ursi: Traditionally used to treat urinary tract infections, Uva Ursi cleanses the kidneys and helps balance urine acidity, which can help prevent the formation of kidney stones.

Alkaline Diet: Dr. Sebi's alkaline diet is designed to reduce the load on the kidneys by minimizing acid waste production. By consuming alkaline-forming foods, the kidneys are less stressed, and their cleansing processes are more effective. The diet includes plenty of fresh fruits and vegetables, particularly leafy greens, which help maintain an alkaline environment in the body.

Hydration: Adequate hydration is crucial for kidney health. Dr. Sebi stressed the importance of drinking plenty of water each day to help the kidneys flush out soluble waste. The water helps keep the kidneys clean and supports their ability to function properly.

Avoiding Toxins: Part of detoxification involves reducing the intake of substances that can harm the kidneys. Dr. Sebi advised against the consumption of processed foods, alcohol, and excessive proteins, all of which can increase the kidneys' workload and contribute to toxin accumulation.

Regular Cleansing Routines: Dr. Sebi recommended periodic detoxification routines that include fasting or consuming specific detoxifying foods and herbal teas. These routines help reset the body's systems, including the kidneys, promoting better health and preventing disease.

Book 8: Dr. Sebi Anxiety Cure

Understanding Anxiety and Its Effects

Dr. Sebi's perspective on anxiety involves understanding it as not just a psychological condition, but as a symptom influenced by overall body health, particularly diet and nutrition. According to Dr. Sebi, anxiety can be significantly impacted by the body's physical state and the substances we consume. Here's a deeper look into his views on understanding anxiety and its effects:

Holistic View of Anxiety: Dr. Sebi saw anxiety as a disorder that is not solely mental but is deeply connected to the body's physiological and biochemical states. He believed that imbalances in the body could manifest as mental health issues, including anxiety. This holistic view considers not only the mind but also the body and spirit in the treatment and understanding of anxiety.

Physical Effects of Anxiety: Anxiety triggers the body's stress response, releasing adrenaline and cortisol, hormones that prepare the body for a 'fight or flight' reaction. While this response can be beneficial in acute situations, chronic activation can have detrimental effects, such as increased heart rate, elevated blood pressure, and a weakened immune system. Over time, these effects can lead to more serious health problems, including heart disease, digestive disorders, and decreased immune function.

Diet and Anxiety: Dr. Sebi emphasized the role of diet in managing anxiety. He advocated for an alkaline diet rich in nutrients that support brain function and reduce inflammation, which can exacerbate anxiety symptoms. Foods high in minerals like magnesium and potassium help to calm the nervous system and reduce the physical reactions to stress.

Detoxification and Anxiety: According to Dr. Sebi, detoxifying the body can help alleviate anxiety by removing toxins that may affect brain function and mood. Herbs like burdock root, which purifies the blood, and dandelion, which supports liver health, are recommended to aid in detoxification processes. Cleansing the body of accumulated toxins helps to restore optimal functioning and balance, reducing the likelihood and severity of anxiety symptoms.

Herbal Remedies for Anxiety: Dr. Sebi also recommended specific herbs known for their calming effects on the mind and body. Herbs such as valerian root, which can help reduce the time it takes to fall asleep and improve sleep quality, and St. John's Wort, known for its potential to treat mild to moderate depression, are examples of natural treatments for managing anxiety.

Natural Treatments for Anxiety

Dr. Sebi's approach to treating anxiety naturally involves a combination of specific diets, herbal remedies, and lifestyle modifications aimed at addressing both the symptoms and underlying causes of anxiety. He focused on restoring balance to the body's biochemistry, reducing inflammation, and enhancing overall mental wellness.

Central to Dr. Sebi's method of treating anxiety is adherence to an alkaline diet rich in whole, plant-based foods. He believed that a diet high in alkaline foods helps reduce inflammation in the body and supports brain health, which is crucial for managing anxiety. Foods such as avocados, kale, almonds, wild rice, and chickpeas are emphasized for their nutrient density and alkaline properties. These foods help stabilize mood and improve overall brain function.

Dr. Sebi also recommended several herbs known for their calming effects to help manage anxiety. Herbs like chamomile, which is well-known for its gentle soothing and sedative properties, and valerian root, often used for its ability to help decrease anxiety and improve sleep quality, are key components of his treatment plan. St. John's Wort is another herb he suggested for its potential benefits in treating mild to moderate depression, which can often co-occur with anxiety disorders.

In addition to dietary changes and herbal treatments, Dr. Sebi advocated for incorporating regular physical activity and adequate rest into daily routines, both of which are essential for reducing stress and improving mental health. Exercise, particularly gentle forms like yoga and walking, can significantly decrease anxiety levels and promote a sense of well-being.

Hydration was another critical element in Dr. Sebi's anxiety treatment protocol. Drinking plenty of spring water throughout the day helps flush out toxins that can affect overall physiological and mental health.

Recommended Herbs and Foods

Dr. Sebi's approach to managing and curing anxiety included a specific focus on herbs and foods that naturally calm the mind, reduce stress, and restore balance to the body's systems. He emphasized the importance of incorporating certain herbs and foods into the diet to help alleviate anxiety symptoms.

Valerian Root was highly recommended due to its sedative properties, which help to calm the nerves and improve sleep quality. It is particularly effective in helping individuals relax and reduce the physiological symptoms of anxiety.

Chamomile was another herb favored by Dr. Sebi for its calming effects. Known for its gentle, soothing properties, chamomile tea can be consumed throughout the day to help manage stress and promote a sense of well-being.

St. John's Wort was included for its potential to treat mild to moderate depression, which can often accompany anxiety disorders. This herb helps to enhance mood and alleviate emotional distress associated with anxiety.

In terms of foods, Dr. Sebi recommended a diet rich in alkaline plant-based foods that support overall brain health and reduce inflammation, a contributor to anxiety. Key foods included:

Avocados, which are high in B vitamins and essential fats that help to nourish the brain and maintain proper nerve function. The natural fats in avocados also contribute to healthy blood flow, which is essential for a healthy brain.

Almonds were suggested for their rich magnesium content, a mineral known for its ability to promote relaxation and reduce anxiety. Magnesium helps in regulating the nervous system and mitigating the stress response.

Wild rice, as a complex carbohydrate, helps in the slow release of glucose into the bloodstream, providing a steady source of energy which can help in stabilizing mood and preventing anxiety spikes.

Leafy greens like kale and spinach are high in magnesium and folate, which are crucial for neurotransmitter function and overall mental well-being.

Relaxation Techniques and Meditation

Dr. Sebi emphasized the importance of relaxation techniques and meditation in his approach to curing anxiety, advocating for their regular practice to help calm the mind, reduce stress, and restore emotional balance. He believed that incorporating these practices into daily life could significantly enhance an individual's ability to manage anxiety and improve overall mental health.

Meditation, in particular, was a cornerstone of Dr. Sebi's recommendations. He encouraged individuals to engage in meditation to foster a deep sense of peace and relaxation. Meditation helps to quiet the mind and can significantly reduce the levels of stress hormones in the body, making it a powerful tool for managing anxiety. Dr. Sebi suggested finding a quiet space each day to practice mindfulness or guided meditation, focusing on deep breathing and the release of mental clutter.

Deep breathing exercises were also a key part of Dr. Sebi's approach. He taught that deep, rhythmic breathing enhances oxygen supply to the brain and helps to activate the parasympathetic nervous system, which is responsible for the body's 'rest and digest' responses as opposed to the 'fight or flight' responses of the sympathetic nervous system. This shift can dramatically reduce anxiety and promote a more balanced emotional state.

In addition to meditation and deep breathing, Dr. Sebi recommended other relaxation techniques such as yoga, which combines physical postures, breathing exercises, and meditation. The practice of yoga helps to improve physical flexibility, reduce stress, and elevate mood, all of which are beneficial for anxiety management.

Dr. Sebi advised making these practices a regular part of one's lifestyle to not only cope with anxiety when it arises but also to cultivate a lasting state of mental and emotional well-being. By regularly engaging in relaxation techniques and meditation, individuals can build resilience against stress and create a solid foundation for mental health, aligning with Dr. Sebi's holistic approach to healing and wellness.

Establishing a Daily Routine for Managing Anxiety

Dr. Sebi believed that establishing a daily routine could play a crucial role in managing anxiety effectively. A consistent routine helps to create a sense of predictability and control, which can significantly reduce feelings of stress and anxiety. He emphasized that this routine should encompass diet, physical activity, and mindfulness practices, all tailored to enhance mental health and emotional equilibrium.

Starting the day with a morning ritual was a key component. Dr. Sebi recommended beginning with herbal teas such as chamomile or ginger, which calm the nervous system and prepare the body and mind for the day ahead. Following this, he advised engaging in some form of physical activity, whether it was yoga, stretching, or a gentle walk. This physical movement helps to release endorphins, improving mood and decreasing anxiety levels.

Nutrition plays a pivotal role in Dr. Sebi's daily routine for managing anxiety. He advocated for a plant-based alkaline diet, rich in nutrients that support brain health and reduce inflammation. Meals should include plenty of leafy greens, fruits, nuts, and seeds, all of which contribute to overall well-being and help mitigate anxiety. Dr. Sebi also emphasized the importance of regular meal times, which help regulate the body's internal clock and reduce stress.

Incorporating meditation and deep breathing exercises into the daily routine is also vital. Dr. Sebi suggested setting aside specific times each day for these practices, particularly during moments of transition such as midday and before bedtime. These practices help to center the mind, ease any accumulated stress, and prepare the body for restful sleep.

Lastly, Dr. Sebi stressed the importance of adequate sleep as part of the daily routine. Establishing a regular bedtime that allows for full, restorative sleep cycles is crucial in managing anxiety. Sleep helps to rejuvenate the body and mind, making it easier to handle stress and maintain emotional balance throughout the day.

Herbal Teas for Stress and Anxiety Relief

Dr. Sebi recognized the therapeutic benefits of herbal teas in managing stress and anxiety. He advocated for the use of specific herbs that have natural calming properties to help soothe the nervous system and alleviate mental discomfort. These herbal teas provide a natural way to relax, reduce tension, and promote a sense of well-being.

Chamomile tea was highly recommended by Dr. Sebi for its well-known sedative effects, making it ideal for reducing stress and anxiety. The compounds in chamomile, particularly apigenin, bind to certain receptors in the brain that decrease anxiety and initiate sleep, helping to calm the mind and body.

Lemon balm tea is another herb favored for its ability to relieve symptoms of stress and anxiety. It has a mild sedative effect and is known for improving mood and cognitive function, which can be particularly beneficial during times of mental stress.

Dr. Sebi also suggested the use of passionflower tea, which studies have shown can help reduce anxiety as effectively as some prescription medications. Passionflower works by increasing levels of gamma-aminobutyric acid (GABA) in the brain, a chemical that lowers brain activity and helps to promote relaxation.

Valerian root tea was included in his recommendations for its potent calming effects that can improve sleep quality and reduce anxiety. Valerian is often used as a sleep aid due to its ability to help relax the central nervous system, promote tranquility, and alleviate anxiety.

These herbal teas are part of Dr. Sebi's holistic approach to health, which integrates natural remedies into daily practices to support overall wellness. By incorporating these teas into a regular routine, individuals can enjoy their soothing effects and potentially reduce the need for pharmaceutical interventions for stress and anxiety.

Role of Exercise in Reducing Anxiety

Dr. Sebi emphasized the importance of exercise as a powerful tool in reducing anxiety. Regular physical activity plays a crucial role in maintaining mental health by helping to alleviate stress, enhance mood, and improve overall emotional well-being. Exercise stimulates the production of endorphins, often referred to as 'feel-good' hormones, which are natural mood lifters. Additionally, engaging in physical activity helps to reduce the levels of the body's stress hormones, such as adrenaline and cortisol.

Dr. Sebi recommended incorporating forms of exercise that not only improve physical health but also promote mental relaxation. Activities such as yoga and tai chi are particularly beneficial because they combine physical movement with breathing techniques and meditation, providing a holistic approach to stress reduction. These practices help focus the mind and are known for their calming effects on the nervous system.

Walking, especially in natural surroundings, was another form of exercise suggested by Dr. Sebi to combat anxiety. The rhythmic nature of walking and the exposure to a peaceful environment can significantly reduce stress levels and improve mental clarity.

Moreover, Dr. Sebi pointed out that regular exercise helps to improve sleep patterns, which can be adversely affected by anxiety. Better sleep not only helps to reduce stress but also improves cognitive function and emotional resilience, making it easier to handle anxiety.

Importance of Sleep in Managing Anxiety

Dr. Sebi highlighted the critical role that sleep plays in managing anxiety, emphasizing its importance in both physical health and mental well-being. Proper sleep is essential for the brain to process emotional information and to recover from the stresses of the day. When sleep is compromised, it can exacerbate or even lead to anxiety disorders, as the body lacks the opportunity to fully relax and regenerate.

Sleep acts as a natural regulator of neurotransmitters, including those that control mood and anxiety levels. A good night's sleep helps to balance the levels of serotonin and dopamine, neurotransmitters that affect mood, appetite, and sleep itself. Inadequate sleep can disrupt this balance, leading to heightened anxiety and mood swings.

Dr. Sebi advocated for establishing a calming bedtime routine to promote high-quality sleep. This might include practices such as disconnecting from electronic devices well before bedtime, as the blue light emitted can interfere with the production of melatonin, the hormone that regulates sleep-wake cycles. He also recommended creating a serene sleep environment—keeping the sleeping area dark, cool, and quiet can significantly improve sleep quality.

Incorporating specific herbs that promote relaxation and induce sleep was another approach Dr. Sebi used to manage anxiety. Herbs like valerian root, chamomile, and lavender are known for their soothing effects on the nervous system, making them beneficial for those struggling to sleep due to anxiety.

Moreover, Dr. Sebi emphasized the importance of aligning sleep patterns with natural circadian rhythms. Going to bed and waking up at the same time every day, even on weekends, helps regulate the body's internal clock and can improve sleep quality over time.

Dr. Sebi taught that adequate, restful sleep is a cornerstone of managing anxiety effectively. By ensuring consistent and quality sleep, individuals can enhance their ability to cope with daily stresses, improve their mental health, and maintain a balanced emotional state.

Book 9: Dr. Sebi Autoimmune Cure

Basics of Autoimmune Diseases

Dr. Sebi approached autoimmune diseases with a holistic perspective, emphasizing the importance of understanding the root causes and mechanisms behind these conditions. Autoimmune diseases occur when the immune system mistakenly attacks the body's own tissues, mistaking them for harmful pathogens. This can lead to a wide range of symptoms and affect various parts of the body, depending on the specific disease.

Understanding Autoimmune Diseases:

Autoimmune diseases stem from an overactive immune response where the body fails to recognize its own cells and tissues as 'self' and instead perceives them as threats, leading to chronic inflammation and tissue damage. Common autoimmune diseases include rheumatoid arthritis, lupus, multiple sclerosis, and type 1 diabetes, each affecting different organs and systems but all rooted in immune system dysfunction.

Contributing Factors:

Dr. Sebi believed that several factors contribute to the development of autoimmune diseases, including genetic predisposition, environmental triggers, and lifestyle choices. He particularly emphasized the role of diet and accumulation of toxins in the body as significant contributors to immune system malfunction. According to him, consuming foods that are unnatural or incompatible with the body can lead to toxic buildup and nutrient deficiencies, which may trigger or exacerbate autoimmune responses.

Diet and Autoimmune Diseases:

In Dr. Sebi's view, a key step in managing or potentially reversing autoimmune diseases involves adopting a strict alkaline diet based on natural plant foods. This diet excludes processed foods, animal products, and synthetic additives, which are believed to promote acidity and inflammation in the body. Instead, the focus is on consuming a variety of fresh fruits, vegetables, nuts, and seeds that alkalize the body and provide essential nutrients and antioxidants.

Detoxification:

Dr. Sebi also stressed the importance of detoxifying the body to remove toxins that could be triggering the autoimmune response. This involves the use of specific herbs and fasting protocols designed to cleanse the blood and organs, thereby reducing immune system hyperactivity and inflammation.

Holistic Healing Approach:

Dr. Sebi's approach to treating autoimmune diseases involves a comprehensive lifestyle overhaul that incorporates dietary changes, detoxification, and stress management to restore balance to the immune system. By addressing the underlying causes of immune dysfunction, rather than just the symptoms, his method aims to promote long-term health and well-being in individuals suffering from autoimmune conditions.

Dr. Sebi's Approach to Autoimmune Disorders

Dr. Sebi's approach to autoimmune disorders is centered on a holistic strategy that addresses the root causes of immune system dysfunction rather than just managing symptoms. He believed that many autoimmune conditions stem from the accumulation of toxins and an acidic environment within the body, which can trigger an abnormal immune response.

Central to Dr. Sebi's method is the adoption of an alkaline diet, which eliminates processed foods, animal products, and artificial additives—all of which contribute to body acidity and inflammation. Instead, he emphasized the importance of eating a variety of fresh fruits, vegetables, nuts, and seeds that help alkalize the body, reduce inflammation, and support immune function. Foods rich in essential minerals and vitamins are crucial, as they play a significant role in regulating immune responses and preventing oxidative stress.

Detoxification is another key aspect of his protocol. Dr. Sebi developed specific herbal cleanses using potent cleansing herbs such as burdock root, dandelion, and sarsaparilla. These herbs are known to purify the blood and cleanse key organs like the liver and kidneys, which are essential for maintaining a healthy immune system.

Alongside dietary changes and detoxification, Dr. Sebi recommended the use of natural herbal supplements to strengthen the body's immune system and combat inflammation. Herbs like sea moss and bladderwrack provide critical nutrients and minerals, such as iodine and selenium, which are vital for thyroid function and overall immune regulation.

Dr. Sebi also believed that managing stress and improving lifestyle habits are integral to treating autoimmune disorders. He recommended practices such as meditation, yoga, and ensuring adequate sleep to help reduce stress and enhance the body's natural healing capabilities. Stress reduction is particularly important, as chronic stress can exacerbate inflammation and immune dysfunction.

Dr. Sebi emphasized the importance of education and empowerment in managing autoimmune disorders. By understanding the impact of diet and lifestyle on health, individuals can make informed decisions that promote long-term well-being.

Treatments and Management Strategies

Dr. Sebi's approach to treating and managing autoimmune diseases emphasizes a comprehensive plan that integrates diet, natural remedies, and lifestyle changes. His strategy aims to cleanse the body, strengthen the immune system, and restore health by addressing the root causes of autoimmune reactions.

At the core of Dr. Sebi's treatment protocol is the adherence to an alkaline diet that reduces acidity in the body, often linked to inflammation and autoimmune responses. This diet focuses on high intake of fresh, raw vegetables and fruits, as well as nuts and seeds that are natural and non-hybrid. Staples of this diet include kale, watercress, cucumbers, avocados, wild rice, and chickpeas, avoiding processed foods and animal products that contribute to acidity and inflammation.

Dr. Sebi also advocated for the use of specific herbs to cleanse the body and support the immune system. Herbs such as burdock root, known for its blood-purifying properties, and elderberry, recognized for its immune-boosting capabilities, are integral to his regimen. Other herbs like sarsaparilla and sea moss are valued for their high mineral content and their ability to remove toxins from the body.

Regular detoxification is another crucial element in Dr. Sebi's approach, helping to alleviate the burden on the immune system and reduce autoimmune reactions. This involves fasting, consuming herbal teas like dandelion or bladderwrack, and using natural diuretics to aid in the elimination of waste.

Recognizing the impact of stress on the immune system, Dr. Sebi recommended incorporating stress reduction techniques into the treatment plan. Practices such as meditation, yoga, deep breathing exercises, and spending time in nature can help mitigate stress and its detrimental effects on health.

Physical activity is also encouraged, with a focus on gentle exercises that promote flexibility and stress relief, such as yoga and Tai Chi, to maintain mobility and reduce stress without over-straining the body.

Proper hydration is emphasized as essential for maintaining cellular health and helping the kidneys flush out toxins effectively. Dr. Sebi suggested drinking plenty of spring water throughout the day to support these processes.

Diet and Lifestyle Changes

Dr. Sebi's treatment protocol for autoimmune diseases places a strong emphasis on diet and lifestyle changes as fundamental elements for healing and restoring balance to the immune system. His approach is rooted in the belief that a natural, holistic lifestyle can significantly mitigate the effects of autoimmune disorders and lead to improved health. Here's an overview of the diet and lifestyle changes recommended by Dr. Sebi:

Dietary Changes: At the heart of Dr. Sebi's approach is the alkaline diet, which is designed to reduce acidity in the body and promote a more balanced pH level. This diet includes:

- High consumption of raw vegetables and fruits: These foods are central to alkalizing the body. Leafy greens, such as kale and spinach, and fruits like apples, bananas, and berries are especially beneficial.

- Exclusion of processed foods and animal products: Dr. Sebi advised against consuming any processed foods, dairy products, and meat as they contribute to acidity and inflammation in the body.

- Inclusion of natural whole foods: Foods like quinoa, wild rice, and alkaline grains are recommended along with nuts and seeds which provide essential fatty acids and proteins without overburdening the digestive system.

Hydration: Maintaining adequate hydration is crucial, as water helps to flush out toxins that can trigger autoimmune responses. Dr. Sebi emphasized the importance of drinking plenty of spring water throughout the day to support detoxification and overall cellular health.

Herbal Supplements: Incorporating specific herbs that support detoxification and strengthen the immune system is a key component of the lifestyle changes Dr. Sebi recommended. Herbs such as burdock root, dandelion, and sarsaparilla are used for their cleansing properties, while elderberry and sea moss provide immune-boosting benefits.

Physical Activity: Dr. Sebi encouraged regular, moderate exercise to help reduce stress, improve circulation, and enhance overall well-being. Activities such as walking, yoga, and other gentle forms of exercise are considered ideal for individuals managing autoimmune conditions.

Stress Management: Stress is a known trigger for autoimmune flare-ups. Dr. Sebi recommended practices such as meditation, deep breathing exercises, and spending time in nature as effective ways to manage stress and reduce its impact on the body.

Adequate Rest: Ensuring sufficient sleep and rest is vital in the management of autoimmune diseases. Sleep is when the body repairs itself, and lack of sleep can exacerbate symptoms and weaken the immune system.

Long-Term Prevention and Control

Dr. Sebi's approach to the long-term prevention and control of autoimmune diseases emphasizes a comprehensive strategy that stresses consistent adherence to a holistic lifestyle. He believed that maintaining an optimal balance in the body through diet, herbal treatments, and lifestyle choices could effectively prevent the progression of autoimmune disorders and control their symptoms over the long term.

A cornerstone of Dr. Sebi's method for long-term management of autoimmune diseases is a strict adherence to an alkaline diet. This diet is designed to reduce acidity in the body, which he believed contributed to inflammation and autoimmune reactions. By consistently consuming alkaline-forming foods like leafy greens, fruits, nuts, and legumes, and avoiding acid-forming foods such as processed foods, dairy, and meat, individuals can help maintain a healthy pH balance and reduce inflammation.

Dr. Sebi recommended regular cleansing and detoxification as a critical part of long-term disease management. Using natural herbs and fasting techniques helps eliminate accumulated toxins from the body, supporting the immune system and reducing unnecessary immune responses that characterize autoimmune diseases.

Continual use of specific herbs that support immune function and reduce inflammation is vital for managing autoimmune conditions. Herbs such as burdock root for blood purification, sarsaparilla for overall tonic benefits, and sea moss for its rich mineral content help nourish and strengthen the body's natural defenses.

Stress management and adequate physical activity are essential for preventing flare-ups and managing symptoms. Dr. Sebi advocated for incorporating regular practices such as yoga, meditation, and mindfulness to manage stress effectively. Additionally, light to moderate exercise helps maintain physical health without overtaxing the body.

Understanding the triggers and mechanisms of autoimmune responses is crucial for long-term management. Dr. Sebi emphasized the importance of education in empowering individuals to make informed choices about their health. Being aware of how different foods, environmental factors, and lifestyle choices affect the body can help individuals avoid triggers and maintain better control over their health.

Dr. Sebi also recognized the importance of community and social support in managing chronic illnesses. Encouraging individuals to connect with others who are facing similar challenges can provide emotional support, exchange of knowledge, and encouragement, which are beneficial for long-term disease management.

Anti-Inflammatory Foods and Their Benefits

Dr. Sebi emphasized the importance of incorporating anti-inflammatory foods into the diet as a crucial component of managing autoimmune diseases. He believed that inflammation is a key factor in the development and progression of autoimmune conditions, and addressing it through diet can significantly alleviate symptoms and potentially halt disease progression. Here's an overview of the anti-inflammatory foods recommended by Dr. Sebi and their benefits:

Leafy Greens: Foods like kale, spinach, and arugula are high in antioxidants and essential nutrients that help reduce inflammation throughout the body. These greens are rich in vitamins A, C, and K, which are crucial for immune function and inflammatory response regulation.

Sea Moss: Dr. Sebi often highlighted the benefits of sea moss, a type of algae that is a powerhouse of nutrients and minerals such as iodine, potassium, calcium, and sulfur. These components are vital for thyroid function, detoxification, and as natural anti-inflammatory agents. Consuming sea moss can help reduce swelling and pain associated with inflammatory conditions.

Berries: Blueberries, strawberries, and raspberries are packed with antioxidants, particularly anthocyanins, which give berries their vibrant color and have strong anti-inflammatory properties. Regular consumption of berries can help reduce inflammation and protect the body against oxidative stress, which can exacerbate autoimmune symptoms.

Walnuts: Rich in omega-3 fatty acids, walnuts are excellent for combating inflammation. Omega-3s are known to reduce the production of molecules and substances linked to inflammation, such as inflammatory eicosanoids and cytokines. Including walnuts in the diet can support heart health and help manage inflammatory markers in the body.

Ginger and Turmeric: These spices are well-known for their anti-inflammatory effects. Ginger helps to reduce inflammation by inhibiting the synthesis of pro-inflammatory cytokines, while turmeric's active compound, curcumin, has potent anti-inflammatory properties that are comparable to some anti-inflammatory drugs, without the side effects.

Garlic: Garlic has been shown to have an anti-inflammatory effect that can help regulate the immune system and reduce inflammation across the body. It contains sulfur compounds that inhibit the pathways that activate inflammatory processes in the body.

Dr. Sebi advised incorporating these foods into a regular diet as part of a holistic approach to treating autoimmune diseases. By reducing inflammation, these foods not only help alleviate symptoms but also contribute to overall health and well-being, supporting the body's natural healing processes and helping to manage or even reverse autoimmune conditions.

Managing Flare-Ups Naturally

Dr. Sebi emphasized the importance of managing autoimmune flare-ups by employing natural methods that align with the body's inherent healing processes. His approach to naturally managing these flare-ups involves a combination of dietary adjustments, herbal remedies, and lifestyle modifications to reduce inflammation and support overall health.

Diet plays a pivotal role in managing flare-ups. Dr. Sebi recommended adhering strictly to an alkaline diet rich in fruits, vegetables, and whole grains that help reduce acidity and inflammation in the body. Specific foods known for their anti-inflammatory properties, such as leafy greens, berries, nuts like walnuts and almonds, and seeds, are particularly beneficial. These foods are packed with antioxidants and essential nutrients that help mitigate the inflammatory responses often seen in autoimmune conditions.

Herbal remedies are also crucial in Dr. Sebi's protocol for flare-up management. Herbs such as ginger, turmeric, and garlic are advocated for their powerful anti-inflammatory effects. Ginger and turmeric, in particular, are effective in reducing inflammation and can be consumed in various forms such as teas, juices, or added to food. Additionally, Dr. Sebi often recommended herbal supplements that support the body's detoxification processes, aiding in the removal of toxins that may trigger or worsen flare-ups.

Lifestyle modifications include reducing stress, which is a known trigger for autoimmune flare-ups. Dr. Sebi advised practices such as meditation, yoga, and other relaxation techniques to help manage stress effectively. Getting adequate sleep is also crucial, as it allows the body to repair and regenerate, thus strengthening the immune system and reducing the likelihood of flare-ups.

Hydration is another key element in managing autoimmune flare-ups naturally. Dr. Sebi stressed the importance of drinking plenty of spring water to help flush out toxins and maintain hydration, which is vital for cellular health and proper immune function.

The Role of Gut Health in Autoimmune Diseases

Dr. Sebi recognized the critical role of gut health in the development and management of autoimmune diseases, underscoring the gut as a central component in the immune system. He believed that a healthy gut microbiome is essential for maintaining overall health and preventing the immune dysregulation that leads to autoimmune conditions.

Connection Between Gut Health and Immune Function: The gastrointestinal tract is home to a large portion of the body's immune cells, and it is where the immune system interacts most frequently with external substances, including food particles, toxins, and microbes. This interaction can influence immune responses; a healthy gut microbiome helps regulate these responses and prevents the immune system from attacking the body's own tissues.

Impact of Diet on Gut Health: Dr. Sebi emphasized that diet directly affects gut health and, consequently, immune function. He advocated for an alkaline diet rich in fiber, antioxidants, and essential nutrients, which supports the growth of beneficial gut bacteria and helps maintain the integrity of the gut lining. This diet includes foods like fruits, vegetables, and alkaline grains, which reduce inflammation and acidity that can damage gut flora and the intestinal wall.

Herbs for Gut Health: Dr. Sebi recommended specific herbs known for their ability to support digestive health and cleanse the gut. These include:

- Burdock Root: Known for its blood and liver cleansing properties, it also fosters a healthy gut by encouraging the growth of good bacteria and enhancing digestive efficiency.

- Sarsaparilla: Used traditionally to treat gastrointestinal issues, it helps purify the organ systems and has properties that soothe the mucous membranes of the intestines.

- Sea Moss: Rich in fiber and prebiotics, it helps to stimulate the growth of beneficial gut bacteria, which is vital for immune modulation and overall health.

Avoiding Gut Irritants: Dr. Sebi advised against the consumption of processed foods, dairy, and meat as these can lead to an imbalance in gut flora, increase gut permeability (leaky gut), and trigger inflammatory responses. These conditions can potentially lead to or exacerbate autoimmune reactions.

Supporting Overall Gut Function: In addition to diet and herbal remedies, Dr. Sebi emphasized the importance of adequate hydration, regular detoxification, and stress management as integral components of maintaining gut health. Water is essential for digestive processes, detoxification helps remove toxins that can burden the gut, and managing stress is critical since stress hormones can compromise gut barrier function and alter gut bacteria.

Book 10: Dr. Sebi Cookbook

Introduction to Alkaline Cooking

In the "Dr. Sebi Cookbook," the introduction to alkaline cooking lays the foundation for understanding how to nourish the body using natural, plant-based ingredients that align with Dr. Sebi's nutritional guide. This section elaborates on the principles behind alkaline cooking and its numerous benefits for maintaining health and wellness.

Alkaline cooking is grounded in Dr. Sebi's philosophy that emphasizes the importance of maintaining an alkaline environment within the body to foster health and prevent disease. The diet focuses on natural, electric foods that help balance the body's pH levels. These foods are primarily plant-based and include a specific list of fruits, vegetables, nuts, seeds, and grains that Dr. Sebi deemed most beneficial, particularly those that are low in starch.

The introduction also highlights the health benefits of adopting an alkaline diet, which include enhanced energy levels, improved digestion, reduced inflammation, and a lowered risk of chronic diseases such as diabetes and heart disease. By eliminating acidic foods like meat, dairy, and processed items, and emphasizing alkaline foods, the body can detoxify more effectively and maintain a healthier state.

Furthermore, the section covers the basic techniques and essential ingredients needed to prepare alkaline meals. It discusses how to use key alkaline ingredients such as sea moss, burdock root, and spelt flour, which are staples in Dr. Sebi's recipes. Techniques such as blending, juicing, and dehydrating are highlighted to help preserve the nutritional integrity of foods.

Recipe guidelines are provided to help readers combine ingredients to create delicious and nutritious meals. The introduction encourages creativity and experimentation in the kitchen while adhering to the approved list of alkaline foods. The recipes are designed to be simple, with clear instructions and tips that make meal preparation both enjoyable and effective in promoting health.

All the following recipes are for 2 people.

Breakfast Recipes

1. Quinoa Berry Porridge

- Ingredients:
  - 1/2 cup quinoa
  - Fresh berries (strawberries, blueberries, raspberries)
  - Pure maple syrup or stevia
- Instructions:

1. Cook quinoa in water or almond milk until fluffy.
2. Serve with fresh berries and drizzle with pure maple syrup or stevia for sweetness.

2. Energizing Green Smoothie

- Ingredients:
  - Fresh spinach
  - Avocado
  - Banana
  - Fresh mint leaves
  - Coconut water or almond milk
  - Chia or flax seeds
- Instructions:
  1. Blend fresh spinach, avocado, banana, and mint leaves with coconut water or almond milk.
  2. Add chia or flax seeds for extra fiber and omega-3.

3. Coconut Flour Banana Pancakes

- Ingredients:
  - Coconut flour
  - Eggs
  - Ripe mashed bananas
  - Cinnamon
- Instructions:
  1. Mix coconut flour with eggs, mashed ripe bananas, and a pinch of cinnamon.
  2. Cook pancakes on a non-stick pan until golden brown.

4. Almond Butter and Banana Toast

- Ingredients:
  - Whole grain bread
  - Almond butter
  - Sliced bananas
- Instructions:
  1. Toast whole grain bread until golden brown.
  2. Spread almond butter on the toast and top with sliced bananas.

5. Chia Seed Pudding
- Ingredients:
  - Chia seeds
  - Almond milk
  - Vanilla extract
  - Fresh fruit for topping
- Instructions:
  1. Mix chia seeds with almond milk and vanilla extract.
  2. Refrigerate overnight until thickened, then top with fresh fruit before serving.

6. Oatmeal with Almond Milk and Mixed Berries

- Ingredients:
  - Rolled oats
  - Almond milk
  - Mixed berries (strawberries, blueberries, raspberries)
- Instructions:
  1. Cook rolled oats with almond milk until creamy.
  2. Top with mixed berries for added flavor and antioxidants.

7. Avocado Toast with Tomato and Sprouts

- Ingredients:
  - Whole grain bread
  - Ripe avocado
  - Sliced tomato
  - Fresh sprouts
- Instructions:
  1. Toast whole grain bread until lightly browned.
  2. Mash ripe avocado onto the toast and top with sliced tomato and fresh sprouts.

8. Green Veggie Omelette

- Ingredients:
  - Eggs
  - Spinach
  - Bell peppers
  - Onions
  - Olive oil
- Instructions:
  1. Sauté spinach, bell peppers, and onions in olive oil until tender.
  2. Pour beaten eggs over the veggies and cook until set to make a nutritious omelette.

9. Coconut Yogurt Parfait with Fresh Fruit

- Ingredients:
  - Coconut yogurt
  - Granola
  - Fresh fruit (such as berries, mango, or pineapple)
- Instructions:
  1. Layer coconut yogurt, granola, and fresh fruit in a glass.
  2. Repeat the layers and serve chilled for a refreshing breakfast option.

10. Almond Flour Banana Muffins

- Ingredients:
  - Almond flour
  - Ripe mashed bananas
  - Eggs
  - Baking powder
- Instructions:

1. Mix almond flour, mashed bananas, eggs, and baking powder until well combined.

2. Pour the batter into muffin cups and bake until golden and cooked through. Enjoy as a wholesome breakfast muffin.

11. Buckwheat Pancakes with Fresh Fruit

- Ingredients:
  - Buckwheat flour
  - Almond milk
  - Banana (mashed)
  - Baking powder
- Instructions:
  1. Combine buckwheat flour, almond milk, mashed banana, and baking powder to make the pancake batter.
  2. Cook pancakes on a non-stick pan until golden brown, then serve with fresh fruit on top.

12. Turmeric Chia Seed Pudding

- Ingredients:
  - Chia seeds
  - Coconut milk
  - Turmeric powder
  - Honey or maple syrup
- Instructions:
  1. Mix chia seeds, coconut milk, turmeric powder, and sweetener of choice in a bowl.
  2. Refrigerate overnight until thickened, then enjoy the pudding topped with nuts or seeds.

13. Veggie Breakfast Burrito

- Ingredients:
  - Whole grain tortilla
  - Scrambled tofu
  - Sautéed veggies (bell peppers, onions, spinach)
  - Avocado slices
- Instructions:
  1. Fill a whole grain tortilla with scrambled tofu and sautéed veggies.
  2. Add avocado slices, roll up the burrito, and enjoy a savory breakfast option.

14. Coconut Flour Banana Bread

- Ingredients:
  - Coconut flour
  - Ripe mashed bananas
  - Eggs
  - Coconut oil
- Instructions:
  1. Combine coconut flour, mashed bananas, eggs, and melted coconut oil to make the banana bread batter.
  2. Bake in a preheated oven until golden and cooked through, then slice and enjoy warm or toasted.

15. Hemp Seed Smoothie Bowl

- Ingredients:
  - Frozen mixed berries
  - Banana
  - Hemp seeds
  - Almond milk
- Instructions:
  1. Blend frozen mixed berries, banana, hemp seeds, and almond milk until smooth.
  2. Pour the smoothie into a bowl and top with additional hemp seeds, sliced fruit, and granola for a nutritious breakfast bowl.

16. Almond Flour Pancakes with Coconut Cream

- Ingredients:
  - Almond flour
  - Eggs
  - Coconut milk
  - Vanilla extract
- Instructions:
  1. Mix almond flour, eggs, coconut milk, and vanilla extract to create the pancake batter.
  2. Cook pancakes on a griddle until golden brown, then serve with a dollop of coconut cream on top.

17. Millet Breakfast Bowl with Berries and Nuts

- Ingredients:
  - Cooked millet
  - Fresh berries (such as strawberries, blueberries)
  - Chopped nuts (such as almonds, walnuts)
- Instructions:
  1. Spoon cooked millet into a bowl.
  2. Top with fresh berries and chopped nuts for a hearty and nutritious breakfast bowl.

18. Spiced Sweet Potato Hash

- Ingredients:
  - Sweet potatoes (diced)
  - Red bell pepper (diced)
  - Red onion (sliced)
  - Olive oil
  - Paprika, cumin, salt, and pepper (to taste)
- Instructions:
  1. Sauté sweet potatoes, red bell pepper, and red onion in olive oil until tender.
  2. Season with paprika, cumin, salt, and pepper, then serve as a flavorful and filling breakfast hash.

19. Chickpea Flour Omelette with Veggies

- Ingredients:

- Chickpea flour
- Water or almond milk
- Sautéed vegetables (such as spinach, tomatoes, mushrooms)
- Olive oil
- Instructions:
  1. Whisk chickpea flour with water or almond milk to make the omelette batter.
  2. Pour the batter into a heated skillet, add sautéed vegetables, fold over, and cook until set for a delicious and protein-rich omelette.

20. Tropical Chia Seed Smoothie

- Ingredients:
  - Frozen pineapple chunks
  - Frozen mango chunks
  - Chia seeds
  - Coconut water
- Instructions:
  1. Blend frozen pineapple chunks, frozen mango chunks, chia seeds, and coconut water until smooth.
  2. Pour into a glass and enjoy a refreshing and energizing tropical smoothie.

Lunch Recipes

1. Quinoa and Avocado Salad

- Ingredients:
  - Cooked quinoa
  - Diced avocado
  - Cubed tomatoes
  - Sliced cucumbers
  - Fresh spinach leaves
  - Dressing: lemon juice, olive oil, salt, and pepper
- Instructions:
  1. Mix cooked quinoa with avocado, tomatoes, cucumbers, and spinach.
  2. Dress with lemon juice, olive oil, salt, and pepper.

2. Vegan Hummus and Veggie Wrap

- Ingredients:
  - Whole grain tortilla
  - Hummus
  - Sliced cucumbers
  - Shredded carrots
  - Sliced bell peppers
  - Mixed greens
- Instructions:

1. Spread hummus on a whole grain tortilla.
2. Layer sliced cucumbers, shredded carrots, sliced bell peppers, and mixed greens on top.
3. Roll up the tortilla and slice in half to serve.

3. Grilled Portobello Mushroom Burger

  - Ingredients:
    - Portobello mushroom caps
    - Olive oil
    - Balsamic vinegar
    - Garlic powder
    - Salt and pepper
    - Whole grain burger buns
    - Toppings: sliced tomatoes, lettuce, avocado
  - Instructions:
    1. Marinate portobello mushroom caps in olive oil, balsamic vinegar, garlic powder, salt, and pepper.
    2. Grill mushrooms until tender and juicy.
    3. Serve on whole grain burger buns with sliced tomatoes, lettuce, and avocado.

4. Chickpea and Vegetable Stir-Fry

  - Ingredients:
    - Cooked chickpeas
    - Sliced bell peppers
    - Sliced zucchini
    - Sliced onions
    - Minced garlic
    - Soy sauce or tamari
    - Olive oil
  - Instructions:
    1. Heat olive oil in a skillet and sauté minced garlic until fragrant.
    2. Add sliced bell peppers, zucchini, and onions, and cook until tender.
    3. Stir in cooked chickpeas and soy sauce or tamari, and cook until heated through.
    4. Serve hot as a flavorful and nutritious stir-fry.

5. Cauliflower Rice Bowl with Black Beans and Salsa

  - Ingredients:
    - Cauliflower rice
    - Cooked black beans
    - Salsa
    - Sliced avocado
    - Chopped cilantro
    - Lime wedges
  - Instructions:
    1. Heat cauliflower rice and cooked black beans in a skillet until warm.
    2. Serve cauliflower rice and black beans in bowls, topped with salsa, sliced avocado, chopped cilantro, and a squeeze of lime juice.

6. Stir-Fried Tofu and Vegetables

- Ingredients:
  - Firm tofu, cubed
  - Mixed vegetables (such as broccoli, bell peppers, snap peas)
  - Minced ginger
  - Soy sauce or tamari
  - Olive oil
- Instructions:
  1. Heat olive oil in a skillet and add minced ginger.
  2. Stir-fry tofu until golden brown, then add mixed vegetables and cook until tender.
  3. Season with soy sauce or tamari and serve hot.

7. Mango and Black Bean Salad

- Ingredients:
  - Cooked black beans
  - Diced mango
  - Chopped red onion
  - Chopped cilantro
  - Lime juice
  - Olive oil
  - Salt and pepper
- Instructions:
  1. Mix cooked black beans with diced mango, chopped red onion, and chopped cilantro.
  2. Dress with lime juice, olive oil, salt, and pepper.

8. Spinach and Chickpea Salad with Tahini Dressing

- Ingredients:
  - Fresh spinach leaves
  - Cooked chickpeas
  - Cherry tomatoes, halved
  - Sliced cucumber
  - Tahini
  - Lemon juice
  - Garlic powder
  - Salt and pepper
- Instructions:
  1. Toss fresh spinach leaves with cooked chickpeas, halved cherry tomatoes, and sliced cucumber.
  2. Drizzle with a dressing made from tahini, lemon juice, garlic powder, salt, and pepper.

9. Zucchini Noodles with Pesto Sauce

- Ingredients:
  - Zucchini, spiralized into noodles
  - Basil pesto (homemade or store-bought)
  - Cherry tomatoes, halved

- Pine nuts, toasted
- Instructions:
  1. Toss zucchini noodles with basil pesto until evenly coated.
  2. Top with halved cherry tomatoes and toasted pine nuts before serving.

10. Lentil and Vegetable Soup

- Ingredients:
  - Green lentils, cooked
  - Chopped carrots, celery, and onions
  - Minced garlic
  - Vegetable broth
  - Diced tomatoes
  - Bay leaves
  - Olive oil
  - Salt and pepper
- Instructions:
  1. Sauté minced garlic, chopped carrots, celery, and onions in olive oil until softened.
  2. Add cooked green lentils, vegetable broth, diced tomatoes, and bay leaves.
  3. Simmer until the vegetables are tender, then season with salt and pepper before serving.

11. Roasted Vegetable Quinoa Bowl

- Ingredients:
  - Cooked quinoa
  - Assorted vegetables (such as bell peppers, zucchini, and eggplant), diced
  - Olive oil
  - Garlic powder
  - Paprika
  - Salt and pepper
- Instructions:
  1. Toss diced vegetables with olive oil, garlic powder, paprika, salt, and pepper.
  2. Roast in the oven until tender and slightly caramelized.
  3. Serve over cooked quinoa for a hearty and nutritious bowl.

12. Black Bean and Corn Salad

- Ingredients:
  - Cooked black beans
  - Corn kernels (fresh or thawed if frozen)
  - Diced bell peppers (various colors)
  - Chopped red onion
  - Chopped fresh cilantro
  - Lime juice
  - Olive oil
  - Cumin
  - Salt and pepper
- Instructions:
  1. Combine black beans, corn, diced bell peppers, chopped red onion, and cilantro in a bowl.

2. Dress with lime juice, olive oil, cumin, salt, and pepper, tossing until well combined.

13. Mushroom and Spinach Quiche with Almond Flour Crust

- Ingredients:
  - Almond flour
  - Eggs
  - Olive oil
  - Sliced mushrooms
  - Fresh spinach
  - Minced garlic
  - Nutritional yeast
  - Salt and pepper
- Instructions:
  1. Mix almond flour with eggs and olive oil to form a dough, then press into a pie dish to form the crust.
  2. Sauté sliced mushrooms, fresh spinach, and minced garlic until cooked.
  3. Pour the mushroom and spinach mixture into the almond flour crust, then sprinkle with nutritional yeast, salt, and pepper.
  4. Bake until set and golden brown.

14. Lentil and Vegetable Stir-Fry

- Ingredients:
  - Cooked lentils
  - Sliced bell peppers
  - Sliced carrots
  - Sliced snow peas
  - Minced ginger
  - Soy sauce or tamari
  - Olive oil
- Instructions:
  1. Heat olive oil in a skillet and add minced ginger.
  2. Stir-fry sliced bell peppers, carrots, and snow peas until tender.
  3. Add cooked lentils and soy sauce or tamari, cooking until heated through.

15. Cauliflower Rice Sushi Rolls

- Ingredients:
  - Cauliflower rice
  - Nori seaweed sheets
  - Sliced avocado
  - Sliced cucumber
  - Sliced bell peppers
  - Sliced carrots
  - Rice vinegar
  - Soy sauce or tamari
- Instructions:
  1. Spread cauliflower rice onto nori seaweed sheets.

2. Layer sliced avocado, cucumber, bell peppers, and carrots on top.

3. Roll tightly and slice into individual sushi rolls.

4. Serve with rice vinegar and soy sauce or tamari for dipping.

16. Sautéed Tofu and Broccoli with Ginger Sauce

- Ingredients:
  - Firm tofu, cubed
  - Broccoli florets
  - Minced ginger
  - Soy sauce or tamari
  - Rice vinegar
  - Olive oil
  - Sesame seeds (for garnish)
- Instructions:
  1. Sauté cubed tofu in olive oil until golden brown.
  2. Add broccoli florets and minced ginger to the skillet and cook until tender-crisp.
  3. Drizzle with a sauce made from soy sauce or tamari and rice vinegar.
  4. Serve hot, garnished with sesame seeds.

17. Coconut Curry Lentil Soup

- Ingredients:
  - Red lentils, rinsed
  - Chopped onion
  - Minced garlic
  - Curry powder
  - Coconut milk
  - Vegetable broth
  - Chopped cilantro (for garnish)
- Instructions:
  1. Sauté chopped onion and minced garlic in a pot until softened.
  2. Stir in curry powder and cook for another minute.
  3. Add red lentils, coconut milk, and vegetable broth to the pot.
  4. Simmer until lentils are tender and soup has thickened.
  5. Serve hot, garnished with chopped cilantro.

18. Portobello Mushroom and Kale Salad

- Ingredients:
  - Portobello mushroom caps
  - Chopped kale
  - Cherry tomatoes, halved
  - Sliced red onion
  - Balsamic vinegar
  - Olive oil
  - Dijon mustard
- Instructions:
  1. Grill or roast portobello mushroom caps until tender.

2. Toss chopped kale, halved cherry tomatoes, and sliced red onion in a bowl.

3. Whisk together balsamic vinegar, olive oil, and Dijon mustard to make the dressing.

4. Slice portobello mushrooms and add to the salad.

5. Drizzle with dressing and toss to combine.

19. Spaghetti Squash Pad Thai

- Ingredients:
  - Spaghetti squash, cooked and shredded
  - Bean sprouts
  - Sliced bell peppers
  - Chopped scallions
  - Chopped peanuts (for garnish)
  - Lime wedges
  - Pad Thai sauce (store-bought or homemade)
- Instructions:
  1. Toss cooked spaghetti squash with bean sprouts, sliced bell peppers, and chopped scallions.
  2. Stir in Pad Thai sauce until evenly coated.
  3. Serve hot, garnished with chopped peanuts and lime wedges.

20. Chickpea and Vegetable Curry

- Ingredients:
  - Cooked chickpeas
  - Chopped cauliflower
  - Diced potatoes
  - Chopped carrots
  - Chopped onion
  - Minced garlic
  - Curry powder
  - Coconut milk
  - Olive oil
- Instructions:
  1. Sauté chopped onion and minced garlic in olive oil until softened.
  2. Add chopped cauliflower, diced potatoes, and chopped carrots to the pot and cook until slightly tender.
  3. Stir in cooked chickpeas, curry powder, and coconut milk.
  4. Simmer until vegetables are cooked through and curry has thickened.
  5. Serve hot, optionally garnished with chopped cilantro.

Dinner Recipes

1. Baked Lemon Herb Salmon

- Ingredients:
  - Salmon fillets

- Lemon juice
- Chopped fresh herbs (such as parsley, dill, or cilantro)
- Minced garlic
- Olive oil
- Salt and pepper
- Instructions:
  1. Preheat the oven to 375°F (190°C).
  2. Place salmon fillets on a baking sheet lined with parchment paper.
  3. Drizzle with lemon juice, olive oil, and sprinkle with chopped herbs and minced garlic.
  4. Season with salt and pepper.
  5. Bake for 12-15 minutes, or until the salmon is cooked through and flakes easily with a fork.

2. Stir-Fried Tofu and Vegetable Quinoa

- Ingredients:
  - Firm tofu, cubed
  - Cooked quinoa
  - Mixed vegetables (such as bell peppers, broccoli, and snap peas)
  - Minced ginger
  - Soy sauce or tamari
  - Sesame oil
  - Olive oil
- Instructions:
  1. Heat olive oil in a skillet over medium-high heat.
  2. Add cubed tofu and cook until golden brown on all sides.
  3. Add mixed vegetables and minced ginger to the skillet and stir-fry until tender-crisp.
  4. Stir in cooked quinoa, soy sauce or tamari, and sesame oil.
  5. Cook for an additional 2-3 minutes, then serve hot.

3. Roasted Vegetable Buddha Bowl

- Ingredients:
  - Assorted vegetables (such as sweet potatoes, cauliflower, and Brussels sprouts), chopped
  - Olive oil
  - Garlic powder
  - Paprika
  - Cooked quinoa or brown rice
  - Avocado slices
  - Tahini dressing
- Instructions:
  1. Preheat the oven to 400°F (200°C).
  2. Toss chopped vegetables with olive oil, garlic powder, and paprika on a baking sheet.
  3. Roast in the oven for 20-25 minutes, or until vegetables are tender and caramelized.
  4. Divide cooked quinoa or brown rice among serving bowls.
  5. Top with roasted vegetables, avocado slices, and drizzle with tahini dressing.

4. Vegetable Stir-Fry with Cashew Nuts

- Ingredients:

- Sliced bell peppers
- Sliced carrots
- Broccoli florets
- Sliced mushrooms
- Snow peas
- Minced garlic
- Soy sauce or tamari
- Cashew nuts
- Olive oil
- Instructions:
  1. Heat olive oil in a wok or large skillet over high heat.
  2. Add sliced bell peppers, carrots, broccoli florets, sliced mushrooms, and snow peas.
  3. Stir-fry until vegetables are tender-crisp.
  4. Add minced garlic and soy sauce or tamari, stirring until fragrant.
  5. Stir in cashew nuts and cook for an additional minute before serving hot.

5. Mushroom and Spinach Lentil Soup

- Ingredients:
  - Green lentils, rinsed
  - Sliced mushrooms
  - Chopped spinach
  - Chopped onion
  - Minced garlic
  - Vegetable broth
  - Olive oil
  - Salt and pepper
- Instructions:
  1. Heat olive oil in a large pot over medium heat.
  2. Add chopped onion and minced garlic, cooking until softened.
  3. Stir in sliced mushrooms and cook until golden brown.
  4. Add green lentils and vegetable broth to the pot, bringing to a simmer.
  5. Cook until lentils are tender, then stir in chopped spinach and season with salt and pepper before serving hot.

6. Spaghetti Squash with Tomato Basil Sauce

- Ingredients:
  - Spaghetti squash
  - Olive oil
  - Garlic, minced
  - Crushed tomatoes
  - Fresh basil, chopped
  - Salt and pepper to taste
- Instructions:
  1. Preheat the oven to 400°F (200°C). Cut the spaghetti squash in half lengthwise and remove the seeds.
  2. Drizzle olive oil over the squash halves and season with salt and pepper. Place them cut side down on a baking sheet.

3. Roast for about 40-50 minutes or until the squash is tender and the strands easily separate.

4. In a saucepan, heat olive oil over medium heat and sauté minced garlic until fragrant.

5. Add crushed tomatoes and chopped basil, then simmer for 10-15 minutes. Serve the sauce over the spaghetti squash strands.

7. Baked Stuffed Bell Peppers

  - Ingredients:
    - Bell peppers, halved and deseeded
    - Cooked quinoa
    - Black beans, drained and rinsed
    - Diced tomatoes
    - Diced onion
    - Minced garlic
    - Cumin, paprika, salt, and pepper to taste
  - Instructions:
    1. Preheat the oven to 375°F (190°C). Place halved bell peppers on a baking sheet.

    2. In a bowl, mix cooked quinoa, black beans, diced tomatoes, diced onion, minced garlic, and seasonings.

    3. Spoon the quinoa mixture into each bell pepper half.

    4. Bake for 25-30 minutes or until the peppers are tender. Serve hot.

8. Lemon Garlic Herb Grilled Chicken

  - Ingredients:
    - Chicken breasts
    - Lemon juice
    - Minced garlic
    - Chopped fresh herbs (such as rosemary, thyme, and parsley)
    - Olive oil
    - Salt and pepper to taste
  - Instructions:
    1. In a bowl, mix lemon juice, minced garlic, chopped herbs, olive oil, salt, and pepper.

    2. Marinate chicken breasts in the mixture for at least 30 minutes.

    3. Preheat grill to medium-high heat. Grill chicken for 6-8 minutes per side or until cooked through.

    4. Serve hot with your choice of side dishes.

9. Cauliflower Fried Rice

  - Ingredients:
    - Cauliflower rice
    - Diced carrots
    - Peas
    - Diced bell peppers
    - Diced onion
    - Minced garlic
    - Soy sauce or tamari
    - Olive oil

- Instructions:

   1. In a large skillet, heat olive oil over medium heat. Add diced onion and minced garlic, cooking until softened.

   2. Stir in diced carrots, peas, and bell peppers, cooking until vegetables are tender.

   3. Add cauliflower rice and soy sauce or tamari, stirring until heated through.

   4. Cook for an additional 3-4 minutes, then serve hot as a flavorful and nutritious alternative to traditional fried rice.

10. Stuffed Portobello Mushrooms

 - Ingredients:
   - Portobello mushroom caps
   - Quinoa, cooked
   - Chopped spinach
   - Diced tomatoes
   - Minced garlic
   - Italian seasoning
   - Salt and pepper to taste
 - Instructions:

   1. Preheat the oven to 375°F (190°C). Remove the stems from portobello mushroom caps and gently scrape out the gills.

   2. In a bowl, mix cooked quinoa, chopped spinach, diced tomatoes, minced garlic, Italian seasoning, salt, and pepper.

   3. Stuff each mushroom cap with the quinoa mixture.

   4. Place stuffed mushrooms on a baking sheet and bake for 20-25 minutes or until mushrooms are tender. Serve hot as a satisfying and nutritious meal.

11. Black Bean and Sweet Potato Tacos

 - Ingredients:
   - Corn tortillas
   - Cooked black beans
   - Roasted sweet potato cubes
   - Sliced avocado
   - Chopped cilantro
   - Lime wedges
   - Salsa or pico de gallo
 - Instructions:

   1. Warm corn tortillas in a skillet or oven.

   2. Fill each tortilla with cooked black beans, roasted sweet potato cubes, sliced avocado, and chopped cilantro.

   3. Serve with lime wedges and salsa or pico de gallo on the side.

12. Eggplant and Chickpea Curry

 - Ingredients:
   - Eggplant, cubed
   - Cooked chickpeas
   - Diced tomatoes

- Chopped onion
  - Minced garlic
  - Curry powder
  - Coconut milk
  - Olive oil
  - Salt and pepper to taste
- Instructions:
    1. In a large pot, heat olive oil over medium heat. Add chopped onion and minced garlic, cooking until softened.
    2. Add cubed eggplant and cook until slightly softened.
    3. Stir in cooked chickpeas, diced tomatoes, curry powder, and coconut milk.
    4. Simmer for 15-20 minutes, or until the eggplant is tender and the curry has thickened. Season with salt and pepper before serving.

13. Zucchini Noodles with Pesto and Cherry Tomatoes

  - Ingredients:
    - Zucchini, spiralized into noodles
    - Homemade or store-bought pesto sauce
    - Cherry tomatoes, halved
    - Pine nuts, toasted
    - Fresh basil leaves
  - Instructions:
    1. In a large skillet, heat zucchini noodles until warmed through.
    2. Toss zucchini noodles with pesto sauce until evenly coated.
    3. Top with halved cherry tomatoes, toasted pine nuts, and fresh basil leaves before serving.

14. Stuffed Bell Peppers with Quinoa and Black Beans

  - Ingredients:
    - Bell peppers, halved and deseeded
    - Cooked quinoa
    - Cooked black beans
    - Diced tomatoes
    - Chopped onion
    - Minced garlic
    - Cumin, paprika, salt, and pepper to taste
  - Instructions:
    1. Preheat the oven to 375°F (190°C). Place halved bell peppers in a baking dish.
    2. In a bowl, mix cooked quinoa, black beans, diced tomatoes, chopped onion, minced garlic, and seasonings.
    3. Spoon the quinoa mixture into each bell pepper half.
    4. Bake for 25-30 minutes or until the peppers are tender. Serve hot.

15. Mushroom and Spinach Stuffed Portobello Mushrooms

  - Ingredients:
    - Portobello mushroom caps
    - Chopped spinach

- Sliced mushrooms
- Diced onion
- Minced garlic
- Balsamic vinegar
- Olive oil
- Salt and pepper to taste
- Instructions:
1. Preheat the oven to 375°F (190°C). Remove the stems from portobello mushroom caps and gently scrape out the gills.
2. In a skillet, heat olive oil over medium heat. Add diced onion and minced garlic, cooking until softened.
3. Add chopped spinach and sliced mushrooms to the skillet, cooking until tender.
4. Stir in balsamic vinegar, salt, and pepper. Remove from heat.
5. Fill each mushroom cap with the spinach and mushroom mixture.
6. Bake for 20-25 minutes or until mushrooms are tender. Serve hot as a flavorful and nutritious meal.

16. Cauliflower Steaks with Chimichurri Sauce

- Ingredients:
  - Cauliflower heads, sliced into steaks
  - Olive oil
  - Salt and pepper
  - Chimichurri sauce (made with parsley, cilantro, garlic, olive oil, red wine vinegar, salt, and pepper)
- Instructions:
1. Preheat the oven to 425°F (220°C). Brush cauliflower steaks with olive oil and season with salt and pepper.
2. Roast in the oven for 25-30 minutes or until tender and golden brown.
3. Serve the cauliflower steaks drizzled with chimichurri sauce.

17. Vegan Lentil Shepherd's Pie

- Ingredients:
  - Cooked lentils
  - Chopped carrots, celery, and onion
  - Minced garlic
  - Tomato paste
  - Vegetable broth
  - Mashed sweet potatoes
  - Olive oil
  - Salt and pepper
- Instructions:
1. Sauté chopped carrots, celery, onion, and minced garlic in olive oil until softened.
2. Stir in cooked lentils, tomato paste, and vegetable broth. Simmer until thickened.
3. Spread the lentil mixture in a baking dish and top with mashed sweet potatoes.
4. Bake at 375°F (190°C) for 25-30 minutes or until golden brown.

18. Zucchini Lasagna with Cashew Ricotta

- Ingredients:
  - Zucchini, thinly sliced lengthwise
  - Cashew ricotta (made with soaked cashews, lemon juice, nutritional yeast, garlic, salt, and pepper)
  - Marinara sauce
  - Fresh basil leaves
- Instructions:
  1. Preheat the oven to 375°F (190°C). Spread a layer of marinara sauce in the bottom of a baking dish.
  2. Layer zucchini slices on top of the sauce, followed by dollops of cashew ricotta and torn basil leaves.
  3. Repeat the layers until all ingredients are used, finishing with a layer of marinara sauce on top.
  4. Bake for 35-40 minutes or until bubbly and golden brown.

19. Quinoa Stuffed Bell Peppers

- Ingredients:
  - Bell peppers, halved and deseeded
  - Cooked quinoa
  - Cooked black beans
  - Diced tomatoes
  - Diced onion
  - Minced garlic
  - Cumin, chili powder, salt, and pepper to taste
- Instructions:
  1. Preheat the oven to 375°F (190°C). Place halved bell peppers in a baking dish.
  2. In a bowl, mix cooked quinoa, black beans, diced tomatoes, diced onion, minced garlic, and seasonings.
  3. Spoon the quinoa mixture into each bell pepper half.
  4. Bake for 25-30 minutes or until the peppers are tender. Serve hot.

20. Sesame Ginger Tofu Stir-Fry

- Ingredients:
  - Firm tofu, cubed
  - Mixed vegetables (such as bell peppers, broccoli, and snap peas)
  - Minced ginger
  - Soy sauce or tamari
  - Sesame oil
  - Olive oil
  - Sesame seeds (for garnish)
- Instructions:
  1. Heat olive oil in a skillet over medium-high heat. Add cubed tofu and cook until golden brown on all sides.
  2. Add mixed vegetables and minced ginger to the skillet and stir-fry until tender-crisp.
  3. Stir in soy sauce or tamari and sesame oil, cooking for an additional 2-3 minutes.
  4. Serve hot, garnished with sesame seeds.

Healthy Snacks and Desserts

1. Chia Seed Pudding

- Ingredients:
  - 1/4 cup chia seeds
  - 1 cup almond milk (or any plant-based milk)
  - 1 tablespoon maple syrup or agave nectar
  - Fresh fruit for topping (such as berries or sliced bananas)
- Instructions:
  1. In a bowl, mix chia seeds, almond milk, and maple syrup/agave nectar.
  2. Let it sit in the refrigerator for at least 2 hours or overnight to thicken.
  3. Serve chilled, topped with fresh fruit.

2. Frozen Banana Bites

- Ingredients:
  - Bananas, peeled and sliced
  - Nut butter of your choice (such as almond butter or peanut butter)
  - Unsweetened shredded coconut or crushed nuts (optional)
- Instructions:
  1. Spread nut butter on banana slices and sandwich them together.
  2. Roll each banana bite in shredded coconut or crushed nuts if desired.
  3. Place the banana bites on a baking sheet lined with parchment paper and freeze until firm.
  4. Enjoy as a delicious frozen treat.

3. Raw Energy Bars

- Ingredients:
  - 1 cup dates, pitted
  - 1 cup nuts of your choice (such as almonds or cashews)
  - 1/4 cup unsweetened cocoa powder or cacao powder
  - 1/4 cup shredded coconut (optional)
  - Pinch of sea salt
- Instructions:
  1. In a food processor, blend dates, nuts, cocoa powder, shredded coconut, and sea salt until a sticky dough forms.
  2. Press the mixture into a lined baking dish and refrigerate for at least 1 hour to set.
  3. Cut into bars and store in the refrigerator for a quick and healthy snack.

4. Baked Apple Chips

- Ingredients:
  - Apples, thinly sliced
  - Cinnamon
- Instructions:
  1. Preheat the oven to 200°F (95°C).
  2. Arrange apple slices on a baking sheet lined with parchment paper.
  3. Sprinkle cinnamon over the apple slices.
  4. Bake for 1.5 to 2 hours, flipping halfway through, until the apples are dried and crispy.
  5. Let cool before serving as a crunchy and satisfying snack.

5. Avocado Chocolate Mousse

- Ingredients:
  - 2 ripe avocados
  - 1/4 cup cocoa powder
  - 1/4 cup maple syrup or agave nectar
  - 1 teaspoon vanilla extract
  - Pinch of sea salt
- Instructions:
  1. Scoop the flesh of the avocados into a blender or food processor.
  2. Add cocoa powder, maple syrup/agave nectar, vanilla extract, and sea salt.
  3. Blend until smooth and creamy, scraping down the sides as needed.
  4. Serve chilled, garnished with fresh berries if desired.

6. Cucumber Slices with Hummus

- Ingredients:
  - Cucumber, sliced
  - Hummus (homemade or store-bought)
- Instructions:
  1. Arrange cucumber slices on a plate.
  2. Serve with a side of hummus for dipping.
  3. Enjoy this refreshing and satisfying snack.

7. Coconut Date Balls
- Ingredients:
  - 1 cup pitted dates
  - 1/2 cup shredded coconut (plus extra for coating)
  - 1/4 cup raw almonds
  - 1 tablespoon coconut oil
- Instructions:
  1. In a food processor, blend dates, shredded coconut, almonds, and coconut oil until a sticky dough forms.
  2. Roll the mixture into balls.
  3. Roll each ball in shredded coconut to coat.
  4. Chill in the refrigerator for at least 30 minutes before serving.

8. Frozen Berry Yogurt Bark

- Ingredients:
  - Greek yogurt (or dairy-free yogurt)
  - Mixed berries (such as strawberries, blueberries, and raspberries)
  - Honey or maple syrup (optional)
- Instructions:
  1. Line a baking sheet with parchment paper.
  2. Spread Greek yogurt evenly onto the parchment paper.
  3. Top with mixed berries and drizzle with honey or maple syrup if desired.
  4. Freeze for 2-3 hours, then break into pieces and serve as a refreshing frozen treat.

9. Carrot Cake Energy Bites

- Ingredients:
  - 1 cup rolled oats
  - 1/2 cup shredded carrots
  - 1/4 cup almond butter
  - 1/4 cup maple syrup
  - 1 teaspoon cinnamon
  - Pinch of nutmeg
- Instructions:
  1. In a bowl, mix rolled oats, shredded carrots, almond butter, maple syrup, cinnamon, and nutmeg until well combined.
  2. Roll the mixture into balls and place on a lined baking sheet.
  3. Chill in the refrigerator for at least 30 minutes before serving.

10. Green Smoothie Popsicles

- Ingredients:
  - Handful of spinach or kale
  - 1 ripe banana
  - 1 cup frozen mixed berries
  - 1/2 cup almond milk (or any plant-based milk)
  - Optional: honey or maple syrup to sweeten
- Instructions:
  1. Blend spinach or kale, banana, mixed berries, and almond milk until smooth.
  2. Taste and sweeten with honey or maple syrup if desired.
  3. Pour the mixture into popsicle molds and insert sticks.
  4. Freeze for at least 4 hours or until solid. Enjoy these nutritious popsicles on a hot day!

11. Almond Butter Banana Slices

- Ingredients:
  - Bananas, sliced
  - Almond butter
  - Unsweetened shredded coconut (optional)
- Instructions:
  1. Spread almond butter onto banana slices.
  2. Optionally, sprinkle shredded coconut on top for added texture.
  3. Enjoy as a quick and satisfying snack.

12. Homemade Trail Mix

- Ingredients:
  - Raw almonds
  - Walnuts
  - Pumpkin seeds
  - Dried cranberries
  - Dried apricots, chopped

- Unsweetened coconut flakes
- Instructions:
  1. Mix all ingredients in a bowl.
  2. Store in an airtight container for a convenient and nutritious snack on the go.

13. Chocolate Avocado Pudding

- Ingredients:
  - Ripe avocados
  - Cocoa powder
  - Maple syrup or agave nectar
  - Vanilla extract
  - Almond milk (or any plant-based milk)
- Instructions:
  1. Blend avocados, cocoa powder, maple syrup/agave nectar, vanilla extract, and almond milk until smooth.
  2. Chill in the refrigerator for at least 30 minutes before serving.
  3. Enjoy this creamy and indulgent dessert guilt-free.

14. Baked Kale Chips

- Ingredients:
  - Fresh kale leaves, torn into bite-sized pieces
  - Olive oil
  - Salt and pepper
- Instructions:
  1. Preheat the oven to 300°F (150°C).
  2. Toss kale leaves with olive oil, salt, and pepper in a bowl until evenly coated.
  3. Spread kale leaves in a single layer on a baking sheet lined with parchment paper.
  4. Bake for 10-15 minutes or until crispy.
  5. Let cool before serving as a crunchy and nutritious snack.

15. Frozen Yogurt Blueberry Bites

- Ingredients:
  - Fresh blueberries
  - Greek yogurt (or dairy-free yogurt)
  - Honey or maple syrup (optional)
- Instructions:
  1. Dip each blueberry into Greek yogurt, coating evenly.
  2. Place the coated blueberries on a baking sheet lined with parchment paper.
  3. Drizzle with honey or maple syrup if desired.
  4. Freeze for 1-2 hours or until the yogurt is set.
  5. Enjoy these refreshing and fruity frozen treats.

16. Crispy Roasted Chickpeas

- Ingredients:
  - Canned chickpeas, drained and rinsed

- Olive oil
- Salt and spices (such as cumin, paprika, or garlic powder)
- Instructions:
  1. Preheat the oven to 400°F (200°C).
  2. Pat dry the chickpeas with a paper towel to remove excess moisture.
  3. Toss chickpeas with olive oil, salt, and desired spices until evenly coated.
  4. Spread chickpeas in a single layer on a baking sheet lined with parchment paper.
  5. Bake for 25-30 minutes or until crispy, shaking the pan halfway through. Let cool before serving.

17. Fruit and Nut Bars

- Ingredients:
  - Dates, pitted
  - Almonds
  - Cashews
  - Dried fruit (such as apricots or figs)
  - Unsweetened shredded coconut
- Instructions:
  1. In a food processor, blend dates, almonds, cashews, dried fruit, and shredded coconut until a sticky dough forms.
  2. Press the mixture into a lined baking dish and refrigerate for at least 1 hour to set.
  3. Cut into bars and store in the refrigerator for a quick and nutritious snack.

18. Baked Apple Slices with Cinnamon

- Ingredients:
  - Apples, thinly sliced
  - Cinnamon
- Instructions:
  1. Preheat the oven to 350°F (175°C).
  2. Arrange apple slices on a baking sheet lined with parchment paper.
  3. Sprinkle cinnamon over the apple slices.
  4. Bake for 15-20 minutes or until the apples are tender and lightly caramelized.
  5. Serve warm as a comforting and naturally sweet dessert.

19. Quinoa and Date Energy Balls

- Ingredients:
  - Cooked quinoa
  - Dates, pitted
  - Almond butter
  - Rolled oats
  - Vanilla extract
- Instructions:
  1. In a food processor, blend dates until they form a sticky paste.
  2. Add cooked quinoa, almond butter, rolled oats, and vanilla extract to the date paste. Blend until well combined.
  3. Roll the mixture into balls and refrigerate for at least 30 minutes before serving.

20. Cherry Almond Chia Pudding

- Ingredients:
  - Chia seeds
  - Almond milk (or any plant-based milk)
  - Maple syrup or agave nectar
  - Almond extract
  - Fresh or frozen cherries, pitted
- Instructions:

1. In a bowl, mix chia seeds, almond milk, maple syrup/agave nectar, and almond extract. Let it sit for 10 minutes.

2. In a blender, blend cherries until smooth.

3. Layer chia pudding and cherry puree in serving glasses.

4. Chill in the refrigerator for at least 1 hour before serving. Enjoy this delightful and nutritious dessert option!

Book 11: Dr. Sebi Fasting Guide

Benefits of Fasting

Dr. Sebi promoted fasting as a powerful tool for healing and detoxification. According to his teachings, fasting not only helps to cleanse the body of toxins but also improves overall health by giving the organs a break, allowing them to repair and rejuvenate. Here are some of the key benefits of fasting according to Dr. Sebi's fasting guide:

Detoxification is one of the primary benefits of fasting. It facilitates deep detoxification as the body, not occupied with digesting food, focuses more on metabolizing and eliminating toxins that have built up in the cells and tissues. Dr. Sebi emphasized that this process helps cleanse the blood, liver, kidneys, and other organs.

Fasting gives the digestive organs a much-needed rest, reducing the strain on the liver, kidneys, and gastrointestinal tract. This pause can help to reset the body's metabolic processes and improve organ efficiency. Dr. Sebi noted that regular fasting could lead to enhanced digestion and more effective nutrient absorption when eating resumes.

Weight loss is another significant benefit of fasting. It can be a safe and effective way to lose weight, as the body turns to fat stores for energy, leading to fat loss. Dr. Sebi pointed out that fasting, when done correctly, can help individuals achieve and maintain a healthy weight.

Mental clarity and emotional balance are often reported by those who engage in fasting. Dr. Sebi believed that fasting could clear the mind and calm the emotions, making it easier to cope with stress and anxiety. The reduction in mental fog and improved concentration can enhance overall well-being.

Increased energy levels can also result from fasting. Initially, one might feel tired, but after the body adjusts, energy levels often increase significantly. This increase is due to the body becoming more efficient at using energy, and also because less energy is devoted to digestion.

Overall, Dr. Sebi advocated for the inclusion of regular fasting into one's lifestyle as a way to purify the body and mind, improve health, and extend life. He emphasized that fasting should be approached with care and ideally under the guidance of health professionals or experienced fasting advocates to ensure it is done safely and effectively.

Types of Fasting According to Dr. Sebi

Dr. Sebi outlined several types of fasting, each with its specific purpose and benefits, allowing individuals to choose a method that fits their health status, lifestyle, and goals. Here's an overview of the types of fasting according to Dr. Sebi's fasting guide:

Water Fasting involves consuming only water for a set period. This type of fasting is one of the most straightforward and effective forms, helping in deep detoxification and giving the digestive system a complete rest. Dr. Sebi recommended water fasting for those looking to thoroughly cleanse their body, as it helps eliminate toxins and repair cells effectively.

Juice Fasting consists of consuming only fresh vegetable and fruit juices. This type of fast provides the body with vitamins and minerals while still promoting detoxification. Dr. Sebi suggested juice fasting as a more nourishing alternative to water fasting, suitable for those who may need more energy during the fast or who are new to fasting.

Intermittent Fasting involves alternating periods of eating and fasting and is typically done daily, such as eating all meals within an 8-hour window and fasting for the remaining 16 hours. Dr. Sebi appreciated intermittent fasting for its flexibility and effectiveness in improving metabolic health, aiding weight loss, and maintaining a healthy lifestyle without the need for extended periods of food deprivation.

Dry Fasting is considered the most extreme form, where one abstains from both food and water for a short period. Dr. Sebi mentioned that dry fasting accelerates detoxification but recommended it only for those experienced in fasting and under careful supervision due to its intense nature.

These various fasting methods offer different levels of intensity and benefits, and Dr. Sebi emphasized the importance of choosing the right type based on individual health needs and fasting experience. He also stressed the need for proper preparation and breaking the fast correctly to maximize the benefits and minimize any adverse effects.

Preparing for a Fast

Preparing for a fast is crucial to ensure its effectiveness and safety, according to Dr. Sebi. Proper preparation helps the body adjust to the absence of regular food intake and can significantly enhance the benefits of fasting. Dr. Sebi recommended several key steps for preparing for a fast:

Gradual reduction of food intake is important in the days leading up to the fast. Dr. Sebi advised eating lighter meals and focusing on foods that are easy to digest. Transitioning from solid foods to soups, smoothies, and then juices can help ease the body into the fasting state.

Eliminating processed and heavy foods such as meats, dairy, and refined sugars from the diet is crucial. Dr. Sebi emphasized the importance of removing these foods, which can cause toxin buildup and digestive stress, to prepare the body for a cleansing fast.

Increasing water intake before starting a fast is essential for hydration, which aids in the detoxification process and prepares the body to handle the fluid shifts that occur during fasting. Drinking plenty of spring water, herbal teas, or Dr. Sebi's recommended alkaline water can help ensure proper hydration.

Mental preparation is as important as physical preparation. Dr. Sebi encouraged individuals to set clear intentions for the fast and to mentally prepare for the challenges that might arise during fasting, such as hunger pangs and emotional fluctuations. Meditation and light physical activities such as walking or yoga can help calm the mind and strengthen resolve.

Planning for more rest than usual is advised since the body will be undergoing deep internal cleansing that can sometimes be taxing. Dr. Sebi advised reducing physical and stressful activities to conserve energy and allow the body to focus on healing.

Preparing the environment by creating a supportive atmosphere can significantly impact the success of the fast. This includes having the necessary supplies such as fresh fruits and vegetables for juicing, herbal teas, and clean water. It's also helpful to inform family members or housemates about the fast to ensure support and understanding during this period.

Especially for those new to fasting or with specific health conditions, Dr. Sebi recommended consulting with a health professional experienced in fasting before beginning any fast to ensure it's done safely and effectively.

Safely Breaking a Fast

Breaking a fast safely is as important as the fast itself, according to Dr. Sebi, who provided specific guidelines on how to reintroduce foods properly to avoid shocking the digestive system. Here's how Dr. Sebi recommended safely breaking a fast:

Begin with a gradual reintroduction of foods, starting with liquids and slowly moving to solids. The initial phase should involve fresh fruit juices or smoothies, which are gentle on the digestive system and begin to reintroduce nutrients and enzymes that help wake up the digestive tract.

After starting with juices or smoothies, the next step involves eating light meals. Suitable foods include raw fruits and steamed vegetables. These foods are high in fiber, which helps to activate bowel movements gently but are not overly taxing on the digestive system.

It is crucial to avoid heavy, processed, or fried foods immediately after a fast. Foods high in fat, protein, or complex carbohydrates can be very difficult for the body to digest after a fasting period. Dr. Sebi advised against reintroducing dairy products, meats, or sugary foods until the digestive system has readjusted.

Dr. Sebi emphasized the importance of chewing food thoroughly to aid digestion. Slow and mindful eating helps ensure that food is well digested and nutrients are absorbed effectively.

After a fast, the stomach contracts, and its capacity to hold food reduces. Dr. Sebi recommended eating smaller portions to avoid overloading the stomach and causing indigestion or discomfort.

Recognizing and respecting the body's signals is crucial. If certain foods cause discomfort or digestive issues when reintroducing them, it may be wise to delay incorporating those foods and focus on those that are easier to digest.

Keeping hydrated continues to be essential even after the fast is broken. Dr. Sebi advised continuing to drink plenty of water, herbal teas, and hydrating vegetables and fruits to support the digestive system as it adjusts back to regular food intake.

Tips for Extended Fasting

Extended fasting, which typically refers to fasting periods longer than 24 hours, requires careful preparation and consideration to ensure it is carried out safely and effectively. Dr. Sebi provided specific tips for those interested in undertaking extended fasts, emphasizing the importance of listening to the body and taking necessary precautions. Here are the tips Dr. Sebi recommended for extended fasting:

Preparation is key before embarking on an extended fast. It is crucial to prepare both mentally and physically. Gradually decrease your food intake a few days prior, focusing on light and easily digestible foods such as fruits and vegetables. This preparation helps ease the body into the fasting state, making the transition smoother and less shocking to your system.

Maintaining hydration is vital during an extended fast. Water is essential, but incorporating herbal teas can also be beneficial. These provide hydration while adding some minerals and antioxidants that support the body during the fasting process.

When fasting for extended periods, it's important to maintain electrolyte balance. Natural sources like coconut water or a homemade electrolyte drink containing lemon, water, and a pinch of salt can help keep electrolyte levels stable.

Extended fasting can significantly lower energy levels, especially in the initial stages. It's important to allow the body to rest and not overexert during this time. Light activities such as walking or gentle yoga can be beneficial, but strenuous activities should be avoided.

Keep a close eye on how your body is responding to the fast. Signs of fatigue, dizziness, or excessive weakness might indicate that it's time to break the fast or that adjustments are needed. Fasting should not cause severe discomfort or pain. If any serious symptoms occur, it's essential to seek medical advice.

Breaking an extended fast should be done very gradually and with care. Start with liquid foods like juices or broths before moving to solids. This approach helps prevent refeeding syndrome, a potentially dangerous condition that can occur if food is reintroduced too quickly after a significant period of fasting.

Fasting and Detoxification

In Dr. Sebi's teachings, fasting is regarded as a powerful method for detoxification, helping to cleanse the body of toxins and rejuvenate its natural functions. He emphasized that fasting not only helps in removing impurities from the bloodstream but also supports the healing processes of the body by giving the organs a much-needed rest. Here's how Dr. Sebi described the relationship between fasting and detoxification:

Fasting initiates a process called autophagy, where the body begins to consume and remove damaged and dysfunctional cells. This natural recycling process helps the body to detoxify and repair itself at a cellular level, promoting better health and longevity.

The liver and kidneys are crucial organs in the body's detoxification system. By fasting, the workload on these organs is significantly reduced, allowing them to repair and recover. During a fast, the liver can efficiently process and eliminate stored toxins, while the kidneys flush out metabolic wastes through increased urine production.

Fasting gives the digestive system a break from its constant work of processing food. This rest period allows the gastrointestinal tract to repair any damages and restore its functions, which is essential for effective detoxification. A healthy digestive system ensures that toxins are properly eliminated from the body.

During fasting, the body's energy is diverted from digestion to other systems, including the immune system. This shift allows the immune system to focus on identifying and eliminating pathogens and damaged cells, enhancing overall immune function and reducing the risk of infections.

Dr. Sebi particularly noted that fasting helps in reducing mucus buildup in the body, which he believed was a root cause of many diseases. By clearing mucus, the body's respiratory and digestive tracts are more efficient in their functions, contributing further to detoxification and overall well-being.

Fasting for Mental Clarity

Dr. Sebi recognized fasting not only as a physical detoxification tool but also as a powerful means to achieve mental clarity and emotional balance. According to his teachings, fasting can clear the mind and sharpen cognitive functions, making it a valuable practice for enhancing mental health. Here's how fasting contributes to mental clarity, as outlined in Dr. Sebi's fasting guide:

During fasting, the body's energy is not diverted to digestion, as it typically would be after eating. This conservation of energy allows the brain to function more efficiently. Dr. Sebi suggested that the absence of new food intake reduces the production of toxins that can lead to mental fog, thus enhancing mental clarity. By minimizing the load on the digestive system, the body can redirect its resources to rejuvenate the brain and other organs.

Fasting also leads to increased production of brain-derived neurotrophic factor (BDNF), a protein that plays a critical role in memory and learning. BDNF supports the survival of existing neurons and encourages the growth of new neurons and synapses. This neurotrophic effect is particularly beneficial for maintaining brain health and cognitive functions.

Moreover, fasting has been shown to increase the levels of norepinephrine, a neurotransmitter associated with alertness and focus. The boost in norepinephrine during fasting helps improve concentration and can also elevate mood, making tasks feel less challenging and more manageable.

Fasting helps in the regulation of blood sugar levels, which stabilizes mood and energy. Stable blood sugar prevents the highs and lows often associated with eating patterns that include refined sugars and high carbohydrate intake. This stability is crucial for maintaining focus and preventing irritability and fatigue.

Emotionally, fasting can also be a grounding experience, fostering a sense of inner peace and mindfulness. This mental state is conducive to reflection and meditation, allowing individuals to develop a deeper sense of self-awareness and emotional resilience.

Incorporating regular fasting into one's lifestyle, as recommended by Dr. Sebi, can be a transformative practice for both the mind and body. It clears mental clutter and enhances cognitive functions, supporting overall mental health and well-being.

Hydration and Electrolyte Balance During Fasting

Hydration and maintaining electrolyte balance are crucial aspects of fasting safely and effectively, as emphasized in Dr. Sebi's fasting guide. During fasting, the body continues to lose water and electrolytes through normal physiological processes like respiration, sweat, and urine. Here's how Dr. Sebi recommended managing hydration and electrolyte balance during fasting:

Dr. Sebi stressed the importance of staying adequately hydrated during a fast. Water is essential for numerous bodily functions, including the detoxification process. It helps flush toxins and waste from the body and supports kidney function. Dr. Sebi advised drinking at least one gallon of spring water daily during fasting to ensure proper hydration.

Electrolytes such as sodium, potassium, magnesium, and calcium are vital for maintaining fluid balance, muscle function, and nerve signaling. Dr. Sebi recommended incorporating natural sources of electrolytes into the fasting regimen. Coconut water is an excellent option, as it contains a balanced mix of electrolytes and is also gentle on the stomach. Other sources include herbal teas such as hibiscus or chamomile, which can provide soothing effects as well as necessary minerals.

During fasting, it's important to avoid substances that can cause dehydration. Dr. Sebi specifically warned against consuming caffeinated beverages and alcohol, as they can increase urine output and lead to a loss of electrolytes.

Dr. Sebi emphasized the importance of listening to your body's signals during fasting. Symptoms such as dizziness, extreme fatigue, or muscle cramps can be signs of dehydration or electrolyte imbalances. If any of these symptoms occur, it's crucial to reassess hydration strategies and consider breaking the fast if necessary.

While drinking water is vital, Dr. Sebi cautioned against overhydration, which can dilute electrolytes and lead to imbalances. He recommended drinking water steadily throughout the day instead of consuming large amounts quickly.

Book 12: Dr. Sebi Female Health

Women's Health and Hormonal Balance

Dr. Sebi emphasized the importance of addressing women's health and hormonal balance through natural and holistic methods. According to his teachings, many of the health issues women face are due to hormonal imbalances that can be managed or corrected through diet, herbs, and lifestyle adjustments. Here's an overview of Dr. Sebi's approach to women's health and hormonal balance:

Alkaline Diet: Central to Dr. Sebi's approach is the adoption of an alkaline diet rich in plant-based, nutrient-dense foods that help regulate the body's pH levels. An alkaline environment supports the proper function of the endocrine system, which regulates hormones. Foods like leafy greens, berries, nuts, and seeds are emphasized for their mineral content, particularly magnesium and calcium, which are crucial for hormonal health.

Herbal Remedies: Dr. Sebi recommended specific herbs that have been known to support women's hormonal health. These include:

- Red Raspberry Leaf: Known for its benefits particularly related to women's reproductive health, red raspberry leaf can help regulate menstrual cycles and decrease cramps. It is also beneficial during pregnancy as it tones the uterus and helps prepare the body for labor.

- Sarsaparilla: This herb contains plant-based hormones that mimic human hormones, which can be beneficial in balancing hormone levels in the body. It's particularly useful for issues like PMS and menopause.

- Nettle: Rich in iron, nettle helps in the production of hemoglobin, which is crucial for women who experience heavy menstrual bleeding. Nettle also supports adrenal and kidney health, which are vital for hormonal balance and detoxification.

- Sea Moss: Dr. Sebi often recommended sea moss because of its high iodine content, which is essential for thyroid health. The thyroid plays a significant role in hormonal regulation.

Hydration and Detoxification: Adequate hydration is essential for maintaining hormonal balance. Dr. Sebi advised drinking plenty of spring water to help flush out toxins and support cellular health. Periodic detoxification, through fasting or consuming detoxifying herbs, helps in clearing hormonal disruptors from the body.

Stress Management: Stress can have a profound effect on hormonal balance. Dr. Sebi advocated for practices such as yoga, meditation, and spending time in nature to reduce stress levels, which in turn supports hormonal health.

Exercise: Regular physical activity is important for maintaining a healthy weight, which can directly impact hormonal balance. Exercise also helps reduce insulin levels and increases insulin sensitivity, which is important for overall hormonal health.

Remedies for Reproductive Health

Dr. Sebi emphasized the importance of natural remedies in supporting female reproductive health. He believed that a combination of specific herbs, a nutrient-rich diet, and lifestyle modifications could significantly improve reproductive functions and address various female health concerns. Here are some of the remedies Dr. Sebi recommended for enhancing reproductive health:

Herbal Remedies:

- Red Raspberry Leaf: Dr. Sebi often recommended red raspberry leaf for its benefits to the female reproductive system. This herb is particularly valued for its ability to strengthen the uterine walls, improve menstrual cycle regularity, and decrease menstrual cramps. It is also traditionally used during pregnancy to ease labor pains and during postpartum recovery.

- Damiana: Known for its aphrodisiac properties, damiana is used to stimulate libido and improve sexual function. It also helps balance hormones and can be particularly beneficial for those suffering from hormonal imbalances that affect reproductive health.

- Sarsaparilla: This herb contains compounds that mimic the hormones naturally produced by the body, making it effective in balancing hormone levels and supporting overall reproductive health.

Diet and Nutrition:

- Alkaline Diet: Following an alkaline diet rich in fruits, vegetables, and whole grains helps maintain an optimal pH balance in the body, which is crucial for reproductive health. Foods high in zinc such as pumpkin seeds, and those rich in omega-3 fatty acids like hemp seeds, are especially beneficial for enhancing fertility and hormone function.

- Sea Moss: Rich in essential minerals and vitamins, sea moss supports thyroid function due to its high iodine content. A healthy thyroid is crucial for regulating reproductive hormones.

Hydration:

- Spring Water: Adequate hydration is vital for all bodily functions, including reproductive health. Dr. Sebi emphasized the importance of drinking plenty of spring water to help transport nutrients to the reproductive organs and support overall cellular health.

Lifestyle Changes:

- Stress Reduction: Chronic stress can have a negative impact on reproductive health by disrupting hormone levels and menstrual cycles. Dr. Sebi recommended practices such as meditation, gentle yoga, and spending time in nature to manage stress effectively.

- Regular Exercise: Moderate exercise improves blood circulation, which is essential for reproductive health. It helps deliver oxygen and nutrients more efficiently to the reproductive organs, supporting their function and health.

These natural remedies and lifestyle changes proposed by Dr. Sebi are designed to nurture the female reproductive system, promoting wellness and vitality through holistic and integrative approaches.

Diet for Menopause

Dr. Sebi's approach to managing menopause focused on using a natural diet to alleviate symptoms and maintain overall health during this transition. His recommendations aimed to support hormonal balance, reduce menopausal symptoms like hot flashes, mood swings, and insomnia, and enhance overall vitality. Here's an overview of the diet Dr. Sebi recommended for managing menopause:

Alkaline Diet: Central to Dr. Sebi's approach for menopause is maintaining an alkaline diet, which helps to reduce bodily inflammation and supports hormonal balance. This diet includes:
- Leafy Greens: Vegetables such as kale, spinach, and arugula are high in calcium and magnesium, which are important for bone health, especially crucial during menopause when the risk of osteoporosis increases.
- Fruits: Berries, apples, and melons are recommended for their antioxidant properties, which combat oxidative stress and help manage menopausal symptoms.
- Whole Grains: Foods like amaranth, quinoa, and wild rice are included for their fiber, which can help manage weight and support digestive health.

Phytoestrogen-rich Foods: Dr. Sebi suggested incorporating foods that naturally contain phytoestrogens, compounds that can mimic the effect of estrogen in the body, thereby helping to balance hormone levels and alleviate menopausal symptoms. Such foods include:
- Nuts and Seeds: Flaxseeds and sesame seeds are particularly high in phytoestrogens. They also provide healthy fats and fiber.
- Herbs: Certain herbs like red clover and black cohosh have been traditionally used to treat menopause symptoms due to their phytoestrogen content.

Avoid Processed Foods: Eliminating processed foods, high in sugars and unhealthy fats, is crucial. These foods can exacerbate menopausal symptoms by destabilizing hormone levels and increasing inflammation.

Hydration: Keeping well-hydrated is essential during menopause. Water helps to manage body temperature and reduce occurrences of hot flashes. Dr. Sebi recommended drinking plenty of spring water throughout the day.

Calcium-Rich Foods: Ensuring adequate calcium intake is vital during menopause to protect bone health. Dr. Sebi encouraged the consumption of alkaline vegetables and certain nuts and seeds, which are good sources of plant-based calcium.

Limit Caffeine and Alcohol: Reducing caffeine and alcohol can help mitigate some menopausal symptoms. Both can trigger hot flashes and disrupt sleep patterns, thus their consumption should be minimized.

Preventing Common Female Ailments

Dr. Sebi's approach to preventing common female ailments focused on holistic health practices, emphasizing the importance of a natural diet, herbal remedies, and lifestyle adjustments to maintain female reproductive health and prevent disorders. Here are key elements of Dr. Sebi's recommendations for preventing common female ailments:

Consistently following an alkaline diet was central to Dr. Sebi's approach for preventing female health issues. This diet helps reduce acidity in the body, which can contribute to inflammation and various reproductive health problems. The diet includes fresh vegetables and fruits that are high in nutrients, antioxidants, and fiber, supporting hormonal balance and detoxification. Whole grains and legumes such as quinoa, wild rice, and chickpeas provide essential B vitamins and minerals that support overall health and help regulate hormonal function.

Dr. Sebi recommended specific herbs known for their benefits to female health, including red raspberry leaf, which is celebrated for its ability to tone the uterus and improve menstrual cycle regularity. Herbs like nettle and dandelion are valued for their high mineral content and supportive effects on the urinary and digestive systems, which are crucial for overall female health.

Maintaining hydration is essential, especially for women, as it supports all bodily functions, including those of the reproductive system. Drinking plenty of water helps keep the body's tissues hydrated and assists in the natural detoxification processes through the kidneys and skin.

Reducing stress is vital in preventing female ailments. Chronic stress can lead to hormonal imbalances that affect the reproductive system. Dr. Sebi advocated for practices such as meditation, deep breathing exercises, and gentle physical activities like yoga to help manage stress effectively.

Regular physical activity not only helps in stress reduction but also promotes better circulation and overall health. It can help maintain a healthy weight, which is important for hormonal balance and preventing conditions like polycystic ovary syndrome (PCOS) and obesity-related issues.

Avoiding toxins and chemicals from processed foods, cosmetics, and environment is crucial. These substances can disrupt hormonal balance and lead to health issues. Dr. Sebi recommended focusing on organic and natural products as much as possible.

Recommended Herbs and Supplements

Dr. Sebi's approach to female health included the use of specific herbs and supplements that target various aspects of women's wellness, from reproductive health to hormonal balance. He believed that certain natural herbs and minerals could significantly support and enhance the female body's functions. Here are some of the herbs and supplements Dr. Sebi recommended for female health:

Red Raspberry Leaf: Highly prized for its benefits to the female reproductive system, red raspberry leaf is known for toning the uterus, improving menstrual cycle regularity, and decreasing menstrual cramps. It is also recommended during pregnancy to help strengthen the uterine muscles, potentially making childbirth easier.

Nettle: Rich in iron, vitamins, and minerals, nettle is excellent for women who may suffer from anemia, especially due to heavy menstrual cycles. It's also a natural diuretic and can support kidney health, which is essential for overall hormonal balance.

Dandelion: Known for its liver-cleansing properties, dandelion is beneficial for detoxifying and metabolic health. It helps in the natural detoxification process and supports liver function, which is crucial for the regulation of hormones.

Sarsaparilla: This herb contains compounds that mimic human hormones, which can be beneficial in balancing hormone levels naturally. Sarsaparilla is often used to treat skin conditions, increase libido, and improve overall energy levels, all of which can be affected by hormonal changes.

Sea Moss: Dr. Sebi frequently recommended sea moss because of its high mineral content, particularly iodine, which is crucial for thyroid health. The thyroid gland plays a significant role in hormonal regulation, and maintaining its health is vital for overall balance.

Burdock Root: Another powerful blood purifier, burdock root helps remove toxins from the blood. It's also beneficial for skin health, which can be problematic for women suffering from hormonal imbalances that cause acne or other skin conditions.

Chondrus Crispus (Irish Moss): Similar to sea moss, Irish moss is loaded with nutrients and minerals that support female reproductive health and general well-being. It's particularly rich in iodine, calcium, potassium, and Vitamin C.

Yellow Dock: This herb is another blood purifier and is specifically useful for its iron content, making it helpful for women prone to iron-deficiency anemia. It also promotes healthy digestion, which is crucial for proper nutrient absorption.

These herbs and supplements can be integrated into daily routines either through dietary consumption or as part of a regimen including teas, capsules, or tinctures. Dr. Sebi's recommendations aim to harness the natural power of herbs to support and enhance women's health holistically, addressing underlying issues rather than just symptoms.

Natural Treatments for PMS And Cramps

Dr. Sebi offered natural treatments for managing premenstrual syndrome (PMS) and menstrual cramps, focusing on alleviating symptoms through dietary adjustments, herbal remedies, and lifestyle changes. His approach emphasized the use of natural products to balance hormones and reduce inflammation, which often contributes to the discomfort associated with PMS and cramps. Here's a detailed look at Dr. Sebi's recommendations for natural treatments for PMS and cramps:

Herbal Remedies:

- Red Raspberry Leaf: This herb is renowned for its uterine toning properties, which can help alleviate menstrual cramps. It also supports overall reproductive health and may reduce PMS symptoms.
- Chamomile Tea: Known for its calming and anti-inflammatory properties, chamomile tea can relieve muscle spasms and reduce the severity of menstrual cramps. It also helps soothe stress and anxiety, which can exacerbate PMS symptoms.
- Ginger: Ginger is effective in reducing inflammation and pain. It can help lessen the severity of cramps and is also beneficial for soothing digestive disturbances often associated with PMS.

Dietary Adjustments:

- Alkaline Diet: Sticking to an alkaline diet helps reduce inflammation in the body and can alleviate some of the symptoms of PMS and menstrual cramps. Foods high in magnesium and calcium, such as leafy greens and almonds, are particularly beneficial as they help in muscle relaxation and nerve function.
- Avoiding Trigger Foods: Reducing intake of caffeine, sugar, and dairy products can help manage PMS symptoms. These foods can increase inflammation and might worsen bloating, mood swings, and irritability.

Supplements:

- Magnesium: This mineral is crucial for muscle relaxation and has been shown to help alleviate menstrual cramps and reduce PMS symptoms such as headaches and mood swings.
- Vitamin B6: Vitamin B6 can help improve mood and reduce symptoms of PMS, including bloating and irritability.
- Calcium: Regular calcium intake has been linked to reductions in PMS symptoms, particularly in mood disturbances and physical discomfort.

Physical Activity:

- Regular Exercise: Engaging in regular, moderate exercise like walking, yoga, or swimming can help reduce the severity of PMS symptoms and menstrual cramps. Exercise helps improve blood flow and can boost mood through the release of endorphins.

Stress Management Techniques:

- Yoga and Meditation: These practices not only help relieve stress but also aid in reducing the physical pain associated with menstrual cramps. Relaxation techniques can help mitigate the emotional symptoms of PMS, such as anxiety and mood swings.

Adequate Hydration:

- Drinking Plenty of Water: Staying well-hydrated is essential, especially during the menstrual period. It helps reduce bloating and alleviate cramps.

Fertility and the Alkaline Diet

Dr. Sebi emphasized the connection between fertility and diet, advocating for an alkaline diet as a key factor in improving reproductive health and enhancing fertility. He believed that a body's acidic environment could negatively affect reproductive function and that an alkaline diet could help create the optimal conditions for fertility. Here's how Dr. Sebi linked fertility and the alkaline diet:

Alkalizing Foods: Dr. Sebi recommended a diet rich in alkaline foods to help balance the body's pH levels. Foods that are high in alkalinity include leafy greens, such as kale and spinach, which are packed with essential vitamins and minerals that support hormone balance and detoxification. Other alkaline-promoting foods include cucumbers, avocados, bell peppers, and alkaline grains like quinoa and amaranth. These foods help cleanse the blood and reproductive organs, creating a healthier environment for conception.

Nutrient-Rich Foods: Fertility can be enhanced by nutrients that support reproductive health. Dr. Sebi advised incorporating foods high in iron, folate, zinc, and omega-3 fatty acids, which are crucial for hormone production, egg health, and overall reproductive wellness. Foods such as hemp seeds, walnuts, and Brazil nuts are recommended for their nutrient density and beneficial effects on hormone regulation.

Herbal Supplements: Dr. Sebi suggested the use of specific herbs to support fertility. For example, Sarsaparilla and Irish moss were recommended due to their high mineral content, particularly zinc, which is vital for both male and female fertility. These herbs not only support hormonal balance but also improve overall vitality, which is important for reproductive health.

Reducing Inflammation: Chronic inflammation can impair fertility by affecting ovulation, hormone production, and implantation. An alkaline diet helps reduce inflammation throughout the body, including the reproductive system. This diet eliminates inflammatory foods such as processed sugars, dairy, and high-fat meats, which are known to adversely affect fertility.

Detoxification: Dr. Sebi stressed the importance of detoxifying the body to remove toxins that can affect the endocrine system and reproductive organs. An alkaline diet promotes the elimination of toxins through enhanced liver function and kidney filtration, which is crucial for maintaining reproductive health.

Hydration: Proper hydration is essential for maintaining cervical fluid, which plays a critical role in helping sperm reach the egg. Dr. Sebi recommended drinking plenty of spring water to ensure adequate hydration, which supports all bodily functions, including reproductive processes.

Hormonal Acne Solutions

Dr. Sebi's approach to treating hormonal acne focused on addressing the root causes rather than just the symptoms. He believed that imbalances in the body, particularly hormonal imbalances and accumulation of toxins, were major contributors to acne. To combat hormonal acne, Dr. Sebi recommended a combination of dietary adjustments, herbal treatments, and lifestyle changes to restore balance and promote skin health.

Dr. Sebi emphasized the importance of an alkaline diet in reducing inflammation and removing toxins that contribute to acne. He advised consuming a diet rich in whole, plant-based foods that alkalize the body, such as leafy greens, fruits, nuts, and seeds. These foods help to cleanse the blood and reduce the acid levels in the body, which can improve skin health and reduce acne outbreaks.

Dr. Sebi suggested avoiding foods that can exacerbate acne, such as dairy products, refined sugars, and processed foods. These foods can lead to increased oil production in the skin and hormonal imbalances, both of which are common triggers for acne.

Several herbs were recommended by Dr. Sebi for their purifying and healing properties. Burdock root, known for its blood-cleansing capabilities, helps to remove toxins that can lead to skin issues. Its anti-inflammatory properties also help to reduce the swelling and redness associated with acne. Sarsaparilla is another herb suggested for its ability to balance hormones and cleanse the blood, making it effective in treating skin conditions related to hormonal imbalances.

In addition to diet and herbal remedies, Dr. Sebi stressed the importance of maintaining proper hydration to help flush out toxins from the body and support skin health. Drinking plenty of spring water is essential for keeping the skin hydrated and for overall detoxification.

Managing stress through relaxation techniques such as yoga and meditation can also help control the hormonal fluctuations that contribute to acne. Stress management is crucial as stress can significantly impact hormone levels and exacerbate skin conditions.

Book 13: Dr. Sebi Female Health

Essential herbs in Dr. Sebi's diet

Dr. Sebi's dietary guidelines incorporated a variety of herbs that he considered essential for maintaining health and treating diseases. These herbs not only support detoxification and healing but also provide vital minerals and vitamins necessary for body functions. Here's a breakdown of some of the essential herbs in Dr. Sebi's diet:

Burdock Root is a powerful blood purifier that helps to remove toxins from the blood. It has diuretic properties which help to detox the kidneys and liver. Rich in iron, it aids in alleviating anemia and supports overall energy levels.

Elderberry is known for its immune-boosting properties. This herb is particularly effective in fighting colds and flu due to its high vitamin C and antioxidant content. Elderberry also supports skin health due to its anti-inflammatory effects.

Sarsaparilla is another key herb in Dr. Sebi's regimen. It is valued for its ability to cleanse the blood and improve overall metabolic health. Sarsaparilla contains compounds that mimic the effects of natural reproductive hormones, which can help balance hormone levels in the body.

Sea Moss is a staple in Dr. Sebi's diet for its rich mineral content. It provides 92 of the 102 minerals that the human body needs, including iodine, calcium, potassium, and sulfur. Sea Moss is excellent for supporting thyroid function, improving metabolism, and promoting healthy skin and hair.

Nettle is highly nutritious and acts as a general tonic to increase energy levels. It is rich in vitamins A, C, K, and several B vitamins, as well as minerals like iron, calcium, magnesium, and potassium. Nettle is beneficial for detoxifying the body and reducing inflammation.

These herbs are integral to Dr. Sebi's dietary recommendations, each selected for their unique properties that contribute to cleansing, healing, and nourishing the body. Incorporating these herbs into a daily regimen is part of Dr. Sebi's holistic approach to achieving and maintaining optimal health.

Specific Benefits of Essential Herbs

Dr. Sebi promoted the use of specific herbs for their unique health benefits, which are crucial in his holistic approach to healing and wellness. Each herb in his regimen serves specific purposes, from detoxifying the body to enhancing immune function. Here are the specific benefits of some of the essential herbs according to Dr. Sebi:

Burdock Root: Burdock root is celebrated for its blood-purifying properties. It helps to clear the bloodstream of toxins, which can improve skin health and reduce the incidence of eczema and acne. It also supports liver health and aids in digestion, making it an all-around detoxifier.

Elderberry: Elderberry is primarily known for its immune-enhancing abilities. It's rich in antioxidants and vitamins that help fight colds, flu, and other viral infections. Elderberry also has anti-inflammatory properties, which can help alleviate symptoms of arthritis and other inflammatory conditions.

Sarsaparilla: This herb is famous for its role in naturally balancing hormones. It contains plant sterols that can mimic human hormones such as estrogen and testosterone, making it useful for those suffering from hormonal imbalances. Sarsaparilla is also beneficial for skin health, helping to treat psoriasis, eczema, and acne.

Sea Moss: Sea Moss is incredibly nutritious, packed with essential minerals like iodine, which is crucial for healthy thyroid function. The thyroid gland regulates metabolism, and proper thyroid function is essential for energy regulation and weight management. Sea Moss also promotes digestive health due to its high fiber content, which can help to prevent constipation and maintain a healthy gut.

Nettle: Nettle is a powerhouse of nutrients, containing a wide array of vitamins and minerals. It is particularly rich in iron, making it excellent for combating anemia and fatigue. Nettle also has natural anti-inflammatory properties, which are beneficial for treating conditions such as arthritis and chronic muscle pain. Additionally, it supports urinary tract function and can help prevent urinary infections.

Each of these herbs plays a crucial role in Dr. Sebi's holistic health approach, addressing specific health concerns and supporting overall well-being. By integrating these herbs into a daily health regimen, individuals can harness their natural properties to maintain and enhance health according to Dr. Sebi's teachings.

How and When to Use These Herbs

Dr. Sebi's recommendations for using herbs emphasized their proper preparation and timing to maximize their health benefits. Here's a guide on how and when to use these essential herbs effectively:

Burdock Root

- How to Use: Burdock root can be consumed in several forms, including teas, tinctures, and capsules. For tea, simmer about one teaspoon of dried root in a cup of water for 10-15 minutes.
- When to Use: Best taken in the morning or early afternoon to support detoxification processes throughout the day without interfering with sleep.

Elderberry

- How to Use: Elderberry is commonly used in syrups, teas, and extracts. For preventive purposes, elderberry syrup can be taken daily during the cold and flu season.
- When to Use: If using to fight off a cold or flu, take elderberry syrup at the first sign of symptoms and continue until symptoms resolve.

Sarsaparilla

- How to Use: Sarsaparilla can be taken as a capsule, tea, or tincture. For tea, steep one teaspoon of the dried root in hot water for about 10 minutes.

- When to Use: Sarsaparilla is best used regularly to help balance hormones and can be taken daily, typically in the morning.

Sea Moss

- How to Use: Sea moss gel is the most common form and can be added to smoothies, teas, or consumed directly. It can also be used as a thickener in soups and desserts.
- When to Use: Sea moss can be consumed daily as part of a balanced diet to ensure consistent intake of its rich mineral content.

Nettle

- How to Use: Nettle is often brewed as a tea or taken as a supplement or tincture. To make nettle tea, steep dried leaves in boiling water for 10-15 minutes.
- When to Use: Nettle tea can be consumed daily, and due to its energizing effects, it's best taken in the morning or early afternoon.

Basic Herb-Based Recipes

Dr. Sebi's approach included using herbs not only for their medicinal properties but also in everyday recipes to incorporate their benefits into daily life seamlessly. Here are some basic herb-based recipes using Dr. Sebi's essential herbs that can be easily made at home:

Burdock Root Tea

- Ingredients:
  - 1-2 teaspoons of dried burdock root
  - 1 liter of water
- Method:
  - Bring the water to a boil in a pot.
  - Add the dried burdock root.
  - Reduce the heat and simmer for about 15 to 30 minutes.
  - Strain the tea into a cup and enjoy.
  - Optionally, add natural sweeteners like agave syrup or date sugar to taste.

Elderberry Syrup

- Ingredients:
  - 1/2 cup dried elderberries
  - 2 cups of water
  - 1 cup raw agave syrup
- Method:
  - Combine elderberries and water in a saucepan.
  - Bring to a boil, reduce heat, and simmer for about 45 minutes or until the liquid has reduced by half.
  - Strain the liquid using a fine mesh sieve, pressing the berries to extract all the juice.
  - Discard the elderberries and let the liquid cool.
  - Stir in the agave syrup until well combined.

- Store in a sealed glass jar in the refrigerator.

Sarsaparilla Tea

- Ingredients:
  - 1 teaspoon of dried sarsaparilla root
  - 1 cup of water
- Method:
  - Boil water in a kettle.
  - Add sarsaparilla root to a tea infuser or directly to the pot.
  - Pour hot water over the herb and let it steep for about 10 minutes.
  - Strain and serve. Sweeten if desired.

Sea Moss Gel

- Ingredients:
  - 1 cup raw sea moss (properly cleaned and soaked)
  - 2-3 cups of spring water
- Method:
  - Rinse the soaked sea moss thoroughly to remove any impurities.
  - Place the sea moss in a blender, add spring water, and blend until smooth.
  - The gel can be stored in a sealed container in the refrigerator for up to three weeks.
  - Use it as a base for smoothies, or add it to teas, soups, and desserts as a nutrient booster.

Nettle Leaf Tea

- Ingredients:
  - 1-2 teaspoons of dried nettle leaves
  - 1 cup of water
- Method:
  - Boil water in a kettle.
  - Add the nettle leaves to a tea infuser or directly into the pot.
  - Pour hot water over the leaves and let it steep for 10 minutes.
  - Strain and drink. Optionally, add lemon or honey for flavor.

Optimal Storage of Herbs

Proper storage of herbs is crucial to maintain their potency and medicinal qualities. Dr. Sebi emphasized the importance of storing herbs correctly to ensure they retain their therapeutic benefits. Here are some guidelines for the optimal storage of herbs:

Keep Herbs Dry: Moisture is one of the main enemies of stored herbs as it can lead to mold and mildew. Ensure that herbs are completely dry before storing. If you have fresh herbs, they can be air-dried or dehydrated before storage.

Use Airtight Containers: Store dried herbs in airtight containers. Glass jars with tight-sealing lids are ideal as they do not allow air to enter, which can degrade the herbs. Avoid using plastic if possible, as it can leach chemicals over time and may affect the flavor and properties of the herbs.

Protect From Light: Light can degrade herbs quickly, reducing their effectiveness. Store herbs in tinted glass containers that block UV rays or keep them in a cupboard or drawer where direct light does not reach them.

Maintain Cool Temperatures: Heat can also degrade herbs, so it's important to store them in a cool place. A pantry or cabinet away from heat sources like stoves, ovens, or direct sunlight is ideal. Avoid storing herbs above appliances that generate heat.

Label Containers: It's essential to label your herb containers with the name of the herb and the date of storage. Herbs can lose potency over time, so knowing how long they have been stored will help you determine their effectiveness.

Keep Them Whole: If possible, store herbs in their whole form and grind or crush them when you are ready to use them. Whole herbs retain their oils and active ingredients longer than powdered forms.

Check Regularly: Periodically check your stored herbs for any signs of spoilage such as mold, a musty smell, or dampness. If you notice any of these signs, it is best to discard the herbs as they may no longer be safe or effective.

Rotate Stock: Use older stocks of herbs first before newer ones to ensure they are used within their optimal period of potency. Most dried herbs can be kept for up to one year, but some may lose their strength quicker depending on how they are processed and stored.

Medicinal Properties of Wild Herbs

Dr. Sebi placed significant emphasis on the value of wild herbs for their potent medicinal properties. Wild herbs often grow in their natural habitat without human intervention, which can make them richer in nutrients and bioactive compounds compared to cultivated counterparts. Here's an overview of the medicinal properties of several key wild herbs that were integral to Dr. Sebi's health recommendations:

Burdock Root: Found growing wild in various parts of the world, burdock root is celebrated for its powerful detoxification properties. It acts as a blood purifier, helps cleanse the liver, and has diuretic effects which aid in removing toxins from the body. Burdock root contains inulin, a prebiotic that can support gut health, and is also rich in antioxidants that protect cells from oxidative stress.

Dandelion: Commonly seen in fields and along roadsides, dandelion is a potent medicinal herb with a wide range of health benefits. The leaves are diuretic, helping to flush toxins from the kidneys and reduce swelling. The roots support liver function and help improve digestion. Dandelion is also rich in vitamins A, C, and K, and minerals such as iron, calcium, magnesium, and potassium.

Nettle: Stinging nettle grows wild in many parts of the world and is highly nutritious. It is used for its anti-inflammatory properties, making it beneficial for treating conditions like arthritis and allergies. Nettle is a natural antihistamine, and it supports the reduction of allergic reaction symptoms. It is also a tonic for the blood, enhancing the creation of red blood cells, and is rich in iron, making it excellent for treating anemia.

Red Clover: This wild herb is known for its ability to balance hormones due to its isoflavone content. Red clover is commonly used to ease menopausal symptoms such as hot flashes and night sweats. It's also a blood purifier and is believed to support cardiovascular health by improving arterial flexibility and helping to lower bad cholesterol levels.

Sarsaparilla: Often found in tropical and temperate regions around the world, sarsaparilla is traditionally used for its detoxifying and purifying properties. It contains compounds that mimic human hormones, which can be beneficial for balancing hormone levels naturally. Sarsaparilla is also known for its ability to bind to endotoxins and remove them from the body, supporting overall immune function.

Irish Moss (Sea Moss): Although not a "wild herb" in the traditional sense, sea moss grows naturally in the ocean and is harvested from its natural environment, making it wild. It is incredibly rich in minerals and vitamins, particularly iodine, which is crucial for thyroid function. Sea moss also acts as a mucilaginous substance, soothing the mucous membranes and aiding digestive health.

Creating Herbal Blends for Specific Conditions

Creating herbal blends involves combining different herbs that synergistically work together to target specific health conditions. Dr. Sebi often emphasized the power of herbal synergy in his teachings, suggesting that the right combinations can enhance the individual effects of each herb for more effective healing and wellness. Here's a guide on how to create herbal blends for specific conditions according to Dr. Sebi's approach:

First, identify the health condition that needs attention, such as digestive problems, hormonal imbalances, respiratory issues, or immune support.

Choose herbs that have known benefits for treating the identified condition. For example:

- For digestive health, consider herbs like peppermint, ginger, and fennel which aid in soothing the stomach, stimulating digestion, and reducing bloating.

- For hormonal balance, red raspberry leaf, sarsaparilla, and maca can be effective. These herbs support hormone regulation and reproductive health.

- For respiratory health, mullein, elderberry, and eucalyptus are beneficial as they help clear mucus, boost immune response, and open breathing passages.

- For immune boosting, elderberry, echinacea, and astragalus make a powerful combination to enhance the body's natural defenses.

Research each herb to understand its properties, benefits, and any potential interactions or contraindications. It's important to know how each herb affects the body and how it might interact with other herbs, medications, or underlying health conditions.

Determine the form in which each herb is most effective, whether it be dried leaves for tea, powdered for capsules, or extracts and tinctures. Some herbs release their active ingredients better in water as teas or decoctions, while others are more effective as tinctures or capsules.

Proportion the herbs correctly to ensure each contributes effectively without overpowering the others. Start with equal parts and adjust based on the strength and desired effect of each herb.

Mix the herbs thoroughly to ensure a homogeneous blend. Store your herbal blend in a cool, dry place in an airtight container to preserve its potency.

Test your herbal blend in small amounts to gauge its effectiveness and make any necessary adjustments to the formulation.

Educate on how to use the herbal blend safely, including dosages, frequency, and any specific instructions on how to prepare and administer the blend.

Safe Herb Consumption Practices

Dr. Sebi stressed the importance of consuming herbs safely to ensure they provide their intended benefits without causing any adverse effects. Here are some key guidelines for safe herb consumption practices based on Dr. Sebi's teachings:

1. Understand the Herbs: Before using any herb, it's essential to thoroughly research its uses, benefits, and potential side effects. Knowledge about each herb can help prevent negative interactions and ensure its suitability for your particular health condition or overall wellness goals.

2. Consult Healthcare Providers: Always consult with a healthcare provider, especially if you have pre-existing conditions, are pregnant, or are currently taking medication. Some herbs can interact with medications or may not be suitable for certain health conditions.

3. Start with Small Doses: When trying a new herb, it's wise to start with small doses to see how your body reacts. Gradually increase the dosage as needed and as you monitor your body's response, ensuring there are no adverse reactions.

4. Listen to Your Body: Pay close attention to how your body responds to herbal treatments. If you experience any discomfort, adverse reactions, or unexpected changes in your health, discontinue use and consult a healthcare professional.

5. Avoid Long-Term Use Without Breaks: Some herbs are not meant for prolonged consumption without breaks. Regularly taking breaks can prevent your body from becoming too accustomed to the herb, which can reduce its efficacy or lead to dependency.

6. Quality and Purity: Use only high-quality, organic herbs from reputable sources. This ensures that the herbs are free from contaminants such as pesticides, heavy metals, and other pollutants that can detract from their health benefits and potentially harm your health.

7. Proper Preparation and Storage: Prepare herbs according to recommended methods to maximize their health benefits and ensure safety. Proper storage is also crucial to maintain their potency and prevent spoilage. Store herbs in a cool, dry place, away from direct sunlight and moisture.

8. Be Aware of Allergic Reactions: Even natural products like herbs can cause allergic reactions in some people. Be alert to any signs of allergy, such as itching, rash, difficulty breathing, or swelling, and seek immediate medical attention if these occur.

9. Respect Traditional Uses: While innovating with herbs can be tempting, respecting their traditional uses and preparation methods can often offer the safest and most effective way to benefit from their properties. Traditional preparations are typically based on long-standing practices that consider the balance and interactions of ingredients.

Book 14: Dr. Sebi Diabetes Cure

Understanding Type 1 and Type 2 Diabetes

Dr. Sebi's approach to understanding and treating diabetes involved a holistic perspective, focusing on natural remedies and dietary changes to manage and potentially reverse the condition. He differentiated between Type 1 and Type 2 diabetes, each having distinct causes and treatments in his methodology:

Type 1 Diabetes

Type 1 diabetes is an autoimmune condition where the body's immune system attacks and destroys insulin-producing cells in the pancreas. As a result, the body produces little to no insulin, which is necessary for transporting glucose from the bloodstream into the cells. Dr. Sebi viewed Type 1 diabetes as primarily genetic and harder to treat but believed that a holistic approach could help manage symptoms and improve quality of life.

For Type 1 diabetes, Dr. Sebi recommended an alkaline diet rich in whole, plant-based foods to help minimize blood sugar spikes and maintain overall health. This includes consuming leafy greens, vegetables, fruits, and nuts that are low on the glycemic index. Herbs that support pancreatic health and insulin sensitivity, such as bilberry and nopal, were suggested to complement dietary changes. Regular exercise and stress management techniques were also emphasized to help improve insulin sensitivity and overall well-being.

Type 2 Diabetes

Type 2 diabetes is often caused by lifestyle factors and develops over time. It involves insulin resistance, where the body's cells do not respond effectively to insulin, and over time, the pancreas may also produce less insulin. Dr. Sebi believed that Type 2 diabetes could be reversed through dietary changes, detoxification, and the use of specific herbs.

Dr. Sebi advocated for a strict alkaline diet to help reverse insulin resistance and promote weight loss, which is often necessary for managing Type 2 diabetes. Foods high in fiber and low in sugar and fat were recommended to help regulate blood sugar levels. Herbs like cinnamon, which is known to improve blood sugar control and enhance insulin sensitivity, were part of the regimen. Regular physical activity was also a critical component of the treatment plan, as it helps to lower blood glucose levels naturally and boost overall health.

In both cases, Dr. Sebi stressed the importance of cleansing the body and maintaining an alkaline environment to improve health outcomes in diabetic patients. His approach was not just about managing symptoms but rather addressing the root causes of diabetes to restore health and vitality.

Dietary Approaches for Managing Diabetes

Dr. Sebi's approach to managing diabetes through dietary means emphasizes a natural, plant-based diet to help regulate blood sugar levels and improve overall health. His recommendations involve strict adherence to foods that create an alkaline environment in the body, which he believed could help mitigate the effects of diabetes, particularly Type 2. Here are the key components of Dr. Sebi's dietary approaches for managing diabetes:

Alkaline Diet: Central to Dr. Sebi's dietary recommendations is the consumption of an alkaline diet. This diet excludes acidic, processed foods and focuses on natural, whole foods that help to alkalize the body's pH level. Recommended foods include leafy greens such as kale, spinach, and arugula, which are high in fiber and essential nutrients without causing blood sugar spikes. Non-starchy vegetables like bell peppers, cucumbers, and zucchini are emphasized for their low glycemic index.

Whole Grains: Incorporating whole grains like quinoa, wild rice, and amaranth is encouraged. These grains provide essential nutrients and fiber, which help maintain steady blood sugar levels and are vital for overall digestive health.

Nuts and Seeds: Almonds, walnuts, and hemp seeds are recommended for their healthy fats and protein. These nutrients are essential for managing hunger and stabilizing blood sugar levels.

Fruits: While fruits are included in the diet, Dr. Sebi advised selecting those lower in sugar and high in fiber. Berries, apples, and pears are excellent choices that can satisfy sweet cravings without causing significant glucose spikes.

Avoiding Harmful Foods: Dr. Sebi strongly advocated for avoiding sugar, artificial sweeteners, dairy products, and meat. These foods can exacerbate diabetes symptoms and contribute to overall health deterioration.

Herbal Teas: Consuming herbal teas such as ginger, cinnamon, and dandelion can help support blood sugar regulation and detoxification. These herbs have properties that benefit insulin sensitivity and liver health, both crucial for diabetic patients.

Hydration: Adequate hydration is crucial, and Dr. Sebi recommended drinking plenty of spring water throughout the day. Proper hydration helps manage blood sugar levels and supports kidney function, which can be compromised in diabetic individuals.

Herbs and Supplements for Diabetes

Dr. Sebi recommended various herbs and natural supplements as part of his holistic approach to managing and potentially reversing diabetes. These herbs and supplements were chosen for their ability to naturally support blood sugar control, enhance insulin sensitivity, and improve overall metabolic health. Here's an overview of the key herbs and supplements Dr. Sebi suggested for diabetes:

Cinnamon: Known for its ability to help lower blood sugar levels and enhance insulin sensitivity. Cinnamon can be added to foods or taken as a supplement to help manage Type 2 diabetes.

Nopal (Prickly Pear Cactus): Nopal is rich in fiber and pectin, which have been shown to help reduce blood glucose by decreasing sugar absorption in the stomach and intestines. It's typically consumed as cooked pads or as a juice.

Fenugreek: This herb has been shown to improve glucose tolerance and lower blood sugar levels due to its high fiber content. Fenugreek seeds can be soaked in water and consumed directly or added to food as a spice.

Gymnema Sylvestre: Often referred to as the "sugar destroyer," Gymnema Sylvestre helps reduce sugar cravings and can help decrease blood sugar levels by promoting the regeneration of pancreas islet cells and enhancing insulin production.

Bitter Melon: Contains at least three active substances with anti-diabetic properties, including charantin, which has been shown to have a blood glucose-lowering effect, vicine, and an insulin-like compound known as polypeptide-p. Bitter melon can be consumed as a vegetable, in juice form, or as a supplement.

Burdock Root: Acts as a blood purifier and can help detoxify the blood and promote blood circulation. This root is also known for its role in restoring liver and pancreas health, which are crucial for proper insulin function.

Irish Moss (Sea Moss): High in essential minerals and vitamins, Irish Moss can help nourish and support the overall health of individuals with diabetes. It is especially useful in maintaining a healthy mucous membrane, which is crucial for proper digestion and nutrient absorption.

Sarsaparilla: Known for its ability to cleanse the blood and improve overall organ health. It contains compounds that may mimic the action of certain human hormones, potentially aiding in balancing the body's metabolic processes affected by diabetes.

Lifestyle Changes for Diabetics

Dr. Sebi emphasized the importance of comprehensive lifestyle changes to effectively manage and potentially reverse diabetes. His recommendations extend beyond dietary adjustments, including several key lifestyle changes that can significantly impact blood sugar control and overall health for individuals with diabetes. Here's a summary of the lifestyle changes Dr. Sebi suggested for diabetics:

Regular physical activity is crucial in managing diabetes. Exercise helps lower blood sugar levels, boosts insulin sensitivity, and aids in weight management. Dr. Sebi recommended engaging in moderate activities such as walking, yoga, or swimming for at least 30 minutes most days of the week.

Keeping the body adequately hydrated is essential for health, particularly for diabetics, as it helps regulate blood sugar levels and supports kidney function. Dr. Sebi advised drinking plenty of spring water throughout the day to promote detoxification and maintain cellular health.

Stress can significantly affect blood sugar levels by increasing the release of stress hormones like cortisol and adrenaline, which can raise blood glucose levels. Dr. Sebi recommended practices such as meditation, deep breathing exercises, and spending time in nature to manage stress effectively. These activities not only reduce stress but also enhance overall well-being.

Adequate sleep is another critical aspect of managing diabetes. Poor sleep can affect insulin sensitivity and hormone regulation, which in turn can influence blood sugar levels. Dr. Sebi stressed the importance of getting 7-8 hours of quality sleep per night to help regulate the body's natural rhythms and support healthy glucose metabolism.

Avoiding toxins and pollutants in the environment is also important. Dr. Sebi pointed out that toxins can affect the body's metabolic processes, including glucose metabolism. He advised using natural cleaning products and personal care items to minimize exposure to harmful chemicals.

Monitoring and Maintaining Blood Sugar Levels

Dr. Sebi emphasized the critical importance of monitoring and maintaining stable blood sugar levels as a key component in managing and potentially reversing diabetes. Here are the strategies he recommended to achieve and maintain healthy blood sugar levels:

Regular monitoring of blood sugar levels is crucial to understand how different foods and activities affect glucose levels. This practice helps individuals identify patterns and make informed decisions about diet, exercise, and lifestyle adjustments.

Central to Dr. Sebi's approach is adherence to an alkaline diet that excludes processed sugars, artificial sweeteners, and high glycemic foods which can spike blood sugar levels. Instead, he recommended a diet rich in whole, plant-based foods that release energy slowly and maintain more stable glucose levels. Foods emphasized include leafy greens, nuts, seeds, and whole grains.

Eating at regular intervals helps prevent dramatic fluctuations in blood sugar levels. Dr. Sebi suggested having a consistent meal schedule and not skipping meals, especially breakfast, which can provide a stable energy source throughout the day.

Stress can significantly impact blood sugar levels by triggering the release of stress hormones like cortisol and adrenaline, which can raise blood glucose levels. Managing stress through techniques such as meditation, deep breathing, and regular physical activity is important for maintaining balanced blood sugar levels.

Adequate hydration is essential for maintaining blood sugar levels as it aids in the metabolism of glucose. Dr. Sebi recommended drinking plenty of spring water throughout the day to help facilitate the body's natural detoxification processes and support overall metabolic function.

The Impact of Alkaline Diet on Insulin Sensitivity

Dr. Sebi's teachings often highlighted the impact of an alkaline diet on improving insulin sensitivity, which is a key factor in managing and potentially reversing diabetes, especially Type 2 diabetes. According to Dr. Sebi, an alkaline diet helps normalize the body's pH levels, reduces inflammation, and can significantly enhance insulin sensitivity. Here's an overview of how an alkaline diet impacts insulin sensitivity based on Dr. Sebi's principles:

Chronic inflammation is linked to reduced insulin sensitivity, which can worsen diabetes. An alkaline diet, rich in anti-inflammatory foods such as leafy greens, cucumbers, avocados, and alkaline fruits, helps reduce inflammation throughout the body. This not only aids in better glucose metabolism but also improves overall health.

Dr. Sebi believed that a buildup of toxins in the body could lead to insulin resistance. An alkaline diet promotes detoxification, helping to cleanse the liver and kidneys, organs crucial for filtering out toxins. Improved function of these detox organs can help enhance insulin sensitivity by reducing the body's toxic load.

Following an alkaline diet often leads to weight loss because it is high in fiber and low in fat and calories. Weight loss is known to improve insulin sensitivity, as it reduces the amount of fatty tissue that can release inflammatory substances that impair insulin action.

Foods that are part of an alkaline diet typically have a low glycemic index and do not cause sudden spikes in blood sugar levels. Consistent blood sugar levels prevent excessive demands on the pancreas for insulin production and can help maintain a more stable metabolic environment conducive to improved insulin sensitivity.

Foods To Avoid for Diabetics

Dr. Sebi's dietary guidelines for diabetics emphasize not only the importance of incorporating healthful foods but also strictly avoiding certain foods that can exacerbate the condition. According to Dr. Sebi, these foods can lead to increased blood sugar levels, insulin resistance, and overall poor health in diabetics. Here are the main types of foods Dr. Sebi advised diabetics to avoid:

Processed sugars and artificial sweeteners, found in foods such as sodas, candies, pastries, and other sweets, can cause rapid spikes in blood glucose levels. Dr. Sebi also recommended avoiding artificial sweeteners as they can have adverse effects on body chemistry and potentially promote insulin resistance.

While fruits are generally healthy, those with a high glycemic index like bananas, grapes, and watermelons should be consumed sparingly to prevent blood sugar spikes.

White bread, pasta, rice, and other refined grains are stripped of their fiber and nutrients during processing, which can lead to quick increases in blood glucose levels. Instead, Dr. Sebi promoted the consumption of whole grains like quinoa, amaranth, and wild rice.

Dr. Sebi argued that dairy products contribute to mucus formation and acidity in the body, which can impact insulin sensitivity. He advised against the consumption of milk, cheese, butter, and other dairy products.

Foods high in animal fat and protein, such as red meat, pork, and poultry, can contribute to insulin resistance and other health issues in diabetics. Dr. Sebi recommended a plant-based diet that avoids these foods.

Fried and greasy foods are not only hard on digestion but also high in unhealthy fats that can worsen insulin resistance and overall health. Dr. Sebi suggested avoiding these types of foods to maintain better control over diabetes.

Daily Routines to Manage Blood Sugar

Managing diabetes effectively involves incorporating specific daily routines that help maintain stable blood sugar levels and promote overall health. Dr. Sebi's approach to diabetes included several key daily practices that could help diabetics manage their condition naturally. Here is an outline of the daily routines recommended by Dr. Sebi to help manage blood sugar levels:

Morning Routine

- Start with Herbal Tea: Begin the day with a cup of herbal tea such as chamomile or ginger, which can help regulate blood sugar levels and aid digestion.
- Consume a Nutrient-Rich Breakfast: Eat a breakfast rich in fiber and low in sugar. Ideal options include alkaline grains like amaranth or quinoa, paired with fresh berries and seeds.

Midday Routine

- Hydration: Continue to drink plenty of spring water throughout the day to stay hydrated. Proper hydration is essential for maintaining blood sugar levels and overall metabolic health.
- Balanced Lunch: Have a lunch that includes a balance of protein, healthy fats, and low-glycemic carbohydrates. A salad with leafy greens, avocado, nuts, and a light dressing made from lime and olive oil can be a good option.

Afternoon Routine

- Physical Activity: Engage in moderate physical activity such as walking, yoga, or swimming. Exercise is crucial as it helps improve insulin sensitivity and manage blood glucose levels.
- Snack Wisely: If needed, have a healthy snack that is low in sugar and high in protein, such as a handful of almonds or a smoothie made with sea moss, cucumber, and apple.

Evening Routine

- Light Dinner: Eat a light dinner early in the evening to ensure that the body has enough time to metabolize the meal before bedtime. A meal similar to lunch, with plenty of vegetables and lean protein, can help prevent nighttime blood sugar spikes.
- Wind Down with Herbal Tea: Conclude the day with a relaxing herbal tea like chamomile, which can aid in digestion and help stabilize blood sugar levels overnight.

Before Bed

- Check Blood Sugar Levels: It's important for diabetics to monitor their blood sugar levels regularly. Checking levels before bed can help ensure they are stable through the night.
- Prepare for Quality Sleep: Ensure a good night's sleep, which is essential for overall health and particularly important for managing blood sugar. Try to maintain a consistent bedtime schedule and create a restful environment.

Book 15: Dr. Sebi Food List

Comprehensive List of Dr. Sebi Approved Foods

Dr. Sebi's dietary recommendations are centered around his alkaline diet, which consists of natural plant-based foods that help maintain the pH balance of the blood and optimize health. The diet excludes foods that create acidity within the body and focuses on those that promote alkalinity. Here is a comprehensive list of Dr. Sebi approved foods:

Vegetables

- Amaranth greens (callaloo)
- Avocado
- Bell peppers
- Chayote (Mexican squash)
- Cucumber
- Dandelion greens
- Garbanzo beans (chickpeas)
- Izote (cactus flower/ cactus leaf)
- Kale
- Lettuce (all except iceberg)
- Mushrooms (all except shiitake)
- Nopales (Mexican cactus)
- Okra
- Olives (and olive oil)
- Onions
- Sea vegetables (wakame/dulse/arame/hijiki/nori)
- Squash
- Tomato (cherry and plum only)
- Turnip greens
- Zucchini
- Watercress

Fruits

- Apples
- Bananas (the smallest one or the Burro/mid-size original banana)
- Berries (all varieties, excluding cranberries)
- Cantaloupe
- Cherries
- Currants
- Dates
- Figs
- Grapes (seeded)

- Limes (key limes preferred with seeds)
- Mango
- Melons (seeded)
- Orange (Seville or sour preferred, difficult to find)
- Papayas
- Peaches
- Pears
- Plums
- Prickly pear (cactus fruit)
- Raisins (seeded)
- Soft jelly coconuts
- Soursop
- Tamarind

Grains

- Amaranth
- Fonio
- Kamut
- Quinoa
- Rye
- Spelt
- Tef
- Wild rice

Nuts and Seeds

- Brazil nuts
- Hemp seeds
- Raw sesame seeds
- Raw sesame "tahini" butter
- Walnuts

Oils

- Olive oil (Do not cook)
- Coconut oil (Do not cook)
- Grapeseed oil
- Sesame oil
- Hempseed oil
- Avocado oil

Herbal Teas

- Anise
- Burdock
- Chamomile
- Elderberry
- Fennel

- Ginger
- Raspberry
- Tila

Nutritional Benefits of Key Foods

Dr. Sebi's food list comprises natural plant-based foods rich in essential nutrients that contribute to overall health and well-being. Here are some of the nutritional benefits of key foods from Dr. Sebi's approved list:

Vegetables:

- Kale: Rich in vitamins K, A, and C, as well as minerals like manganese, kale is a powerful antioxidant that helps fight oxidative stress and inflammation.
- Avocado: High in healthy monounsaturated fats, avocados are beneficial for heart health and contain potassium, which is vital for blood pressure regulation.
- Dandelion greens: These greens are an excellent source of vitamins A, C, and K, and they contain iron and calcium. They are also known for their detoxifying properties.

Fruits:

- Berries (all varieties): Berries are high in fiber, vitamin C, and antioxidant polyphenols, which are linked to reduced inflammation and lower risk of chronic disease.
- Mango: Provides a high amount of vitamin C, which boosts immune function, as well as fiber, which aids in digestion and overall gut health.
- Soursop: Known for its potential anti-cancer properties, soursop is also a good source of Vitamin C and B vitamins that are essential for maintaining energy levels and cellular health.

Grains:

- Quinoa: A complete protein, quinoa provides all nine essential amino acids that the body cannot produce on its own. It's also high in fiber and iron.
- Spelt: Spelt is an ancient grain rich in vitamins and minerals such as magnesium, which is important for bone health and metabolic function.
- Wild rice: Offers a substantial amount of protein and dietary fiber, promoting satiety and aiding in digestive health.

Nuts and Seeds:

- Hemp seeds: These seeds are a great source of plant-based protein and omega-3 fatty acids, which are crucial for brain health and reducing inflammation.
- Walnuts: High in omega-3 fatty acids, walnuts are known for their ability to support heart health and improve cognitive function.
- Brazil nuts: One of the best natural sources of selenium, a mineral that plays a key role in metabolism and thyroid function.

Oils:

- Olive oil: Known for its heart-health benefits, olive oil is rich in monounsaturated fats and antioxidants, particularly vitamin E.
- Coconut oil: Contains medium-chain triglycerides (MCTs) that are metabolized differently, providing a quick source of energy and potentially helping in weight management.

Herbal Teas:

- Ginger tea: Ginger has powerful anti-inflammatory properties and can help with nausea and digestion.
- Chamomile tea: Renowned for its calming effects, chamomile can aid in sleep and relaxation, and it may help reduce inflammation.

The foods on Dr. Sebi's list not only offer high nutritional value but are also chosen for their minimal impact on the body's acidity levels. By incorporating these foods into your diet, you can enjoy their health benefits while adhering to Dr. Sebi's principles of natural, alkaline eating.

How to Incorporate These Foods into Daily Meals

Incorporating foods from Dr. Sebi's food list into your daily meals can help you adhere to his alkaline diet principles, ensuring you consume nutrient-rich, natural foods that support overall health. Here are some practical ways to include these foods into your everyday eating habits:

Breakfast Options:

- Amaranth porridge topped with fresh berries and a sprinkle of hemp seeds. Amaranth is a gluten-free grain that is high in protein and fiber.
- Smoothies made with alkaline fruits like apples, pears, and berries, along with a handful of kale or spinach and some sea moss gel for added minerals.
- Spelt pancakes served with agave syrup and slices of fresh soursop or mango.

Lunch Ideas:

- Quinoa salad with chopped cucumbers, cherry tomatoes, avocado, and a dressing of lime juice and olive oil. Quinoa is excellent for providing a high-protein base that's also rich in fiber.
- Wild rice and vegetable stir-fry using Dr. Sebi-approved vegetables like bell peppers, onions, and mushrooms. Add some fresh herbs for flavor, such as cilantro or basil.
- Chickpea soup with kale and dandelion greens, seasoned with sea salt and cayenne pepper for an extra kick.

Dinner Suggestions:

- Grilled portobello mushrooms served with a side of sautéed asparagus and mashed butternut squash. Portobello mushrooms are a hearty, meaty option for an evening meal.
- Stuffed bell peppers with a filling of wild rice, herbs, and chopped vegetables, topped with a drizzle of grapeseed oil.
- Kale and avocado salad with slices of cucumber, olives, and a dressing made from tahini and lime juice.

Snacks and Small Bites:

- Raw nuts and seeds, such as walnuts and Brazil nuts, are great for snacking throughout the day. They provide healthy fats and are filling.
- Fruit slices like apple or pear paired with a small handful of almonds for a balanced snack.
- Sea moss gel can be added to teas or smoothies for a nutrient boost without altering the flavor significantly.

Herbal Teas and Beverages:

- Ginger tea in the morning to stimulate digestion and energize the body.
- Elderberry tea in the evening, known for its immune-boosting properties.
- Lime water throughout the day for hydration and added vitamin C.

Avoiding Non-Approved Foods

Adhering to Dr. Sebi's dietary guidelines involves not only incorporating the recommended alkaline foods but also diligently avoiding foods that are not approved on his list. These non-approved foods can disrupt the body's pH balance and negate the benefits of an alkaline diet. Here's how to avoid non-approved foods according to Dr. Sebi's dietary principles:

Familiarize yourself with Dr. Sebi's food list thoroughly. Knowing which foods are approved will make it easier to identify and avoid those that are not. Keeping a copy of the list handy, such as on your refrigerator or in your wallet, can be a helpful reminder when shopping or dining out.

Always read labels carefully when shopping. Processed and packaged foods often contain ingredients that are not approved by Dr. Sebi, such as artificial additives, preservatives, and harmful chemicals. Check labels to ensure the food you buy is free of these substances and consists only of natural, whole ingredients.

Prepare meals at home as much as possible. Cooking your meals can ensure that you are using only ingredients that adhere to Dr. Sebi's food list. This control is lost when eating out, as many restaurants may not use ingredients that fit the alkaline diet.

Educate yourself on the types of foods that typically contain non-approved ingredients. Common culprits include commercial salad dressings, sauces, baked goods, and snack foods. Opt for making your dressings and sauces with approved oils and seasonings to avoid hidden additives.

Be cautious when dining out. Choose restaurants that offer fresh, whole foods and are accommodating to customizing dishes to suit dietary needs. Don't hesitate to ask about the ingredients used in your meals and request substitutions when necessary to adhere to Dr. Sebi's guidelines.

Stay informed and updated as food lists and health guidelines can evolve. Dr. Sebi's official website and trusted resources related to his dietary teachings are good places to find updates and additional advice on following his food list effectively.

Shopping and Meal Planning Tips

Shopping and meal planning according to Dr. Sebi's food list can help ensure that you adhere to his alkaline diet principles efficiently and effectively. Here are some tips to assist with shopping and meal planning while following Dr. Sebi's dietary recommendations:

1. Make a Meal Plan: Before you shop, plan your meals for the week. This helps to ensure that you purchase only the items you need, reducing waste and impulse buys that might not align with Dr. Sebi's guidelines. Include a variety of recipes that utilize the diverse foods listed by Dr. Sebi to maintain an interesting and balanced diet.

2. Create a Shopping List: Based on your meal plan, create a detailed shopping list. Stick to this list when you shop to avoid purchasing non-approved items. This can also help streamline your shopping process and reduce time spent in stores.

3. Shop the Perimeter: Most grocery stores are designed with fresh produce, nuts, seeds, and whole grains around the perimeter of the store. Stick to these outer aisles as much as possible since they typically contain the healthiest and least processed foods.

4. Buy Organic and Non-GMO: Whenever possible, choose organic and non-GMO foods to minimize your exposure to pesticides and other chemicals that are not in line with Dr. Sebi's natural, toxin-free approach.

5. Bulk Buying: For non-perishable items such as grains and nuts, consider buying in bulk. This can be more economical and ensures you have a steady supply of essential items for your meals.

6. Read Labels Carefully: When buying packaged foods, always read the labels to check for hidden non-approved ingredients. Look out for added sugars, artificial additives, and preservatives.

7. Embrace Seasonal Eating: Purchase fruits and vegetables that are in season. Not only are they more affordable and at their nutritional peak, but they also align with the natural eating philosophy advocated by Dr. Sebi.

8. Frequent Local Farmers' Markets: Farmers' markets are great places to find fresh, locally-sourced produce that adheres to alkaline diet principles. This also supports local farmers and reduces the carbon footprint associated with long-distance food transportation.

9. Prep Meals in Advance: To save time and ensure adherence to the diet throughout the week, consider preparing meals in advance. Batch cooking and storing meals in the fridge or freezer can help you stay on track, especially during busy days.

10. Be Flexible and Experiment: While it's important to plan, be flexible enough to swap out ingredients based on availability or to experiment with new recipes. This keeps your diet interesting and allows you to explore a variety of nutritional benefits from Dr. Sebi's approved foods list.

Understanding Food Labels

Understanding food labels is crucial when following Dr. Sebi's food list to ensure the products you purchase align with his guidelines for an alkaline, natural diet. Here's a guide on how to read and understand food labels to help maintain adherence to Dr. Sebi's dietary principles:

The ingredients list is the most important section to check. Dr. Sebi emphasized consuming natural, whole foods free from artificial additives, preservatives, and chemicals. Look for short ingredient lists with recognizable items. Avoid products with artificial flavorings, colorings, preservatives, or any ingredients that are difficult to pronounce.

Check the sugar content on labels, and be wary of different names for sugar, including sucrose, high-fructose corn syrup, dextrose, and maltose. Dr. Sebi recommended avoiding processed sugars as they can disrupt the body's natural pH balance. Opt for foods that are naturally low in sugars or have no added sugars.

Look at the nutritional information to understand the content of fats, proteins, and carbohydrates. Dr. Sebi advocated for a diet low in saturated fats and high in natural, plant-based foods that provide essential nutrients. Ensure that the food aligns with this principle by checking the types of fat listed and opting for those with healthy fats like olive oil or coconut oil.

Sodium levels are also crucial to consider, as high sodium intake can be detrimental to health. Dr. Sebi's diet suggests minimizing salt intake to maintain the body's natural mineral balance. Look for low sodium options or foods where no salt is added.

Check for any allergens or substances that Dr. Sebi specifically advised against, such as dairy or gluten, if you are sensitive. These can often be found listed at the end of the ingredient list or in a separate allergen statement.

Organizing an Alkaline Pantry

Organizing an alkaline pantry according to Dr. Sebi's food list involves selecting and arranging foods that support an alkaline diet, which is central to his nutritional approach. An alkaline pantry will help maintain the body's natural balance and promote overall health. Here are steps and tips on how to organize an alkaline pantry effectively:

Begin by removing foods that do not comply with Dr. Sebi's guidelines. This includes products containing artificial ingredients, preservatives, high sodium, refined sugars, animal products, and non-alkaline grains.

Stock up on approved grains like amaranth, quinoa, spelt, and wild rice. These grains are excellent bases for meals and are versatile for both sweet and savory dishes.

Fill your pantry with a variety of alkaline-promoting nuts and seeds such as hemp seeds, walnuts, Brazil nuts, and raw sesame seeds. These are great for snacking or adding to meals for extra protein and healthy fats.

Include a selection of Dr. Sebi approved oils for cooking and dressing foods. Olive oil, grapeseed oil, and coconut oil are good choices. Remember to store oils in a cool, dark place to preserve their nutritional quality.

Keep a variety of dried or fresh herbs and spices to enhance the flavor of your meals without adding acidity. Focus on herbs like basil, oregano, cilantro, and spices such as cayenne pepper and sea salt.

Add a range of alkaline vegetables such as kale, avocado, cucumbers, and bell peppers. If fresh produce is difficult to keep stocked, consider some high-quality, organic frozen options.

For snacks and other quick meal components, stock up on chickpeas, lentils, and other approved legumes. These can be used to make salads, soups, and stews.

Dedicate a section for herbal teas and natural sweeteners like agave syrup or date sugar, which are better alternatives to refined sugar.

Use clear containers to store grains, nuts, seeds, and dried herbs. Label them for easy identification and to keep track of freshness dates.

Maintain organization by grouping similar items together and placing frequently used items within easy reach. This not only saves time while cooking but also helps in keeping track of what needs to be replenished.

Seasonal Variations in Food Selection

Adhering to Dr. Sebi's food list while considering seasonal variations can enhance the nutritional benefits of your diet and ensure you consume the freshest produce available. Seasonal eating is not only economically beneficial but also aligns with natural growth cycles, which can be better for the environment and your health. Here's how to incorporate seasonal variations in food selection according to Dr. Sebi's dietary guidelines:

In spring, focus on leafy greens which are plentiful, such as amaranth greens, dandelion greens, and kale. These greens are detoxifying and help to refresh the system after the heavier meals often consumed during winter. Incorporate spring herbs like basil and oregano, which start to flourish in this season. These can be used fresh to enhance the flavor and nutritional value of meals.

During summer, take advantage of a variety of fruits that come into season, such as berries, melons, and peaches. These fruits are high in antioxidants and provide hydration during the hotter months. Include light vegetables like cucumbers, bell peppers, and zucchini, which are also abundant in summer. These can be used in salads, smoothies, or light sautés to create refreshing meals.

In fall, utilize root vegetables such as burdock root and squashes, which are harvested during the fall. These are excellent for grounding and hearty dishes that align with cooler weather. Fall is also a good time to incorporate nuts and seeds like walnuts and hemp seeds into your diet, which provide essential fats and proteins that can help prepare the body for winter.

Book 16: Dr. Sebi Mucus Cleanse

The Role of Mucus in the Body

Dr. Sebi emphasized the role of mucus in the body as both a protector and a potential source of disease when it becomes excessive or stagnates. According to his teachings, understanding the role of mucus is crucial for maintaining health and effectively addressing various ailments through cleansing. Here's a detailed explanation of the role of mucus in the body according to Dr. Sebi's perspective:

Protective Barrier: Mucus serves a fundamental role in protecting the linings of various organs and structures within the body. It is produced by mucous membranes and acts as a barrier against environmental toxins, pathogens, and irritants. For example, mucus in the respiratory system traps dust, pollen, and other airborne particles, preventing them from entering the lungs.

Lubrication: Mucus helps to keep tissues moist and lubricated, which is essential for the proper functioning of the digestive, respiratory, and reproductive systems. In the stomach, mucus forms a protective layer that shields the lining from acidic digestive juices and prevents ulceration.

Immune Defense: Mucus contains antibodies and enzymes that help to neutralize harmful bacteria and viruses, contributing to the body's immune response. In the airways, for instance, mucus traps and helps to remove microbes and small particles from the body through coughing or sneezing.

Disease Connection: Dr. Sebi argued that excess mucus production is often a response to inflammation or toxicity in the body and can lead to disease if not addressed. He believed that many common diseases, including bronchitis, sinusitis, and even more chronic conditions like diabetes and hypertension, are linked to the buildup of mucus in specific organs.

Mucus Buildup and Cleansing: According to Dr. Sebi, an excessive buildup of mucus, especially in the lungs and digestive tract, creates an environment where bacteria and viruses can thrive, leading to illness. His mucus cleanse involves dietary changes that minimize mucus production—focusing on an alkaline diet devoid of mucus-producing foods such as dairy, refined grains, and processed foods. He also recommended herbs like burdock root, elderberry, and ginger, which are believed to help reduce mucus buildup and support the body's natural detoxification processes.

Mucus Cleanse Benefits: The purpose of a mucus cleanse, as advocated by Dr. Sebi, is to reduce mucus production, clear out accumulated mucus, and restore optimal function to affected organs. This is thought to not only improve respiratory and digestive health but also enhance overall vitality and immune function.

How to Reduce Mucus Production

Reducing mucus production is a key aspect of Dr. Sebi's approach to healing and wellness, particularly for individuals who suffer from conditions exacerbated by excess mucus. According to Dr. Sebi, certain dietary and lifestyle changes can significantly help in minimizing mucus production. Here's a detailed guide on how to reduce mucus production based on Dr. Sebi's teachings:

Follow an alkaline diet that avoids mucus-forming foods. This includes eliminating all forms of dairy, processed foods, refined sugars, and wheat. Instead, focus on consuming a wide variety of alkaline-forming foods such as leafy greens, vegetables like cucumbers and bell peppers, fruits like apples and berries, and grains like quinoa and amaranth.

Increase hydration by drinking ample amounts of spring water throughout the day. This helps to thin mucus and facilitates its expulsion from the body. Hydration is crucial for keeping the mucosal linings moist and reducing the stickiness of mucus, which can trap pathogens and particulate matter.

Incorporate herbal teas known for their mucolytic properties. Herbs such as ginger, peppermint, and mullein are effective in breaking down and expelling mucus. Drinking these teas regularly can aid in clearing the respiratory and digestive tracts.

Consume foods rich in antioxidants and anti-inflammatory compounds. Foods like garlic, onions, turmeric, and citrus fruits not only support immune function but also reduce inflammation, which can trigger mucus production.

Practice deep breathing exercises and mild physical activity. Both activities help in improving circulation and lymphatic drainage, aiding in the removal of toxins and excess mucus from the body.

Maintain a clean living environment to reduce allergen exposure, which can stimulate mucus production. Regularly clean dust, use air purifiers, and keep pets groomed to minimize dander.

Detox and Cleanse Programs

Dr. Sebi's approach to healing emphasized the importance of detoxification and cleansing, especially when addressing issues related to excessive mucus production. His mucus cleanse programs are designed to purify the body, eliminating toxins and mucus that can block the natural healing process. Here's an overview of the detox and cleanse programs recommended by Dr. Sebi as part of his mucus cleanse:

The foundation of Dr. Sebi's detox programs is a strict alkaline diet that eliminates acidic, mucus-producing foods. This diet focuses on consuming raw and cooked fruits, vegetables, nuts, seeds, and alkaline grains like amaranth, quinoa, and spelt. The goal is to restore the body's natural alkaline state and reduce inflammation.

Dr. Sebi developed a range of herbal supplements that are integral to his cleanse programs. These herbs are selected for their purifying properties and their ability to support various organs such as the liver, kidneys, and lymphatic system, which play crucial roles in detoxification. Common herbs used in these supplements include burdock root, dandelion, elderberry, and sarsaparilla.

Intermittent fasting or short-term fasting is often recommended as part of the cleansing process. Fasting helps reset the body's systems and aids in the deeper elimination of accumulated waste and mucus. During fasting periods, individuals may consume herbal teas and plenty of spring water to stay hydrated and support the body's cleansing processes.

Increasing fluid intake is critical during any detox program. Dr. Sebi emphasized the importance of drinking plenty of spring water and herbal teas to help flush toxins and mucus from the body. Adequate hydration also ensures that the body can effectively process and remove waste products.

Foods that Help Minimize Mucus

Dr. Sebi's dietary approach for minimizing mucus production revolves around selecting foods that naturally reduce mucus and inflammation in the body. These foods support the detoxification process, enhance the immune system, and help maintain a healthy alkaline environment. Here are some key foods recommended by Dr. Sebi that help minimize mucus:

Leafy Greens: Vegetables such as kale, spinach, and dandelion greens are high in chlorophyll, which helps cleanse the blood and reduce mucus production. These greens are also alkaline-forming, which helps maintain the body's pH balance.

Cucumbers: High in water content, cucumbers help hydrate the body and flush out toxins and mucus. They are also cooling and soothing to the gastrointestinal tract, which can help reduce mucus production related to digestive issues.

Garlic and Onions: Both garlic and onions are renowned for their natural antibiotic properties. They help combat infections, reduce inflammation, and decrease mucus production. They are effective in clearing up respiratory ailments where excess mucus is a problem.

Seamoss: Dr. Sebi was a strong proponent of sea moss, which is rich in essential minerals and a natural mucilaginous food. Its soothing properties help to dissolve mucus and inflammation in the mucous membranes.

Ginger: Ginger is another powerful anti-inflammatory that can help break down and remove mucus. Consuming ginger tea or adding fresh ginger to foods can help stimulate circulation and detoxification.

Turmeric: With its strong anti-inflammatory properties, turmeric helps reduce inflammation in the body and mucus production. It can be used in cooking or consumed as a tea.

Apples: Apples contain a type of soluble fiber called pectin, which helps cleanse and release mucus from the intestinal tract. Eating apples regularly can aid in reducing mucus buildup.

Pineapple: Rich in bromelain, an enzyme that helps digest protein and reduce inflammation, pineapple is especially effective in treating respiratory issues and reducing mucus in the throat and lungs.

Berries: Berries such as raspberries, blackberries, and blueberries are high in antioxidants and vitamins that support the immune system and reduce inflammation, helping to minimize mucus production.

Daily Practices to Maintain Low Mucus Levels

Maintaining low mucus levels in the body is a fundamental aspect of Dr. Sebi's approach to health and wellness, particularly for those prone to excessive mucus production which can lead to various health issues. Here are daily practices recommended by Dr. Sebi to help maintain low mucus levels:

Follow an alkaline diet as outlined by Dr. Sebi, which focuses on consuming plenty of fruits, vegetables, nuts, and seeds that do not contribute to mucus formation. Avoid mucus-forming foods such as dairy, wheat, soy, and processed sugars.

Start each day with a glass of warm lime or lemon water. This helps to alkalize the body and can stimulate digestion and the expulsion of toxins and mucus from the body.

Incorporate herbal teas known for their mucus-reducing properties into your daily routine. Herbs like mullein, fenugreek, ginger, and peppermint are excellent for reducing mucus buildup.

Stay hydrated throughout the day by drinking plenty of spring water. Hydration is key to thinning mucus and facilitating its removal from the body.

Practice deep breathing exercises or engage in regular physical activity. Both help improve circulation and lung capacity, aiding in the expulsion of mucus from the respiratory tract.

Use steam inhalation or take hot showers to help open airways and loosen mucus in the nasal passages and lungs.

Ensure sufficient sleep each night, as sleep is crucial for the body's recovery and removal of toxins, including excess mucus.

Symptoms of Excess Mucus and How to Address Them

Excess mucus in the body can lead to a variety of symptoms and health issues, as it impedes normal bodily functions and can harbor pathogens. Dr. Sebi emphasized the importance of recognizing these symptoms and addressing them through natural means. Here's an overview of common symptoms associated with excess mucus and Dr. Sebi's recommendations on how to address them:

Symptoms of Excess Mucus:

- Congestion in the Sinuses or Lungs: Feeling of stuffiness, difficulty breathing, or a persistent cough.

- Digestive Issues: Bloating, gas, constipation, or diarrhea can occur when mucus coats the lining of the stomach and intestines, affecting the absorption and digestion of nutrients.

- Frequent Infections: Excess mucus can become a breeding ground for bacteria and viruses, leading to recurrent respiratory or sinus infections.

- Fatigue: Excessive mucus production requires energy from the body and can lead to a feeling of constant tiredness or lethargy.

- Allergic Reactions: Increased sensitivity to allergens with symptoms such as sneezing, itchy eyes, and runny nose.

How to Address Excess Mucus:

- Adopt an Alkaline Diet: Focus on consuming foods that reduce mucus production. Dr. Sebi recommended fruits, vegetables, and whole grains that support the body's alkalinity and help reduce mucus build-up.

- Hydration: Increase water intake to help thin the mucus, making it easier for the body to expel it. Drinking herbal teas like ginger or peppermint can also be beneficial.

- Herbal Supplements: Incorporate herbs known for their mucolytic (mucus-breaking) properties, such as elderberry, burdock root, and mullein. These herbs help in clearing mucus from the body.

- Steam Inhalation: Breathing in steam from a bowl of hot water can help loosen the mucus in the sinuses and lungs, facilitating easier breathing.

- Regular Exercise: Physical activity helps increase blood circulation and lymphatic drainage, aiding in the elimination of toxins and mucus from the body.

- Avoid Mucus-Producing Foods: Eliminate dairy products, refined sugars, and other foods known to increase mucus production from your diet.

- Clean Living Environment: Reduce exposure to dust, pollen, and pet dander, as these can exacerbate mucus production and allergies.

The Relationship Between Mucus and Respiratory Health

Dr. Sebi emphasized the significant impact of mucus on respiratory health, highlighting the complex relationship between mucus production and respiratory disorders. According to Dr. Sebi, excessive mucus accumulation in the respiratory tract can lead to various health issues, such as chronic bronchitis, asthma, and even pneumonia. Here's an overview of the relationship between mucus and respiratory health as outlined in Dr. Sebi's teachings:

Mucus serves an essential function in the respiratory system by trapping dust, allergens, and pathogens to prevent them from entering the lungs. Under normal conditions, mucus is cleared from the respiratory tract through ciliary movement and coughing. However, problems arise when there is an overproduction or inadequate clearance of mucus.

Excessive mucus in the airways can obstruct airflow, making breathing difficult. This can lead to symptoms such as wheezing, coughing, and shortness of breath. Over time, if not properly managed, it can contribute to more severe respiratory conditions like asthma or chronic obstructive pulmonary disease (COPD).

Persistent mucus production often signals underlying inflammation in the respiratory tract. Inflammatory responses can be triggered by infections, allergens, or exposure to pollutants, all of which increase mucus production as the body tries to protect and heal the respiratory lining.

To address and manage respiratory health issues related to mucus, Dr. Sebi recommended a combination of dietary adjustments, herbal treatments, and lifestyle changes:

Adopting an alkaline diet low in mucus-producing foods, such as dairy and processed sugars, and rich in fruits and vegetables that help reduce inflammation and cleanse the body of excess mucus.

Using herbal remedies that have natural expectorant properties, such as mullein, elderberry, and ginger, can help in thinning and expelling mucus, facilitating clearer breathing.

Maintaining hydration is crucial as it helps thin the mucus, making it easier to expel. Regular intake of fluids, especially warm herbal teas and spring water, is recommended.

Implementing breathing exercises and practices like steam inhalation can also aid in loosening mucus in the respiratory tract, improving overall respiratory function.

Cleansing Herbs and Their Uses

Dr. Sebi's approach to holistic health often included the use of specific cleansing herbs that aid in removing mucus and toxins from the body, particularly from the respiratory and digestive systems. These herbs not only help cleanse the body but also strengthen it against further accumulation of toxins and mucus. Here's an overview of some key cleansing herbs and their uses as recommended in Dr. Sebi's Mucus Cleanse:

1. Burdock Root:
   - Uses: Burdock root is highly regarded for its blood purifying properties. It helps to eliminate toxins through its diuretic effects, encouraging the detoxification of the liver and improving kidney function. It also has a substantial inulin content, a prebiotic that supports the health of the gut microbiome.
   - Preparation: Can be consumed as a tea, tincture, or in capsule form. For tea, simmer the dried root in water for about 20-30 minutes.

2. Elderberry:
   - Uses: Elderberry is well-known for its immune-boosting capabilities, thanks to its high vitamin C and antioxidant levels. It's especially effective in treating respiratory illnesses by reducing mucus buildup and helping to clear congestion.
   - Preparation: Commonly taken as a syrup or tea. To make elderberry tea, simmer dried berries in water for 15-20 minutes and strain.

3. Mullein:
   - Uses: Mullein is excellent for the respiratory system. It acts as an expectorant, helping to break up respiratory congestion and promote the expulsion of mucus.
   - Preparation: Mullein leaves can be used to make a soothing tea by steeping them in hot water for about 10 minutes.

4. Sarsaparilla:
   - Uses: This root has potent detoxifying properties and is often used for purifying the blood. It also has anti-inflammatory properties, making it beneficial for joint health and skin conditions.
   - Preparation: Sarsaparilla can be consumed as a tea, tincture, or in capsules. As a tea, it should be simmered similarly to burdock root.

5. Sea Moss (Irish Moss):
   - Uses: Sea moss is rich in minerals and vitamins, which are essential for maintaining good health and supporting the immune system. It acts as a natural mucilaginous agent, soothing the mucus membranes and helping to remove mucus from the body.
   - Preparation: Typically made into a gel by soaking the dried moss and then blending it with water. The gel can be added to smoothies, teas, or other dishes.

6. Ginger:
   - Uses: Ginger has strong anti-inflammatory properties and can help in reducing mucus production and relieving congestion.
   - Preparation: Ginger can be consumed fresh in juices or teas, or used as a powdered supplement.

Book 17: Dr. Sebi Cancer Cure

Dr. Sebi's Views on Cancer and Its Causes

Dr. Sebi's views on cancer were rooted in his broader perspective on disease and holistic health, emphasizing that disease arises when the body is out of balance, particularly from excessive acidity and the accumulation of toxins and mucus. He believed that cancer, like many other chronic illnesses, is largely caused by environmental factors that disrupt the body's natural alkaline state. Here's an outline of Dr. Sebi's views on cancer and its causes:

Dr. Sebi argued that a diet high in acidic foods, such as processed foods, meats, dairy products, and refined grains, leads to an acidic body environment. He maintained that cancer cells thrive in acidic conditions and that an alkaline diet could help prevent and combat cancer by creating an environment where cancer cells cannot survive.

According to Dr. Sebi, mucus buildup from consuming mucus-forming foods (like dairy) blocks the body's natural filtration systems and leads to the accumulation of toxins in the body. He believed that this environment could foster the development of cancerous cells.

Dr. Sebi also pointed to environmental toxins—including pollutants, chemical additives in foods, and pesticides—as significant contributors to cancer. He believed that these toxins could damage cells and lead to mutations that develop into cancer.

While Dr. Sebi acknowledged that genetic predispositions could play a role in the development of cancer, he emphasized that a person's environment and diet could significantly influence whether genetic traits related to cancer would express themselves.

Dr. Sebi also considered emotional well-being as part of the holistic view of health. He noted that chronic stress and poor emotional health could weaken the immune system and alter cellular functions, potentially leading to the development of cancer.

He argued that deficiencies in essential vitamins and minerals could compromise the body's ability to fight off cancerous changes. An alkaline diet rich in nutrients from natural plant sources was central to his recommendations for cancer prevention and treatment.

Dr. Sebi advocated for addressing the root causes of cancer holistically—through detoxifying the body, adopting an alkaline diet rich in plant-based, natural foods, and eliminating toxic exposures from one's environment and lifestyle. He believed in the body's inherent ability to heal itself when supported with the right nutrients and a clean environment.

Alkaline Diet and Cancer Prevention

Dr. Sebi's approach to cancer prevention is heavily anchored in the principles of an alkaline diet, which he believed was crucial in maintaining the body's health and warding off diseases, including cancer. According to Dr. Sebi, this diet helps create a bodily environment that is less favorable for the growth and proliferation of cancer cells.

Dr. Sebi taught that cancer cells thrive in acidic environments but struggle to survive in alkaline conditions. By consuming foods that increase the body's alkalinity, you reduce the acidity that can foster the growth and spread of cancer cells. An alkaline diet also aids in reducing mucus and toxins in the body, which Dr. Sebi believed could lead to cellular dysfunction and mutation, potentially resulting in cancer. Alkaline foods such as leafy greens, fruits, and vegetables help cleanse the body and support the functioning of vital organs, such as the liver and kidneys, which play a role in detoxification.

Furthermore, alkaline foods are generally high in essential vitamins, minerals, and antioxidants that are crucial for maintaining robust immune function and preventing DNA damage that can lead to cancer. These nutrients include vitamin C, vitamin E, selenium, and beta-carotene, all known for their cancer-protective properties. A strong immune system is vital for identifying and destroying cancerous cells. An alkaline diet, rich in nutrients from fresh fruits and vegetables, provides the necessary support to boost the immune system's capabilities.

The alkaline diet also promotes healthy digestion by maintaining a balanced gut flora and encouraging regular bowel movements. This aids in the efficient elimination of toxins and minimizes the chances of waste products contributing to cancer development. By adhering to this diet, individuals can enhance their overall health and significantly lower the risks associated with cancer.

Specific Herbs for Cancer Treatment

Dr. Sebi emphasized the use of specific herbs as part of his holistic approach to cancer treatment, believing in their potent medicinal properties to help combat the disease naturally. Among these, some key herbs were particularly valued for their ability to cleanse, detoxify, and nourish the body at a cellular level, thereby helping to fight cancer.

Burdock root is one of the cornerstone herbs in Dr. Sebi's approach to cancer treatment. Known for its powerful blood-purifying properties, burdock root helps to eliminate toxins that can lead to cancerous conditions. It is rich in antioxidants, which protect cells from damage by free radicals, substances that are linked to cancer development.

Soursop, also known as Graviola, is another herb Dr. Sebi frequently recommended for cancer. Research suggests that soursop contains compounds that may be effective in targeting and killing cancer cells. It is especially noted for its use in alternative cancer treatments due to its potential to target cancer cells without harming healthy cells.

Dandelion is another herb used for its cancer-fighting properties. It has been studied for its potential in inducing apoptosis (cell death) in cancer cells, effectively helping to reduce tumor growth without affecting the surrounding healthy cells.

Red clover is valued for its isoflavone content, plant-based chemicals that mimic the effects of estrogen in the body. These properties make it particularly useful in treating cancers that are sensitive to hormonal changes, such as breast cancer. Red clover is also used to cleanse the blood and improve circulation, helping to detoxify the body.

Lastly, Irish moss, or sea moss, was often recommended by Dr. Sebi for its rich mineral content and mucilaginous properties. It nourishes the body at a fundamental level, supporting the immune system and providing essential nutrients that can help the body fight cancer.

Dr. Sebi advocated using these herbs in conjunction with an alkaline diet as part of a comprehensive treatment approach to combat cancer and enhance overall health.

Lifestyle Adjustments for Cancer Patients

Dr. Sebi advocated for significant lifestyle adjustments for cancer patients, emphasizing the importance of holistic healing practices that encompass dietary changes, mental health, and physical well-being. According to Dr. Sebi, these lifestyle adjustments are crucial for supporting the body's natural healing processes and improving the effectiveness of treatments.

Firstly, Dr. Sebi stressed the importance of adopting an alkaline diet, which is central to his approach. This diet excludes acidic foods that contribute to mucus buildup and inflammation, which can exacerbate cancer. Instead, it focuses on consuming a wide variety of fresh fruits and vegetables, alkaline grains, and nuts, which help to detoxify the body and provide essential nutrients that strengthen the immune system.

Physical activity is also a critical component of the lifestyle adjustments recommended by Dr. Sebi. Regular exercise, even mild activities like walking or gentle yoga, helps improve circulation, boosts mood, and enhances the overall energy level, which is often compromised in cancer patients. Physical activity also aids in detoxification through sweat and can help manage the side effects of cancer treatments such as fatigue and constipation.

Mental and emotional well-being is another area that Dr. Sebi emphasized. Managing stress through meditation, deep breathing exercises, or engaging in hobbies can significantly impact the overall health and recovery process. Stress reduction is key to lowering inflammation and boosting the immune system, both of which are vital for cancer patients.

Adequate rest and sleep are equally important. Dr. Sebi advised cancer patients to ensure they get enough sleep, as it is a time when the body undergoes repair and rejuvenation. A restful sleep cycle supports hormonal balance, reduces stress, and strengthens the body's defenses against illness.

Success Stories and Feedback

Dr. Sebi's approach to treating cancer with his unique herbal remedies and strict dietary protocols has garnered a variety of responses, including numerous anecdotal success stories from individuals who have adopted his methods. Many of these stories highlight remarkable improvements in health and well-being, offering hope to those seeking alternative treatments for cancer.

Among the success stories, individuals have reported significant reductions in tumor sizes, improvements in cancer markers, and, in some cases, complete remission of the disease after following Dr. Sebi's nutritional guidelines and using his herbal supplements. These stories often emphasize not only the physical benefits of the regimen but also enhancements in energy levels, mental clarity, and overall vitality.

Feedback from patients who have followed Dr. Sebi's cancer cure often includes appreciation for the holistic and natural approach, which contrasts with conventional treatments that can have severe side effects. Many express gratitude for the diet's role in improving their quality of life, enabling them to feel more in control of their health.

However, it is important to note that while there are numerous positive testimonials, these accounts are anecdotal and individual results vary. The scientific community generally remains skeptical due to the lack of rigorous clinical trials backing Dr. Sebi's methods. Critics argue that while an alkaline diet and herbal treatments may improve general health, they have not been proven as effective in curing cancer scientifically.

Despite this, the success stories and positive feedback from many who have followed Dr. Sebi's teachings continue to inspire others looking for non-conventional ways to fight cancer. These stories contribute to the legacy of Dr. Sebi's approach, encouraging a dialogue about alternative health practices and the potential benefits of natural remedies and dietary changes in cancer treatment.

Supporting Immune System during Cancer Treatment

Supporting the immune system is a fundamental aspect of Dr. Sebi's approach to cancer treatment. He believed that a strong immune system is vital in helping the body fight cancer and recover from the intense treatments often associated with conventional cancer therapies. According to Dr. Sebi, bolstering the immune system involves a combination of dietary adjustments, herbal supplements, and lifestyle practices.

Dr. Sebi recommended adhering to a strict alkaline diet, which focuses on consuming foods that naturally enhance the body's immune response. This diet primarily includes fresh fruits, vegetables, nuts, and seeds, all rich in essential nutrients, antioxidants, and minerals that support immune health. Foods particularly emphasized are those high in vitamin C, such as berries and citrus fruits, known for their immune-boosting properties.

Herbal supplements also play a crucial role in Dr. Sebi's regimen. He advocated the use of natural herbs such as elderberry, sea moss, and burdock root, which have been traditionally known to strengthen the immune system. Elderberry, for instance, is recognized for its antiviral and antibacterial properties, making it excellent for fighting infections that cancer patients are particularly susceptible to.

In addition to diet and herbal remedies, Dr. Sebi stressed the importance of maintaining a healthy lifestyle to support the immune system. This includes ensuring adequate sleep, managing stress, and engaging in moderate physical activity. Sleep is crucial for immune function as it helps regulate the production of cytokines, a type of protein that targets infection and inflammation, effectively creating an immune response. Stress management, through practices such as yoga and meditation, is vital as stress can weaken the immune system and hamper the body's ability to fight cancer.

Anti-Cancer Properties of Specific Foods

Dr. Sebi emphasized the healing properties of certain foods, particularly their role in preventing and combating cancer. His approach highlighted the importance of an alkaline diet rich in specific foods known for their anti-cancer properties. According to Dr. Sebi, these foods help neutralize acidity in the body, which he believed was a breeding ground for disease, including cancer.

Among the foods often recommended by Dr. Sebi for their anti-cancer properties are leafy greens such as kale and dandelion greens. These vegetables are not only highly alkaline but also packed with vitamins, minerals, and antioxidants that support detoxification and immune function—both critical in fighting cancer.

Berries, particularly blueberries, raspberries, and blackberries, are also integral to Dr. Sebi's cancer-fighting diet. These fruits are rich in antioxidants such as vitamin C and flavonoids, which protect cells from oxidative stress and reduce the risk of chronic diseases including cancer. Berries help inhibit the growth and spread of cancer cells while promoting the death of cancerous cells.

Sea moss, a type of seaweed, was another cornerstone of Dr. Sebi's nutritional approach to cancer. It's rich in iodine and selenium, minerals known for their role in regulating hormone function and protecting against cancer, particularly of the thyroid and breast.

Soursop, also known as Graviola, is frequently highlighted for its potential anti-cancer effects. Soursop contains compounds that have been shown in studies to target and kill cancer cells without harming healthy cells, offering promising therapeutic benefits.

Dr. Sebi also recommended nuts like Brazil nuts and walnuts, which are high in selenium and omega-3 fatty acids, respectively. Selenium is a powerful antioxidant that plays a key role in detoxification and cancer protection, while omega-3 fatty acids help reduce inflammation in the body, which can lower the risk of cancer development.

Emotional and Mental Support Strategies for Cancer Patients

Dr. Sebi recognized that fighting cancer isn't just a physical battle but also an emotional and mental one. To support holistic healing, he emphasized the importance of integrating emotional and mental support strategies alongside physical remedies. Here are some of the approaches he recommended to support emotional and mental well-being in cancer patients:

Stress Reduction: Dr. Sebi stressed the importance of managing stress as part of the treatment for cancer. Chronic stress can suppress the immune system and interfere with the body's ability to fight cancer. Techniques such as meditation, yoga, and deep breathing exercises can significantly reduce stress, help maintain mental clarity, and promote a positive outlook.

Community and Social Support: Building a strong support network is crucial for those battling cancer. Dr. Sebi advised patients to seek support from family, friends, or support groups where they can share experiences and receive emotional encouragement. Being surrounded by a community that understands what you are going through can provide comfort and alleviate feelings of isolation or depression.

Nature Connection: Spending time in nature was another strategy Dr. Sebi recommended for emotional and mental healing. The tranquility of natural surroundings has a therapeutic effect, helping to reduce anxiety and improve mood. Activities like walking in a park, gardening, or simply sitting under a tree can help reconnect with oneself and the healing rhythms of nature.

Positive Visualization and Affirmations: Dr. Sebi believed in the power of the mind to influence physical health. He encouraged practices such as positive visualization and affirmations to foster a mindset conducive to healing. Visualizing one's body healing and affirming one's intentions to overcome illness can be powerful tools in cancer treatment.

Journaling: Writing down thoughts and feelings can be a cathartic activity for many cancer patients. Dr. Sebi suggested that keeping a journal to express emotions, fears, and hopes can help process feelings constructively and contribute to mental well-being.

Holistic Therapies: Incorporating holistic therapies like music therapy, art therapy, or aromatherapy can also play a significant role in emotional and mental support. These therapies can help distract from pain and discomfort, reduce stress, and provide a non-verbal outlet for emotions.

Dr. Sebi's approach was to nurture the whole person—body, mind, and spirit. He believed that a well-supported emotional and mental state not only aids in coping with the illness but can also actively contribute to the healing process.

Book 18: Dr. Sebi Hair Loss Cure

Causes of Hair Loss and Natural Solutions

Dr. Sebi approached hair loss by focusing on the underlying causes, which he attributed to nutritional deficiencies, toxin buildup, poor scalp circulation, and hormonal imbalances. He believed that addressing these root causes naturally could help prevent and reverse hair loss effectively.

According to Dr. Sebi, inadequate nutrition plays a significant role in hair health. A lack of essential vitamins and minerals such as iron, zinc, and the B vitamins can lead to weakened hair follicles and increased hair shedding. To combat this, he recommended adhering to an alkaline diet rich in leafy greens, fruits, vegetables, nuts, and seeds, which are loaded with the nutrients necessary for maintaining healthy hair.

Toxin buildup is another factor that Dr. Sebi identified as contributing to hair loss. He argued that toxins from an unhealthy diet, environmental pollution, and poor digestive health could lead to clogged hair follicles and ultimately, hair loss. To detoxify the body and promote hair health, Dr. Sebi suggested incorporating herbal supplements like burdock root, yellow dock, and sarsaparilla, which are known for their blood-purifying properties.

Poor scalp circulation can also starve hair follicles of essential oxygen and nutrients, hindering hair growth. Dr. Sebi recommended stimulating scalp circulation through regular scalp massages, using natural oils such as coconut oil, castor oil, or jojoba oil to nourish the scalp and strengthen hair. Enhancing blood flow to the scalp ensures that nutrients are efficiently delivered to hair roots.

Hormonal imbalances, especially those involving thyroid function or changes in androgen levels, are significant contributors to hair loss. Dr. Sebi emphasized the importance of balancing hormones naturally through diet and holistic health practices to mitigate hair loss.

In addition to these specific interventions, Dr. Sebi also highlighted the importance of maintaining adequate hydration by drinking plenty of spring water. This helps flush out toxins that could negatively affect hair health. Managing stress through meditation, yoga, and adequate rest was also recommended, as stress can further exacerbate hair loss.

Scalp Treatments and Care Routines

Dr. Sebi emphasized the use of specific herbs and nutrients to encourage hair regrowth, focusing on their natural ability to nourish the body and stimulate healthy hair development. Understanding the beneficial properties of these herbs and nutrients can help individuals seeking natural remedies for hair loss.

Herbs such as horsetail and nettle are rich in silica and sulfur, minerals that are essential for strengthening hair and improving its texture and growth. Horsetail, in particular, has been traditionally used to enhance blood circulation to the scalp, thereby nourishing hair follicles and promoting hair growth. Nettle, on the other hand, is known for its ability to combat hair loss by reducing inflammation in the scalp and blocking DHT, a hormone associated with hair loss.

Dr. Sebi also recommended the use of aloe vera, both topically and internally, for its enzyme-rich composition that repairs dead skin cells on the scalp. Aloe vera also acts as a great conditioner and leaves hair all smooth and shiny. It promotes hair growth, prevents itching on the scalp, reduces dandruff, and conditions your hair.

Sea moss is another key nutrient in Dr. Sebi's hair care regimen. Packed with essential minerals and vitamins, sea moss helps to nourish the hair follicles and support the production of collagen, which is crucial for maintaining healthy hair structure.

For internal nourishment, Dr. Sebi advised increasing the intake of alkaline foods rich in vitamins and minerals essential for hair health. These include foods high in iron, zinc, and vitamins A and C, which support sebum production, provide antioxidants, and aid in collagen formation, respectively.

Additionally, he highlighted the importance of adequate protein intake, as hair is primarily made up of protein. Incorporating plant-based proteins such as quinoa, chickpeas, and almonds can help provide the necessary nutrients for hair strength and growth.

Incorporating these herbs and nutrients into daily routines, whether through dietary adjustments or topical applications, aligns with Dr. Sebi's holistic approach to health and can significantly contribute to reducing hair loss and promoting healthy hair regrowth.

Diet for Healthy Hair

Dr. Sebi's approach to maintaining healthy hair through diet centers on consuming nutrient-rich, alkaline foods that nourish the body and promote optimal hair growth. He believed that a healthy scalp and strong hair are direct reflections of the overall health of the body, and that specific dietary practices could significantly enhance hair quality.

A key aspect of Dr. Sebi's dietary recommendations for healthy hair is the emphasis on hydration. Drinking sufficient amounts of spring water each day helps hydrate the body and scalp, aiding in the regulation of the natural oils in the scalp and keeping the hair moisturized.

The diet Dr. Sebi recommended includes a generous amount of fresh fruits and vegetables, which are high in vitamins and antioxidants that protect the hair and scalp from oxidative stress. Foods like blueberries, oranges, and bell peppers are rich in Vitamin C, which is crucial for collagen production. Collagen strengthens the capillaries that supply the hair shafts with nutrients.

Leafy greens such as kale and spinach are essential in Dr. Sebi's diet for healthy hair due to their high content of iron, folate, and vitamins A and C, all of which contribute to hair health. Iron ensures that your hair follicles get enough oxygen, while vitamin A aids in the production of sebum, which keeps hair moisturized.

Dr. Sebi also highlighted the importance of consuming nuts and seeds, which are good sources of zinc and selenium, minerals known for their roles in hair growth and repair. Almonds, walnuts, and flaxseeds, for example, provide omega-3 fatty acids that nourish the hair and support thickening.

Additionally, whole grains like quinoa and amaranth are recommended for their high protein content, as hair is primarily composed of protein. These grains also provide other hair-supportive nutrients such as biotin, which helps to prevent hair loss.

Preventative Measures for Maintaining Hair Health

Dr. Sebi's approach to maintaining hair health centers on preventive measures that nurture the scalp and hair through natural, holistic means. His methodology emphasizes the importance of diet, proper scalp care, and the use of natural products to prevent hair loss and promote healthy hair growth. Here's an outline of the preventative measures recommended by Dr. Sebi for maintaining hair health:

Dietary Focus: Dr. Sebi stressed the importance of an alkaline diet rich in minerals, vitamins, and hydration to support hair health. He recommended consuming plenty of leafy greens, fruits, nuts, and seeds, which provide essential nutrients such as iron, zinc, vitamin A, vitamin C, and omega-3 fatty acids. These nutrients are crucial for maintaining strong hair follicles, promoting blood circulation to the scalp, and producing natural oils that keep the hair moisturized and healthy.

Scalp Hygiene and Care: Keeping the scalp clean and well-nourished is essential for preventing buildup and ensuring the hair follicles are not clogged with product residue or excess oil. Dr. Sebi advised using natural cleansing agents like herbal shampoos or rinses made from plants such as aloe vera or rosemary, which cleanse without stripping the hair of its natural oils.

Avoid Chemical Treatments: Dr. Sebi cautioned against the use of harsh chemical treatments, such as dyes and relaxers, which can damage the hair and scalp. He advocated for natural styling techniques that do not involve heat or chemicals, thus minimizing potential harm and breakage to the hair.

Regular Scalp Massages: Regularly massaging the scalp helps stimulate blood circulation, promoting hair growth and vitality. Dr. Sebi suggested using natural oils like coconut or castor oil during scalp massages to nourish the scalp and strengthen the hair roots.

Minimize Stress: Stress can significantly impact hair health, potentially leading to hair thinning and loss. Dr. Sebi recommended practices such as meditation, yoga, and deep breathing exercises to manage stress effectively and maintain overall well-being, which in turn supports hair health.

Adequate Water Intake: Hydration is vital for overall health and is particularly important for maintaining hair health. Dr. Sebi emphasized the importance of drinking plenty of spring water to ensure that the body and scalp are well-hydrated, which supports the strength and elasticity of the hair.

Addressing Underlying Health Issues Causing Hair Loss

Dr. Sebi's holistic approach to treating hair loss involved addressing the underlying health issues that contribute to hair thinning and shedding. He believed that most bodily ailments, including hair loss, stem from systemic imbalances that need to be corrected to restore health fully.

A primary focus in Dr. Sebi's methodology is on cleansing and detoxifying the body to remove toxins and mucus, which he identified as major contributors to disease and dysfunction. By following a strict alkaline diet and using specific herbal supplements, he aimed to cleanse the blood and organs, thereby improving overall bodily functions, including hair growth. This diet avoids foods that contribute to acidity and mucus production, such as processed foods, dairy, and meat, while emphasizing natural, mineral-rich foods that support the body's healing process.

Dr. Sebi also pointed out the importance of the body's mineral balance, particularly the levels of iron, zinc, and magnesium, which are crucial for healthy hair growth. Deficiencies in these minerals can lead to poor scalp health and hair loss. Through dietary recommendations and herbal supplements, such as sea moss, which is rich in essential minerals, he aimed to correct these deficiencies.

Hormonal imbalances are another area of concern addressed in Dr. Sebi's hair loss cure. Hormones such as thyroid hormones and sex hormones can significantly impact hair growth and health. Dr. Sebi recommended natural ways to balance hormones through diet and herbal remedies, thereby helping to manage conditions like thyroid disorders or PCOS, which can contribute to hair loss.

Chronic stress can lead to conditions such as telogen effluvium, where significant stress pushes large numbers of hair follicles into a resting phase, followed by hair shedding. Dr. Sebi advocated for stress reduction techniques such as meditation, deep breathing exercises, and adequate rest to help mitigate these effects.

Natural Styling Tips that Prevent Hair Damage

Dr. Sebi's philosophy on maintaining hair health extended into natural styling techniques designed to prevent hair damage and promote healthy growth. Understanding that hair damage often results from harsh styling practices and chemical treatments, he advocated for gentle, natural methods that nurture the hair rather than deplete it.

A key aspect of Dr. Sebi's advice was to avoid using heat styling tools such as straighteners, curling irons, and blow dryers, which can lead to significant hair damage, including dryness, breakage, and split ends. Instead, he encouraged natural drying techniques, allowing hair to air dry whenever possible to preserve its natural moisture and resilience.

Dr. Sebi also advised against tight hairstyles that pull on the scalp, such as tight ponytails, braids, and dreadlocks, which can cause tension alopecia—a form of hair loss resulting from the constant pull on the hair roots. He recommended looser styles that do not stress the hair follicles, helping to maintain a healthy scalp and prevent hair loss.

For those who wanted to enhance their hair's texture or appearance, Dr. Sebi suggested using natural products like aloe vera gel or coconut oil, which provide hold and sheen without the harsh chemicals found in commercial hair styling products. These natural products not only style the hair effectively but also nourish the scalp and hair strands.

Additionally, Dr. Sebi was a proponent of regular scalp massages to stimulate blood circulation and promote hair growth. Using oils such as castor oil, which is rich in ricinoleic acid and omega-6 fatty acids, during these massages can strengthen the roots and encourage healthier hair growth.

Essential Oils for Hair Care

Dr. Sebi recognized the potent benefits of essential oils for hair care, emphasizing their natural ability to nourish the scalp, strengthen hair, and promote healthy growth. Incorporating essential oils into your hair care routine can provide therapeutic properties that enhance the health and appearance of your hair.

Peppermint Oil: Known for its invigorating properties, peppermint oil stimulates the scalp, promoting blood circulation which is crucial for healthy hair growth. The tingling sensation it creates is not just soothing but also effective in awakening dormant hair follicles.

Lavender Oil: Lavender oil is celebrated for its ability to improve hair growth and thickness. It has antimicrobial properties, which can help prevent bacteria and fungi from growing on the scalp, reducing itchy scalp and dandruff. It's also known for its stress-relieving scent, which can indirectly benefit those experiencing stress-related hair loss.

Rosemary Oil: Rosemary is one of the top essential oils for hair care, often associated with hair thickness and growth. It works by enhancing cellular metabolism that stimulates hair growth. Clinical studies have shown that it can be as effective as minoxidil, a common hair growth treatment, but without the side effects.

Tea Tree Oil: With powerful cleansing, antibacterial, and antimicrobial properties, tea tree oil can help unclog hair follicles and nourish the roots. It's excellent for treating dandruff and scalp irritation, creating a healthy environment for hair growth.

Castor Oil: Although not an essential oil, castor oil is frequently recommended by Dr. Sebi for its rich ricinoleic acid content, which helps increase scalp circulation and improve hair growth. Castor oil is also a humectant, meaning it helps to lock in moisture and protect hair from becoming dry and brittle.

Jojoba Oil: Jojoba oil's structure closely resembles the sebum naturally produced by our scalp, which makes it an excellent product for balancing oil production. Using jojoba oil can help prevent hair breakage and enhance hair thickness.

To use essential oils effectively, they should be diluted with a carrier oil such as coconut oil, jojoba oil, or olive oil to prevent irritation. Typically, adding a few drops of essential oil to a carrier oil before applying it to the scalp and hair can provide a nourishing hair treatment. Massaging the oil mixture into the scalp and leaving it on for a period before washing can maximize absorption and effectiveness.

Book 19: Dr. Sebi Smoothie Diet

Benefits of Smoothies in an Alkaline Diet

Smoothies are a cornerstone of the alkaline diet promoted by Dr. Sebi, serving as a powerful tool for delivering dense nutritional content in an easily digestible form. Incorporating smoothies into your diet provides numerous health benefits, especially when adhering to an alkaline dietary approach.

Smoothies made from Dr. Sebi-approved fruits, vegetables, and supplements naturally increase your intake of alkaline-forming ingredients. These help to maintain the body's pH balance, which Dr. Sebi believed was essential for optimal health and preventing disease. By blending ingredients into a smoothie, you maximize nutrient absorption as the body can more easily assimilate the vitamins, minerals, and enzymes from the liquefied foods.

The fiber in smoothies, particularly from whole fruits and vegetables, supports digestive health by facilitating regular bowel movements and aiding in detoxification. Fiber helps to sweep the digestive tract of toxins and waste, which is a key component of Dr. Sebi's health philosophy. Unlike juices, smoothies retain all the fiber from the produce, making them more filling and beneficial for digestive health.

Smoothies are also a convenient way to boost your intake of antioxidants, which are crucial for combating oxidative stress and inflammation in the body. Ingredients like berries, leafy greens, and seeds that are high in antioxidants can be easily incorporated into smoothies, enhancing their disease-fighting capabilities.

For individuals following Dr. Sebi's dietary recommendations, smoothies are a practical method to include a variety of essential minerals and vitamins in their diet. They allow for the combination of multiple alkaline ingredients that might be more challenging to consume in large quantities when eaten whole. For example, blending greens like kale or spinach with fruits like apples and bananas can improve the taste while ensuring you receive a broad spectrum of nutrients.

Moreover, smoothies are an excellent vehicle for incorporating Dr. Sebi's recommended supplements, such as sea moss gel, which is rich in minerals and supports overall vitality. Adding such supplements to smoothies enhances their nutritional value without compromising taste.

Smoothies are a versatile, delicious, and effective way to adhere to an alkaline diet and ensure your body receives an abundance of nutrients necessary for maintaining health and preventing illness, aligning perfectly with Dr. Sebi's holistic approach to wellness.

Recipes for Nutrient-Rich Smoothies

Dr. Sebi's smoothie diet is designed to maximize nutrient intake through delicious and healthful smoothies, incorporating a variety of Dr. Sebi-approved alkaline foods. Here are a few recipes for nutrient-rich smoothies that align with Dr. Sebi's dietary guidelines, providing essential vitamins, minerals, and antioxidants:

Green Vitality Smoothie

Blend a handful of fresh kale or spinach with one green apple and half a cucumber for a refreshing and cleansing drink. Add a piece of fresh ginger for a spicy kick and a squeeze of key lime for some tang. This smoothie is rich in iron from the leafy greens, while the apple and cucumber provide hydration and additional nutrients.

Berry Alkaline Boost

Combine a cup of mixed berries such as raspberries, blackberries, and strawberries with a ripe banana for sweetness. Add a tablespoon of hemp seeds for protein and a bit of spring water or coconut water to blend smoothly. Berries are high in antioxidants and vitamin C, and the hemp seeds offer omega-3 fatty acids and additional protein.

Tropical Sea Moss Energizer

Mix one cup of chopped pineapple with one mango (peeled and pitted) and a tablespoon of sea moss gel. Include a squeeze of fresh lime juice and a bit of spring water to achieve the desired consistency. Pineapple and mango provide a wealth of vitamins A and C, while sea moss gel adds a boost of nearly 92 minerals that support overall health.

Spiced Almond Delight

Blend one ripe banana with a cup of homemade almond milk, a teaspoon of cinnamon, and a tablespoon of agave syrup for sweetness. Add a dash of nutmeg and a small piece of vanilla bean or a drop of vanilla extract for enhanced flavor. This smoothie offers a comforting and warming taste, with cinnamon helping to regulate blood sugar levels.

Avocado Lime Smoothie

Use one ripe avocado, the juice of two key limes, and a tablespoon of agave to blend together with ice or a little spring water. Avocados are rich in healthy fats and fiber, making this smoothie very filling. The lime adds zest and aids digestion, making this a perfect smoothie for a nourishing breakfast or a satisfying afternoon snack.

These smoothie recipes are not only aligned with Dr. Sebi's alkaline diet but are also designed to be easy to prepare, delicious, and highly nutritious, supporting overall health and wellness while pleasing the palate.

How to Use Smoothies for Detoxification

In Dr. Sebi's approach to holistic health, smoothies play a significant role, particularly in detoxification. He advocated using smoothies as a tool to cleanse the body of toxins and restore its natural alkaline state, which is essential for optimal health. Here's how smoothies can be effectively used for detoxification according to Dr. Sebi's dietary principles:

Smoothies provide a concentrated dose of nutrients and phytochemicals, which are essential for supporting the body's natural detox pathways. By blending a variety of Dr. Sebi-approved fruits and vegetables, you create a powerful detox drink that helps to flush out toxins while nourishing the body. The high fiber content in these smoothies also aids in promoting regular bowel movements, which are crucial for expelling toxins from the digestive tract.

To maximize the detoxification benefits, it's recommended to include ingredients that are particularly known for their cleansing properties. For example, leafy greens like kale and dandelion greens are rich in chlorophyll, which helps in purifying the blood. Cucumbers and celery are high in water and can help hydrate the body and flush out toxins. Adding a bit of ginger or turmeric to your smoothies can boost anti-inflammatory and antioxidant benefits, further supporting detoxification.

Moreover, incorporating sea moss into your smoothies can be particularly effective. Sea moss is a type of seaweed that is rich in minerals and vitamins essential for maintaining proper cell function and detoxification. It's especially known for its ability to remove heavy metals from the body's tissues.

For those using smoothies for detoxification, it's important to consume them regularly, ideally as part of a balanced diet that is low in processed foods and high in whole, natural foods. Starting the day with a detoxifying smoothie can help kickstart the body's natural cleansing processes. Additionally, replacing one meal a day with a nutrient-rich smoothie can reduce the digestive load on the body, allowing it to focus more on detoxification and healing.

Hydration is key to effective detoxification. Drinking adequate amounts of spring water throughout the day, in addition to consuming detox smoothies, ensures that the body can properly flush out toxins. This combination of hydration, nutrient-dense smoothies, and an overall alkaline diet creates an ideal environment for the body to cleanse itself and promote long-term health.

Best Ingredients for Alkaline Smoothies

When crafting alkaline smoothies according to Dr. Sebi's guidelines, selecting the right ingredients is crucial to ensure they not only taste great but also support the body's natural pH balance. Dr. Sebi emphasized the importance of using fresh, natural, and minimally processed ingredients that contribute to alkalinity. Here are some of the best ingredients to include in alkaline smoothies:

Leafy Greens: Greens such as kale, spinach, and dandelion are staple ingredients in alkaline smoothies. They are high in vitamins, minerals, and chlorophyll, which helps increase blood alkalinity and remove toxins from the body.

Alkaline Fruits: Incorporating fruits like apples, bananas, berries, and melons can add natural sweetness to smoothies while contributing to their alkaline properties. Avocados, which are also a fruit, are excellent for creating a creamy texture and are packed with healthy fats and nutrients that support overall health.

Cucumbers and Celery: These vegetables are high in water content, making them perfect for adding hydration to your smoothies. They also help flush toxins from the body and contribute to alkaline balance.

Herbs and Roots: Ginger and turmeric are great for their anti-inflammatory properties and can add a kick to any smoothie. They aid digestion and enhance the immune system. Fresh herbs like mint and parsley can also boost the flavor and nutrient profile of your smoothies.

Seeds: Hemp, flax, and chia seeds are alkaline and high in omega-3 fatty acids, which are beneficial for heart health and cognitive functions. They also add a nice texture and are good thickeners for smoothies.

Nuts: Almonds can be used in smoothies, particularly through homemade almond milk, which is a preferable alternative to dairy milk and adds creaminess along with essential nutrients like calcium.

Sea Moss: A favorite of Dr. Sebi, sea moss gel can be added to any smoothie to enrich it with minerals and vitamins. It is known for its high iodine content and its ability to support thyroid function, which is crucial for maintaining a healthy metabolism.

Natural Sweeteners: To add extra sweetness without using refined sugar, natural sweeteners like agave syrup or dates can be used. They provide sweetness and additional nutrients without spiking your blood sugar levels.

These smoothies can be a powerful part of your daily routine, helping to detoxify the body, support nutritional intake, and maintain an optimal state of health.

Tips for Smoothie-Based Meal Plans

Dr. Sebi's Smoothie Diet emphasizes incorporating nourishing, alkaline-forming ingredients into daily meal plans through smoothies. These drinks can serve as a powerful tool for detoxification, nutrient intake, and overall health maintenance. Here are some tips for integrating smoothies into meal plans effectively, following Dr. Sebi's nutritional guidelines.

Prioritize Alkaline Ingredients: Focus on including a variety of alkaline fruits and vegetables in your smoothies, such as kale, spinach, cucumber, apples, and berries. These ingredients help maintain the body's pH balance, which is central to Dr. Sebi's dietary philosophy.

Incorporate Nutrient-Dense Superfoods: Enhance the nutritional value of your smoothies with superfoods like sea moss, which is rich in minerals and helps support thyroid function, and spirulina, known for its high protein content and antioxidant properties. These superfoods boost the smoothie's ability to nourish the body deeply.

Balance Macronutrients: Ensure each smoothie has a good balance of carbohydrates, proteins, and healthy fats. Add nuts or seeds such as hemp, flax, or chia to incorporate essential fatty acids and protein, which will help you feel full and satisfied. Avocado can be used to add healthy fats and create a creamy texture.

Use Natural Sweeteners Sparingly: If additional sweetness is desired, opt for natural sweeteners like dates or agave syrup. These sweeteners are better alternatives to refined sugar and align with Dr. Sebi's emphasis on natural, unprocessed foods.

Stay Hydrated: While smoothies contain a lot of water, especially when made with juicy fruits or added liquids like coconut water, it's still important to drink plenty of spring water throughout the day to aid digestion and further support detoxification processes.

Plan for Variety: To prevent nutritional deficiencies and keep the diet interesting, rotate the ingredients in your smoothies regularly. Trying different combinations of fruits, vegetables, and superfoods can help ensure a broad range of vitamins and minerals are consumed.

Prepare in Advance: For convenience, pre-package portions of cut fruits, vegetables, and other smoothie ingredients in your freezer. This preparation makes it easy to blend a nutritious smoothie quickly, especially useful on busy mornings or when you need a quick nutrient boost.

By following these tips, smoothies can become a cornerstone of a healthy, satisfying meal plan that adheres to Dr. Sebi's nutritional guidelines. They provide a delicious and effective way to consume a concentrated amount of nutrients while enjoying a variety of flavors and textures.

Balancing Macronutrients in Smoothies

Balancing macronutrients in smoothies is crucial for making them not just delicious and refreshing, but also nutritionally complete. Dr. Sebi's approach emphasized the importance of creating smoothies that provide a balanced blend of proteins, carbohydrates, and fats to support overall health and maintain the body's natural alkaline state.

Carbohydrates are typically the primary macronutrient in smoothies, mainly derived from fruits and sometimes vegetables. These natural sources provide essential fibers, vitamins, and sugars that offer energy and support digestive health. For a more balanced smoothie, it's beneficial to choose low-glycemic fruits such as berries, apples, and pears, which provide sustained energy without a significant sugar spike.

Proteins are vital for repair and growth of tissues, and including them in smoothies can make the beverages more satiating. Dr. Sebi recommended plant-based protein sources that align with his alkaline diet. Options such as hemp seeds, chia seeds, or alkaline-friendly protein powders can be added to smoothies to increase their protein content. These not only offer essential amino acids but also contribute additional fiber and omega-3 fatty acids, which are beneficial for heart health.

Fats are often overlooked in smoothies but are essential for nutrient absorption and providing sustained energy. Adding sources of healthy fats like avocado, coconut oil, or soaked nuts can enrich the smoothie's texture, making it creamier and more filling. These fats are crucial for absorbing fat-soluble vitamins present in other ingredients, enhancing the overall nutritional value of the smoothie.

In addition to these macronutrients, it's also important to incorporate various greens and superfoods to maximize the health benefits. Ingredients like kale, spinach, and sea moss not only boost the mineral and vitamin content but also help increase the alkalinity of the smoothies, supporting Dr. Sebi's dietary principles.

Superfoods to Enhance Smoothie Benefits

In the Dr. Sebi Smoothie Diet, superfoods play a critical role in enhancing the nutritional benefits of each smoothie, offering a concentrated source of vitamins, minerals, and other nutrients that can significantly boost health and well-being. Dr. Sebi highlighted several superfoods that are especially beneficial when incorporated into smoothies, due to their high nutrient density and alignment with his principles of natural, alkaline eating.

Sea moss is one of the most esteemed superfoods in Dr. Sebi's diet. Packed with over 90 essential minerals, sea moss supports thyroid function due to its high iodine content, boosts immunity with its rich vitamin and antioxidant profile, and promotes good digestion due to its mucilaginous texture. Adding sea moss gel to smoothies enhances their texture and boosts their nutrient content without altering the taste.

Spirulina, a type of blue-green algae, is another powerful superfood recommended by Dr. Sebi. It is exceptionally high in protein and a good source of antioxidants, B-vitamins, and other nutrients. Its intense color reflects its rich chlorophyll content, which helps detoxify the body. A small spoonful of spirulina powder can transform any smoothie into a nutrient powerhouse, enhancing energy levels and overall vitality.

Chia seeds are highly beneficial for their omega-3 fatty acid content, fiber, and protein, making them an ideal addition to smoothies for enhanced satiety and energy. They also help in maintaining hydration, as they can absorb many times their weight in water, prolonging hydration and nutrient absorption when consumed in a smoothie.

Hemp seeds offer a balanced ratio of omega-3 to omega-6 fatty acids, which is rare in many plant foods. They are also a complete protein source, containing all nine essential amino acids. A tablespoon of hemp seeds added to a smoothie can provide a nutty flavor and a boost of protein.

Moringa powder, made from the dried leaves of the moringa tree, is another nutrient-dense superfood used in Dr. Sebi's diet. It's a rich source of iron, calcium, vitamin A, and antioxidants. Incorporating moringa into a smoothie can help combat fatigue, support bone health, and boost the immune system.

Preparing Smoothies for Energy Boost

Preparing smoothies for an energy boost is a central theme in Dr. Sebi's Smoothie Diet, emphasizing the use of natural, plant-based ingredients that provide sustained energy throughout the day. Dr. Sebi's approach to energizing smoothies involves combining foods that are high in vitamins, minerals, and other essential nutrients that help increase vitality and combat fatigue.

To create an energizing smoothie, start with a base of high-electrolyte fluids like coconut water or alkaline water, which hydrates the body and provides a quick source of natural sugars and minerals. This base helps facilitate the transport of nutrients in the bloodstream and enhances overall energy levels.

For the body of the smoothie, incorporating fruits like bananas or apples is excellent as they offer natural sugars for quick energy, along with fiber for sustained release. These fruits also provide essential nutrients like potassium and vitamin C, which support cellular functions and energy production.

Leafy greens such as kale and spinach are perfect additions to any energy-boosting smoothie. These greens are not only nutrient-dense but also packed with chlorophyll, which helps oxygenate the blood, enhancing energy production and overall vitality. The high iron content in these greens is crucial for preventing fatigue, especially in those who might be iron deficient.

To further enhance the energy-boosting properties, adding superfoods like maca powder can be particularly effective. Maca is known for its ability to increase stamina and endurance, making it a favorite among athletes. It also helps regulate hormones and can boost overall energy levels.

A scoop of protein-rich seeds like hemp or chia can also be beneficial in an energy smoothie. These seeds provide not only protein but also essential fatty acids that are vital for brain health and sustained energy levels. The protein content helps rebuild muscle and sustain energy without causing a sugar crash.

For an extra burst of energy and a hint of spice, a small piece of ginger or a sprinkle of cinnamon can be added. Ginger increases circulation, which helps awaken the body and boost metabolism, while cinnamon helps regulate blood sugar levels, ensuring that your energy levels are stable throughout the day.

Book 20: Dr. Sebi Smoothie Recipes

Welcome to "Dr. Sebi Smoothie Recipes" – a delightful compilation of nourishing blends designed to invigorate your senses and revitalize your health. Within these pages, you'll discover a treasure trove of smoothie creations inspired by the timeless wisdom of Dr. Sebi's nutritional philosophy.

Dr. Sebi's holistic approach to wellness emphasized the importance of consuming foods that harmonize with the body's natural alkaline state, fostering balance and vitality from within. With this guiding principle in mind, we've meticulously crafted each smoothie recipe to include an array of nutrient-dense ingredients that not only tantalize the taste buds but also support your overall well-being.

Whether you're embarking on a journey to improve your health, seeking to boost your energy levels, or simply craving a delicious and convenient way to incorporate more fruits and vegetables into your diet, our collection of smoothie recipes has something for everyone. From refreshing fruit medleys bursting with antioxidants to creamy blends packed with leafy greens and plant-based proteins, each recipe is a celebration of the vibrant flavors and health-boosting properties found in nature.

Whether you're sipping on a revitalizing breakfast smoothie to kickstart your day or indulging in a post-workout refresher to replenish your energy stores, our recipes are designed to nourish your body and lift your spirits. So dust off your blender, gather your ingredients, and join us on a journey toward vibrant health and well-being. Here's to embracing the transformative power of whole foods and savoring every sip along the way.

1. **Alkalizing Green Glow Smoothie**

   - Ingredients:
     - 1 cup spinach
     - 1/2 cucumber, peeled and chopped
     - 1/2 green apple, cored and diced
     - 1/4 avocado, pitted and peeled
     - 1 tablespoon fresh lemon juice
     - 1 cup coconut water
   - Instructions:
     1. Combine all ingredients in a blender.
     2. Blend until smooth and creamy.
     3. Pour into a glass and enjoy the refreshing, alkalizing goodness.

2. **Berry Blast Antioxidant Smoothie**

   - Ingredients:
     - 1/2 cup mixed berries (strawberries, blueberries, raspberries)
     - 1/2 cup kale leaves, stemmed and torn
     - 1/2 banana, frozen
     - 1 tablespoon chia seeds

- 1 cup almond milk (or any plant-based milk)
- Instructions:
  1. Place all ingredients in a blender.
  2. Blend until smooth and creamy.
  3. Pour into a glass and relish the burst of antioxidants.

3. Mango Tango Immunity Booster

- Ingredients:
  - 1 ripe mango, peeled and diced
  - 1/2 cup pineapple chunks
  - 1/2 banana, frozen
  - 1 tablespoon fresh ginger, grated
  - 1 teaspoon turmeric powder
  - 1 cup coconut water
- Instructions:
  1. Add all ingredients to a blender.
  2. Blend until smooth and velvety.
  3. Serve in a glass and savor the tropical flavors while boosting your immunity.

4. Creamy Coconut Paradise Smoothie

- Ingredients:
  - 1/2 cup coconut meat
  - 1/2 cup pineapple chunks
  - 1/2 banana, frozen
  - 1 tablespoon coconut oil
  - 1/4 teaspoon vanilla extract
  - 1 cup coconut water
- Instructions:
  1. Blend all ingredients until creamy and well combined.
  2. Pour into a glass and transport yourself to a tropical paradise with every sip.

5. Protein Powerhouse Almond Butter Smoothie

- Ingredients:
  - 2 tablespoons almond butter
  - 1/2 banana, frozen
  - 1 tablespoon hemp seeds
  - 1 tablespoon flaxseed meal
  - 1 tablespoon raw honey or maple syrup (optional)
  - 1 cup almond milk (or any plant-based milk)
- Instructions:
  1. Combine all ingredients in a blender.
  2. Blend until smooth and creamy.
  3. Pour into a glass and enjoy the protein-packed goodness to fuel your day.

6. Vibrant Beetroot Berry Smoothie

- Ingredients:
  - 1/2 cup cooked beetroots, chopped
  - 1/2 cup mixed berries (such as strawberries, raspberries, and blueberries)
  - 1/2 banana, frozen
  - 1 tablespoon hemp seeds
  - 1 cup coconut water
- Instructions:
  1. Place all ingredients in a blender.
  2. Blend until smooth and velvety.
  3. Pour into a glass and relish the beautiful hue and delightful flavor.

7. **Citrus Sunshine Smoothie**

- Ingredients:
  - 1 orange, peeled and segmented
  - 1/2 cup pineapple chunks
  - 1/2 banana, frozen
  - 1 tablespoon fresh lime juice
  - 1 tablespoon grated ginger
  - 1 cup coconut water
- Instructions:
  1. Add all ingredients to a blender.
  2. Blend until smooth and creamy.
  3. Serve in a glass and enjoy the refreshing burst of citrus flavors.

8. **Creamy Papaya Coconut Smoothie**

- Ingredients:
  - 1/2 cup ripe papaya, diced
  - 1/4 cup coconut meat
  - 1/2 banana, frozen
  - 1 tablespoon coconut flakes
  - 1/4 teaspoon ground cinnamon
  - 1 cup coconut milk (or any plant-based milk)
- Instructions:
  1. Blend all ingredients until smooth and creamy.
  2. Pour into a glass and savor the tropical creaminess with every sip.

9. **Detoxifying Green Tea Smoothie**

- Ingredients:
  - 1/2 cup brewed green tea, cooled
  - 1/2 cup kale leaves, stemmed and torn
  - 1/2 cucumber, peeled and chopped
  - 1/4 avocado, pitted and peeled
  - 1 tablespoon fresh lemon juice
  - 1 teaspoon raw honey or maple syrup (optional)
- Instructions:
  1. Combine all ingredients in a blender.

2. Blend until smooth and well combined.
3. Pour into a glass and enjoy the refreshing and detoxifying benefits.

10. Chocolate Banana Almond Smoothie

- Ingredients:
  - 1 banana, frozen
  - 1 tablespoon almond butter
  - 1 tablespoon cocoa powder
  - 1 tablespoon flaxseed meal
  - 1 cup almond milk (or any plant-based milk)
  - 1 teaspoon raw honey or maple syrup (optional)
- Instructions:
  1. Blend all ingredients until smooth and creamy.
  2. Pour into a glass and indulge in the rich and satisfying flavors of chocolate and banana.

11. Pineapple Mint Refresher

- Ingredients:
  - 1 cup pineapple chunks
  - Handful of fresh mint leaves
  - 1/2 cucumber, peeled and chopped
  - 1/2 lime, juiced
  - 1 tablespoon raw honey or agave syrup (optional)
  - 1 cup coconut water
- Instructions:
  1. Combine all ingredients in a blender.
  2. Blend until smooth and refreshing.
  3. Pour into glasses and garnish with mint leaves for an extra burst of flavor.

12. Turmeric Mango Smoothie

- Ingredients:
  - 1 ripe mango, peeled and diced
  - 1/2 banana, frozen
  - 1/2 teaspoon ground turmeric
  - Pinch of black pepper
  - 1 tablespoon hemp seeds
  - 1 cup almond milk (or any plant-based milk)
- Instructions:
  1. Blend all ingredients until smooth and creamy.
  2. Pour into glasses and enjoy the tropical sweetness with a hint of spice.

13. Berry-licious Spinach Smoothie

- Ingredients:
  - 1/2 cup mixed berries (strawberries, blueberries, raspberries)
  - Handful of spinach leaves
  - 1/2 banana, frozen

- 1 tablespoon almond butter
- 1 tablespoon chia seeds
- 1 cup coconut water
- Instructions:
  1. Blend all ingredients until smooth and vibrant.
  2. Pour into glasses and relish the combination of sweet berries and nutrient-packed spinach.

14. Peachy Keen Oatmeal Smoothie

- Ingredients:
  - 1 ripe peach, pitted and diced
  - 1/4 cup rolled oats
  - 1/2 banana, frozen
  - 1 tablespoon almond butter
  - 1 teaspoon vanilla extract
  - 1 cup almond milk (or any plant-based milk)
- Instructions:
  1. Blend all ingredients until smooth and creamy.
  2. Pour into glasses and enjoy the creamy texture and fruity sweetness.

15. Coconut Pineapple Greens Smoothie

- Ingredients:
  - 1/2 cup pineapple chunks
  - Handful of kale leaves, stemmed and torn
  - 1/2 cucumber, peeled and chopped
  - 1/4 avocado, pitted and peeled
  - 1 tablespoon coconut flakes
  - 1 cup coconut water
- Instructions:
  1. Combine all ingredients in a blender.
  2. Blend until smooth and luscious.
  3. Pour into glasses and transport yourself to a tropical oasis with every sip.

16. Golden Glow Turmeric Smoothie

- Ingredients:
  - 1/2 cup frozen pineapple chunks
  - 1/2 teaspoon ground turmeric
  - 1/2 teaspoon grated ginger
  - 1/4 teaspoon ground cinnamon
  - 1 tablespoon hemp seeds
  - 1 cup coconut water
- Instructions:
  1. Blend all ingredients until smooth and creamy.
  2. Pour into glasses and savor the vibrant golden hue and warming flavors.

17. Minty Watermelon Cooler

- Ingredients:
  - 1 cup cubed watermelon
  - Handful of fresh mint leaves
  - 1/2 cucumber, peeled and chopped
  - Juice of 1 lime
  - 1 tablespoon raw honey or agave syrup (optional)
  - 1 cup coconut water
- Instructions:
  1. Combine all ingredients in a blender.
  2. Blend until smooth and refreshing.
  3. Pour into glasses and garnish with mint leaves for an extra burst of freshness.

18. Cocoa Banana Protein Smoothie

- Ingredients:
  - 1 ripe banana, frozen
  - 1 tablespoon cocoa powder
  - 1 tablespoon almond butter
  - 1 tablespoon chia seeds
  - 1/2 teaspoon vanilla extract
  - 1 cup almond milk (or any plant-based milk)
- Instructions:
  1. Blend all ingredients until smooth and creamy.
  2. Pour into glasses and enjoy the rich chocolatey flavor with a boost of protein.

19. Pineapple Coconut Green Smoothie

- Ingredients:
  - 1/2 cup frozen pineapple chunks
  - Handful of spinach leaves
  - 1/4 avocado, pitted and peeled
  - 1 tablespoon coconut flakes
  - Juice of 1 lime
  - 1 cup coconut water
- Instructions:
  1. Blend all ingredients until smooth and velvety.
  2. Pour into glasses and revel in the tropical fusion of flavors.

20. Creamy Blueberry Almond Smoothie

- Ingredients:
  - 1/2 cup frozen blueberries
  - 1/2 banana, frozen
  - 1 tablespoon almond butter
  - 1 tablespoon flaxseed meal
  - 1/2 teaspoon vanilla extract
  - 1 cup almond milk (or any plant-based milk)
- Instructions:
  1. Blend all ingredients until smooth and luxurious.

2. Pour into glasses and indulge in the creamy goodness of blueberries and almonds.

21. Mango Pineapple Bliss Smoothie

- Ingredients:
  - 1/2 cup mango chunks
  - 1/2 cup pineapple chunks
  - 1/2 banana, frozen
  - 1 tablespoon shredded coconut
  - 1 tablespoon hemp seeds
  - 1 cup coconut water
- Instructions:
  1. Combine all ingredients in a blender.
  2. Blend until smooth and creamy.
  3. Pour into glasses and enjoy the tropical paradise in a sip.

22. Citrus Beet Detox Smoothie

- Ingredients:
  - 1/2 cup cooked beetroots, chopped
  - 1 orange, peeled and segmented
  - 1/2 banana, frozen
  - 1 tablespoon fresh lemon juice
  - 1 tablespoon grated ginger
  - 1 cup coconut water
- Instructions:
  1. Add all ingredients to a blender.
  2. Blend until smooth and vibrant.
  3. Serve in glasses and cleanse your body with this zesty detox elixir.

23. Peach Raspberry Delight Smoothie

- Ingredients:
  - 1 ripe peach, pitted and diced
  - 1/2 cup raspberries
  - 1/2 banana, frozen
  - 1 tablespoon almond butter
  - 1 tablespoon chia seeds
  - 1 cup almond milk (or any plant-based milk)
- Instructions:
  1. Blend all ingredients until smooth and luscious.
  2. Pour into glasses and enjoy the sweet and tangy flavor combination.

24. Cucumber Melon Mint Refresher

- Ingredients:
  - 1/2 cucumber, peeled and chopped
  - 1/2 cup honeydew melon, diced
  - Handful of fresh mint leaves

- Juice of 1 lime
- 1 tablespoon raw honey or agave syrup (optional)
- 1 cup coconut water
- Instructions:
    1. Combine all ingredients in a blender.
    2. Blend until smooth and rejuvenating.
    3. Pour into glasses and garnish with mint leaves for a refreshing twist.

25. Blueberry Spinach Protein Smoothie

- Ingredients:
    - 1/2 cup frozen blueberries
    - Handful of spinach leaves
    - 1/2 banana, frozen
    - 1 tablespoon almond butter
    - 1 tablespoon hemp seeds
    - 1 cup almond milk (or any plant-based milk)
- Instructions:
    1. Blend all ingredients until smooth and creamy.
    2. Pour into glasses and relish the nutritious blend of blueberries, spinach, and protein-rich ingredients.

26. Tropical Mango Coconut Smoothie

- Ingredients:
    - 1/2 cup mango chunks
    - 1/4 cup coconut meat
    - 1/2 banana, frozen
    - 1 tablespoon coconut flakes
    - 1 tablespoon hemp seeds
    - 1 cup coconut water
- Instructions:
    1. Blend all ingredients until smooth and creamy.
    2. Pour into glasses and enjoy the taste of the tropics.

27. Pineapple Kale Sunshine Smoothie

- Ingredients:
    - 1/2 cup pineapple chunks
    - Handful of kale leaves, stemmed
    - 1/2 banana, frozen
    - Juice of 1 orange
    - 1 tablespoon chia seeds
    - 1 cup coconut water
- Instructions:
    1. Combine all ingredients in a blender.
    2. Blend until smooth and radiant.
    3. Pour into glasses and bask in the sunshine with each sip.

28. Berry Beet Antioxidant Smoothie

- Ingredients:
  - 1/2 cup mixed berries (strawberries, raspberries, blueberries)
  - 1/2 cup cooked beetroots, chopped
  - 1/2 banana, frozen
  - 1 tablespoon flaxseed meal
  - 1 tablespoon raw honey or agave syrup (optional)
  - 1 cup almond milk (or any plant-based milk)
- Instructions:
  1. Blend all ingredients until smooth and vibrant.
  2. Pour into glasses and relish the antioxidant-rich goodness.

29. Creamy Papaya Banana Smoothie

- Ingredients:
  - 1/2 cup ripe papaya, diced
  - 1/2 banana, frozen
  - 1/4 avocado, pitted and peeled
  - 1 tablespoon almond butter
  - 1 tablespoon hemp seeds
  - 1 cup almond milk (or any plant-based milk)
- Instructions:
  1. Blend all ingredients until smooth and creamy.
  2. Pour into glasses and enjoy the creamy texture and tropical flavors.

30. Green Tea Berry Detox Smoothie

- Ingredients:
  - 1/2 cup brewed green tea, cooled
  - 1/2 cup mixed berries (strawberries, blueberries, raspberries)
  - Handful of spinach leaves
  - 1/2 banana, frozen
  - Juice of 1 lemon
  - 1 tablespoon raw honey or agave syrup (optional)
- Instructions:
  1. Combine all ingredients in a blender.
  2. Blend until smooth and detoxifying.
  3. Pour into glasses and cleanse your body with this antioxidant-packed smoothie.

31. Cherry Almond Bliss Smoothie

- Ingredients:
  - 1/2 cup cherries, pitted
  - 1/2 banana, frozen
  - 1 tablespoon almond butter
  - 1 tablespoon flaxseed meal
  - 1 tablespoon hemp seeds
  - 1 cup almond milk (or any plant-based milk)

- Instructions:
  1. Blend all ingredients until smooth and creamy.
  2. Pour into glasses and savor the sweet and nutty flavor combination.

32. Peachy Mango Mint Smoothie

- Ingredients:
  - 1 ripe peach, pitted and diced
  - 1/2 cup mango chunks
  - Handful of fresh mint leaves
  - 1/2 banana, frozen
  - 1 tablespoon chia seeds
  - 1 cup coconut water
- Instructions:
  1. Combine all ingredients in a blender.
  2. Blend until smooth and refreshing.
  3. Pour into glasses and enjoy the tropical peachy goodness.

33. Raspberry Lemonade Smoothie

- Ingredients:
  - 1/2 cup raspberries
  - Juice of 1 lemon
  - 1/2 banana, frozen
  - 1 tablespoon coconut flakes
  - 1 tablespoon raw honey or agave syrup (optional)
  - 1 cup coconut water
- Instructions:
  1. Blend all ingredients until smooth and tangy.
  2. Pour into glasses and enjoy the zesty raspberry lemonade flavor.

34. Mint Chocolate Chip Smoothie

- Ingredients:
  - Handful of spinach leaves
  - 1/2 banana, frozen
  - 1 tablespoon cocoa powder
  - Handful of fresh mint leaves
  - 1 tablespoon hemp seeds
  - 1 cup almond milk (or any plant-based milk)
- Instructions:
  1. Blend all ingredients until smooth and creamy.
  2. Pour into glasses and indulge in the refreshing minty chocolate goodness.

35. Orange Carrot Turmeric Smoothie

- Ingredients:
  - 1 orange, peeled and segmented
  - 1/2 cup carrot, chopped

- 1/2 banana, frozen
- 1/2 teaspoon ground turmeric
- Pinch of black pepper
- 1 cup coconut water
- Instructions:
   1. Combine all ingredients in a blender.
   2. Blend until smooth and vibrant.
   3. Pour into glasses and enjoy the immune-boosting properties of this orange carrot turmeric smoothie.

36. Pineapple Ginger Energizer Smoothie

- Ingredients:
   - 1 cup pineapple chunks
   - 1/2 teaspoon grated ginger
   - Handful of spinach leaves
   - 1/2 banana, frozen
   - 1 tablespoon chia seeds
   - 1 cup coconut water
- Instructions:
   1. Blend all ingredients until smooth and refreshing.
   2. Pour into glasses and enjoy the zesty pineapple and invigorating ginger flavors.

37. Mango Avocado Green Dream Smoothie

- Ingredients:
   - 1/2 cup mango chunks
   - 1/4 avocado, pitted and peeled
   - Handful of kale leaves, stemmed
   - 1/2 banana, frozen
   - 1 tablespoon hemp seeds
   - 1 cup almond milk (or any plant-based milk)
- Instructions:
   1. Combine all ingredients in a blender.
   2. Blend until smooth and creamy.
   3. Pour into glasses and relish the dreamy combination of mango, avocado, and greens.

38. Blueberry Basil Beauty Smoothie

- Ingredients:
   - 1/2 cup blueberries
   - Handful of basil leaves
   - 1/2 banana, frozen
   - 1 tablespoon almond butter
   - 1 tablespoon flaxseed meal
   - 1 cup almond milk (or any plant-based milk)
- Instructions:
   1. Blend all ingredients until smooth and vibrant.
   2. Pour into glasses and enjoy the antioxidant-rich blueberries and refreshing basil.

39. Tropical Turmeric Twist Smoothie

- Ingredients:
  - 1/2 cup pineapple chunks
  - 1/2 cup mango chunks
  - 1/2 banana, frozen
  - 1/2 teaspoon ground turmeric
  - 1 tablespoon coconut flakes
  - 1 cup coconut water
- Instructions:
  1. Blend all ingredients until smooth and tropical.
  2. Pour into glasses and savor the golden goodness of turmeric combined with tropical fruits.

40. Berry Basil Blast Smoothie

- Ingredients:
  - 1/2 cup mixed berries (strawberries, blueberries, raspberries)
  - Handful of basil leaves
  - 1/2 banana, frozen
  - 1 tablespoon chia seeds
  - 1 tablespoon raw honey or agave syrup (optional)
  - 1 cup almond milk (or any plant-based milk)
- Instructions:
  1. Combine all ingredients in a blender.
  2. Blend until smooth and bursting with berry-basil goodness.
  3. Pour into glasses and enjoy the refreshing twist of basil with sweet berries.

41. Creamy Coconut Pineapple Kale Smoothie

- Ingredients:
  - 1/2 cup pineapple chunks
  - Handful of kale leaves, stemmed
  - 1/4 cup coconut meat
  - 1/2 banana, frozen
  - 1 tablespoon hemp seeds
  - 1 cup coconut water
- Instructions:
  1. Blend all ingredients until smooth and creamy.
  2. Pour into glasses and enjoy the tropical fusion of coconut, pineapple, and kale.

42. Strawberry Kiwi Lime Refresher

- Ingredients:
  - 1/2 cup strawberries
  - 1 kiwi, peeled and diced
  - Juice of 1 lime
  - 1/2 banana, frozen
  - 1 tablespoon raw honey or agave syrup (optional)

- 1 cup coconut water
- Instructions:
  1. Combine all ingredients in a blender.
  2. Blend until smooth and refreshing.
  3. Pour into glasses and enjoy the tangy sweetness of strawberries, kiwi, and lime.

43. Peach Raspberry Basil Smoothie

- Ingredients:
  - 1 ripe peach, pitted and diced
  - 1/2 cup raspberries
  - Handful of basil leaves
  - 1/2 banana, frozen
  - 1 tablespoon chia seeds
  - 1 cup almond milk (or any plant-based milk)
- Instructions:
  1. Blend all ingredients until smooth and vibrant.
  2. Pour into glasses and savor the delightful combination of peach, raspberry, and basil.

44. Orange Mango Carrot Glow Smoothie

- Ingredients:
  - 1 orange, peeled and segmented
  - 1/2 cup mango chunks
  - 1/4 cup carrot, chopped
  - 1/2 banana, frozen
  - 1 tablespoon coconut flakes
  - 1 cup coconut water
- Instructions:
  1. Blend all ingredients until smooth and glowing.
  2. Pour into glasses and enjoy the refreshing burst of orange, mango, and carrot.

45. Chocolate Cherry Almond Joy Smoothie

- Ingredients:
  - 1/2 cup cherries, pitted
  - 1 tablespoon cocoa powder
  - 1 tablespoon almond butter
  - 1 tablespoon shredded coconut
  - 1 tablespoon hemp seeds
  - 1 cup almond milk (or any plant-based milk)
- Instructions:
  1. Blend all ingredients until smooth and indulgent.
  2. Pour into glasses and relish the rich chocolatey flavor with a hint of cherry and almond joy.

46. Pineapple Mango Turmeric Sunshine Smoothie

- Ingredients:
  - 1/2 cup pineapple chunks

- 1/2 cup mango chunks
- 1/2 teaspoon ground turmeric
- 1/2 banana, frozen
- 1 tablespoon coconut flakes
- 1 cup coconut water
- Instructions:
  1. Blend all ingredients until smooth and vibrant.
  2. Pour into glasses and enjoy the tropical sunshine in every sip.

47. Blueberry Spinach Avocado Power Smoothie

- Ingredients:
  - 1/2 cup blueberries
  - Handful of spinach leaves
  - 1/4 avocado, pitted and peeled
  - 1/2 banana, frozen
  - 1 tablespoon chia seeds
  - 1 cup almond milk (or any plant-based milk)
- Instructions:
  1. Combine all ingredients in a blender.
  2. Blend until smooth and powerful.
  3. Pour into glasses and fuel your day with this nutrient-packed smoothie.

48. Peach Coconut Kale Dream Smoothie

- Ingredients:
  - 1 ripe peach, pitted and diced
  - 1/4 cup coconut meat
  - Handful of kale leaves, stemmed
  - 1/2 banana, frozen
  - 1 tablespoon hemp seeds
  - 1 cup coconut water
- Instructions:
  1. Blend all ingredients until smooth and dreamy.
  2. Pour into glasses and enjoy the creamy texture and sweet peachy flavor.

49. Raspberry Beet Basil Elixir

- Ingredients:
  - 1/2 cup raspberries
  - 1/2 cup cooked beetroots, chopped
  - Handful of basil leaves
  - 1/2 banana, frozen
  - 1 tablespoon flaxseed meal
  - 1 cup almond milk (or any plant-based milk)
- Instructions:
  1. Blend all ingredients until smooth and revitalizing.
  2. Pour into glasses and indulge in the earthy sweetness of beets and the refreshing taste of raspberries and basil.

50. Minty Melon Cucumber Cooler

- Ingredients:
  - 1/2 cup honeydew melon, diced
  - 1/2 cucumber, peeled and chopped
  - Handful of fresh mint leaves
  - Juice of 1 lime
  - 1/2 banana, frozen
  - 1 cup coconut water
- Instructions:
  1. Combine all ingredients in a blender.
  2. Blend until smooth and cooling.
  3. Pour into glasses and enjoy the refreshing taste of melon, cucumber, and mint.

51. Mango Pineapple Basil Bliss Smoothie

- Ingredients:
  - 1/2 cup mango chunks
  - 1/2 cup pineapple chunks
  - Handful of basil leaves
  - 1/2 banana, frozen
  - 1 tablespoon chia seeds
  - 1 cup coconut water
- Instructions:
  1. Blend all ingredients until smooth and blissful.
  2. Pour into glasses and enjoy the tropical fusion of mango, pineapple, and basil.

52. Strawberry Papaya Coconut Refresher

- Ingredients:
  - 1/2 cup strawberries
  - 1/2 cup ripe papaya, diced
  - 1/4 cup coconut meat
  - 1/2 banana, frozen
  - 1 tablespoon coconut flakes
  - 1 cup coconut water
- Instructions:
  1. Combine all ingredients in a blender.
  2. Blend until smooth and refreshing.
  3. Pour into glasses and savor the tropical delight.

53. Blueberry Banana Kale Power Smoothie

- Ingredients:
  - 1/2 cup blueberries
  - 1/2 banana, frozen
  - Handful of kale leaves, stemmed
  - 1 tablespoon almond butter

- 1 tablespoon hemp seeds
- 1 cup almond milk (or any plant-based milk)
- Instructions:
  1. Blend all ingredients until smooth and powerful.
  2. Pour into glasses and enjoy the nutritious boost of blueberries, banana, and kale.

54. Peach Raspberry Turmeric Elixir

- Ingredients:
  - 1 ripe peach, pitted and diced
  - 1/2 cup raspberries
  - 1/2 teaspoon ground turmeric
  - Pinch of black pepper
  - 1/2 banana, frozen
  - 1 cup coconut water
- Instructions:
  1. Blend all ingredients until smooth and revitalizing.
  2. Pour into glasses and enjoy the vibrant flavor and health benefits.

55. Orange Carrot Ginger Glow Smoothie

- Ingredients:
  - 1 orange, peeled and segmented
  - 1/4 cup carrot, chopped
  - 1/2-inch piece of fresh ginger, peeled
  - 1/2 banana, frozen
  - 1 tablespoon raw honey or agave syrup (optional)
  - 1 cup coconut water
- Instructions:
  1. Combine all ingredients in a blender.
  2. Blend until smooth and glowing.
  3. Pour into glasses and enjoy the refreshing and immune-boosting blend.

56. Pineapple Mango Spinach Glow Smoothie

- Ingredients:
  - 1/2 cup pineapple chunks
  - 1/2 cup mango chunks
  - Handful of spinach leaves
  - 1/2 banana, frozen
  - 1 tablespoon chia seeds
  - 1 cup coconut water
- Instructions:
  1. Blend all ingredients until smooth and glowing.
  2. Pour into glasses and enjoy the tropical sweetness with a nutritious boost.

57. Blueberry Basil Lemon Zest Smoothie

- Ingredients:

- 1/2 cup blueberries
- Handful of basil leaves
- Juice of 1 lemon
- 1/2 banana, frozen
- 1 tablespoon flaxseed meal
- 1 cup almond milk (or any plant-based milk)
- Instructions:
  1. Combine all ingredients in a blender.
  2. Blend until smooth and zestful.
  3. Pour into glasses and enjoy the refreshing burst of blueberries, basil, and lemon.

58. Mango Papaya Coconut Dream Smoothie

- Ingredients:
  - 1/2 cup mango chunks
  - 1/2 cup ripe papaya, diced
  - 1/4 cup coconut meat
  - 1/2 banana, frozen
  - 1 tablespoon coconut flakes
  - 1 cup coconut water
- Instructions:
  1. Blend all ingredients until smooth and dreamy.
  2. Pour into glasses and savor the tropical paradise in each sip.

59. Strawberry Kiwi Spinach Vitality Smoothie

- Ingredients:
  - 1/2 cup strawberries
  - 1 kiwi, peeled and diced
  - Handful of spinach leaves
  - 1/2 banana, frozen
  - 1 tablespoon hemp seeds
  - 1 cup coconut water
- Instructions:
  1. Blend all ingredients until smooth and revitalizing.
  2. Pour into glasses and enjoy the vibrant flavor and nutritional boost.

60. Raspberry Beet Carrot Radiance Smoothie

- Ingredients:
  - 1/2 cup raspberries
  - 1/4 cup cooked beetroots, chopped
  - 1/4 cup carrot, chopped
  - 1/2 banana, frozen
  - 1 tablespoon raw honey or agave syrup (optional)
  - 1 cup coconut water
- Instructions:
  1. Combine all ingredients in a blender.
  2. Blend until smooth and radiant.

3. Pour into glasses and enjoy the beautiful color and nourishing blend

Book 21: Dr. Sebi Digestive Remedies

This book delves into a comprehensive exploration of holistic approaches to digestive health. Rooted in the principles of natural healing and herbal medicine, this encyclopedia serves as a guide to understanding and nurturing the digestive system. Dr. Sebi's philosophy emphasizes the interconnectedness of body, mind, and spirit, recognizing the digestive system as a vital component of overall well-being.

Within these pages, readers will uncover an array of remedies curated to support optimal digestive function. From herbal infusions to dietary recommendations, each remedy is carefully crafted to address various digestive concerns, ranging from indigestion and bloating to more complex issues like irritable bowel syndrome (IBS) and gastritis.

Drawing upon the wisdom of traditional healing practices from around the world, this book offers accessible and practical solutions for individuals seeking to restore balance and vitality to their digestive health. Whether it's incorporating healing herbs into daily rituals or adopting mindful eating habits, this encyclopedia empowers readers to take proactive steps towards achieving digestive wellness.

1. Aloe Vera and Mint Infusion for Digestion

- Ingredients:
  - 1 cup water
  - 1 tablespoon fresh aloe vera gel
  - Handful of fresh mint leaves
- Instructions:
  1. Bring water to a boil and remove from heat.
  2. Add fresh aloe vera gel and mint leaves to the hot water.
  3. Cover and let steep for 5-10 minutes.
  4. Strain the infusion and drink it warm to support digestion and soothe the stomach.

2. Turmeric and Ginger Anti-inflammatory Tea

- Ingredients:
  - 1 cup hot water
  - 1/2 teaspoon ground turmeric
  - 1/2 teaspoon grated ginger
  - Juice of 1/2 lemon
  - 1 teaspoon raw honey (optional)
- Instructions:
  1. Combine hot water, turmeric, ginger, and lemon juice in a cup.
  2. Stir well and let it steep for 5 minutes.
  3. Add honey if desired and enjoy this anti-inflammatory tea to ease digestive discomfort and boost immunity.

3. Chamomile and Lavender Relaxation Tonic

- Ingredients:
  - 1 cup water
  - 1 chamomile tea bag
  - 1 teaspoon dried lavender flowers
  - 1 teaspoon raw honey (optional)
- Instructions:
  1. Heat water to near boiling and pour it over the chamomile tea bag and lavender flowers in a mug.
  2. Cover and let steep for 5-10 minutes.
  3. Remove the tea bag and strain out the lavender flowers.
  4. Sweeten with honey if desired and sip slowly to relax the mind and soothe digestion.

4. Fennel Seed and Peppermint Digestive Elixir

- Ingredients:
  - 1 cup hot water
  - 1 teaspoon fennel seeds
  - 1 teaspoon dried peppermint leaves
- Instructions:
  1. Steep fennel seeds and peppermint leaves in hot water for 5-10 minutes.
  2. Strain the mixture and drink it warm to alleviate gas, bloating, and indigestion.

5. Apple Cider Vinegar Digestive Tonic

- Ingredients:
  - 1 tablespoon raw, unfiltered apple cider vinegar
  - 1 cup warm water
  - 1 teaspoon raw honey (optional)
- Instructions:
  1. Mix apple cider vinegar into warm water.
  2. Add honey if desired and drink it before meals to stimulate digestion and balance stomach acidity.

6. Psyllium Husk Fiber Smoothie

- Ingredients:
  - 1 tablespoon psyllium husk powder
  - 1 cup almond milk (or any plant-based milk)
  - 1/2 cup frozen berries
  - 1/2 banana
- Instructions:
  1. Blend all ingredients until smooth.
  2. Drink immediately to promote healthy bowel movements and improve digestive regularity.

7. Licorice Root Digestive Tea

- Ingredients:
  - 1 cup water
  - 1 teaspoon dried licorice root
- Instructions:
  1. Boil water and add dried licorice root.
  2. Let it simmer for 10-15 minutes.
  3. Strain and drink the tea to soothe inflammation and support gastrointestinal health.

8. Dandelion Root Detox Tea

- Ingredients:
  - 1 cup water
  - 1 teaspoon dried dandelion root
- Instructions:
  1. Boil water and add dried dandelion root.
  2. Simmer for 10-15 minutes.
  3. Strain and enjoy the detoxifying benefits of this herbal tea for liver and digestive health.

9. Ginger and Lemon Balm Digestive Elixir

- Ingredients:
  - 1 cup hot water
  - 1 teaspoon grated ginger
  - 1 teaspoon dried lemon balm leaves
- Instructions:
  1. Steep grated ginger and dried lemon balm leaves in hot water for 5-10 minutes.
  2. Strain and drink it warm to ease stomach discomfort and promote digestion.

10. Cumin and Coriander Seed Digestive Tonic

- Ingredients:
  - 1 cup hot water
  - 1 teaspoon cumin seeds
  - 1 teaspoon coriander seeds
- Instructions:
  1. Crush cumin and coriander seeds lightly and steep them in hot water for 10-15 minutes.
  2. Strain and drink this aromatic tonic to relieve gas, bloating, and improve overall digestion.

11. Peppermint and Lemon Verbena Digestive Tea

- Ingredients:
  - 1 cup hot water
  - 1 teaspoon dried peppermint leaves
  - 1 teaspoon dried lemon verbena leaves
- Instructions:
  1. Steep peppermint and lemon verbena leaves in hot water for 5-10 minutes.
  2. Strain and enjoy this soothing tea to alleviate digestive discomfort and promote relaxation.

12. Chia Seed and Coconut Water Hydration Drink

- Ingredients:
  - 1 cup coconut water
  - 1 tablespoon chia seeds
  - Juice of 1/2 lime
  - 1 teaspoon raw honey (optional)
- Instructions:
  1. Mix chia seeds with coconut water and let it sit for 10 minutes to allow chia seeds to absorb liquid.
  2. Stir in lime juice and honey, if desired, and drink to stay hydrated and support healthy digestion.

13. Cinnamon and Clove Gut Soothing Elixir

- Ingredients:
  - 1 cup hot water
  - 1/2 teaspoon ground cinnamon
  - 2-3 whole cloves
  - 1 teaspoon raw honey (optional)
- Instructions:
  1. Steep ground cinnamon and whole cloves in hot water for 5-10 minutes.
  2. Strain and sweeten with honey, if desired, to enjoy this comforting elixir for soothing digestive discomfort.

14. Ginger and Lemongrass Digestive Tonic

- Ingredients:
  - 1 cup hot water
  - 1 teaspoon grated ginger
  - 1 stalk lemongrass, chopped
- Instructions:
  1. Steep grated ginger and chopped lemongrass in hot water for 5-10 minutes.
  2. Strain and drink this aromatic tonic to ease nausea, bloating, and support healthy digestion.

15. Fennel and Cardamom Seed Digestive Infusion

- Ingredients:
  - 1 cup hot water
  - 1 teaspoon fennel seeds
  - 2-3 whole cardamom pods, lightly crushed
- Instructions:
  1. Steep fennel seeds and crushed cardamom pods in hot water for 5-10 minutes.
  2. Strain and enjoy this fragrant infusion to relieve gas, bloating, and improve overall digestion.

16. Marshmallow Root and Slippery Elm Soothing Drink

- Ingredients:
  - 1 cup warm water
  - 1 teaspoon marshmallow root powder
  - 1 teaspoon slippery elm powder

- Instructions:

1. Mix marshmallow root and slippery elm powders in warm water until well combined.

2. Drink this soothing concoction to coat the digestive tract and alleviate irritation and inflammation.

17. Dill and Lemon Digestive Detox Water

- Ingredients:
- 1 cup cold water
- 1 tablespoon fresh dill leaves, chopped
- Juice of 1/2 lemon
- Instructions:

1. Mix chopped dill leaves and lemon juice in cold water.

2. Let it infuse for a few hours in the refrigerator and sip throughout the day to support detoxification and aid digestion.

18. Papaya and Pineapple Enzyme Smoothie

- Ingredients:
- 1/2 cup ripe papaya, diced
- 1/2 cup pineapple chunks
- 1/2 banana, frozen
- 1/2 cup coconut water
- Instructions:

1. Blend all ingredients until smooth and enjoy this enzyme-rich smoothie to aid digestion and promote gut health.

19. Burdock Root and Dandelion Tea

- Ingredients:
- 1 cup hot water
- 1 teaspoon dried burdock root
- 1 teaspoon dried dandelion root
- Instructions:

1. Steep dried burdock root and dandelion root in hot water for 10-15 minutes.

2. Strain and drink this herbal tea to support liver function, aid digestion, and detoxify the body.

20. Mint and Coriander Digestive Cooler

- Ingredients:
- 1 cup cold water
- Handful of fresh mint leaves
- Handful of fresh coriander leaves
- Juice of 1/2 lime
- Instructions:

1. Blend mint leaves, coriander leaves, lime juice, and cold water until well combined.

2. Strain and drink this refreshing cooler to soothe the stomach and aid digestion.

21. Chamomile and Ginger Soothing Tea

- Ingredients:
  - 1 cup hot water
  - 1 chamomile tea bag
  - 1 teaspoon grated ginger
  - 1 teaspoon raw honey (optional)
- Instructions:
  1. Steep chamomile tea bag and grated ginger in hot water for 5-10 minutes.
  2. Remove the tea bag and stir in honey, if desired. Drink this calming tea to ease digestive discomfort and promote relaxation.

22. Cabbage Juice for Gut Healing

- Ingredients:
  - 1/2 head of cabbage
  - 1 cup water
- Instructions:
  1. Blend cabbage with water until smooth.
  2. Strain the juice and drink it to help heal and soothe the digestive tract, reduce inflammation, and promote gut health.

23. Pumpkin Seed and Cinnamon Snack

- Ingredients:
  - 1/4 cup pumpkin seeds
  - 1/2 teaspoon ground cinnamon
- Instructions:
  1. Toss pumpkin seeds with ground cinnamon.
  2. Roast them in the oven until golden brown.
  3. Enjoy as a crunchy and nutritious snack that supports digestion and provides essential nutrients.

24. Oatmeal with Flaxseed and Berries

- Ingredients:
  - 1/2 cup rolled oats
  - 1 cup almond milk (or any plant-based milk)
  - 1 tablespoon ground flaxseed
  - Handful of berries (such as blueberries or raspberries)
- Instructions:
  1. Cook oats with almond milk according to package instructions.
  2. Stir in ground flaxseed and top with berries.
  3. Enjoy this fiber-rich breakfast that promotes digestive health and provides sustained energy.

25. Probiotic-Rich Coconut Yogurt Parfait

- Ingredients:
  - 1/2 cup coconut yogurt
  - Handful of mixed nuts and seeds (such as almonds, walnuts, and pumpkin seeds)
  - 1/4 cup fresh fruit (such as sliced banana or berries)

- Instructions:
    1. Layer coconut yogurt, nuts, seeds, and fruit in a glass.
    2. Repeat layers as desired.
    3. Enjoy this probiotic-packed parfait that supports gut health and provides essential nutrients.

26. Quinoa Salad with Leafy Greens and Lemon Dressing

- Ingredients:
    - 1 cup cooked quinoa
    - Mixed leafy greens (such as spinach, kale, or arugula)
    - Juice of 1 lemon
    - Drizzle of olive oil
    - Salt and pepper to taste
- Instructions:
    1. Toss cooked quinoa and mixed greens together in a bowl.
    2. Drizzle with lemon juice and olive oil.
    3. Season with salt and pepper to taste.
    4. Enjoy this nutritious salad that supports digestion and provides essential vitamins and minerals.

27. Ginger and Turmeric Roasted Vegetables

- Ingredients:
    - Assorted vegetables (such as carrots, sweet potatoes, and Brussels sprouts)
    - 1 tablespoon grated ginger
    - 1 teaspoon ground turmeric
    - Drizzle of olive oil
    - Salt and pepper to taste
- Instructions:
    1. Preheat oven to 400°F (200°C).
    2. Toss vegetables with grated ginger, ground turmeric, olive oil, salt, and pepper.
    3. Roast in the oven until tender and golden brown.
    4. Enjoy these flavorful roasted vegetables that aid digestion and provide anti-inflammatory benefits.

28. Coconut Water Kefir

- Ingredients:
    - 1 quart coconut water
    - 2 tablespoons kefir grains
- Instructions:
    1. Combine coconut water and kefir grains in a glass jar.
    2. Cover the jar with a breathable cloth and secure with a rubber band.
    3. Allow the mixture to ferment at room temperature for 24-48 hours, until tangy and slightly effervescent.
    4. Strain out the kefir grains and refrigerate the coconut water kefir.
    5. Enjoy this probiotic-rich beverage that supports gut health and aids digestion.

29. Sauerkraut and Kimchi Fermented Vegetables

- Ingredients:
  - 1 head cabbage, shredded
  - 2 tablespoons sea salt
  - Optional: spices (such as caraway seeds, ginger, or garlic)
- Instructions:
  1. Massage shredded cabbage with sea salt until it starts to release liquid.
  2. Pack the cabbage tightly into a clean glass jar, ensuring it is fully submerged in its own liquid.
  3. Add spices if desired.
  4. Cover the jar with a lid and let it ferment at room temperature for 3-7 days, depending on desired level of fermentation.
  5. Once fermented, transfer the jar to the refrigerator to store.
  6. Enjoy sauerkraut and kimchi as a tasty and probiotic-rich addition to meals that supports digestion and gut health.

30. Lemon Water Morning Detox

- Ingredients:
  - 1 cup warm water
  - Juice of 1/2 lemon
  - Optional: raw honey or maple syrup
- Instructions:
  1. Mix warm water with freshly squeezed lemon juice.
  2. Add honey or maple syrup if desired.
  3. Drink this cleansing tonic first thing in the morning on an empty stomach to kickstart digestion, hydrate the body, and support detoxification.

31. Papaya and Pineapple Enzyme Smoothie

- Ingredients:
  - 1/2 cup ripe papaya, diced
  - 1/2 cup pineapple chunks
  - 1/2 banana, frozen
  - 1/2 cup coconut water or almond milk
- Instructions:
  1. Blend all ingredients until smooth.
  2. Enjoy this enzyme-rich smoothie to aid digestion and reduce bloating.

32. Ginger and Lemon Infused Water

- Ingredients:
  - 1 cup water
  - 1 teaspoon grated ginger
  - Juice of 1/2 lemon
  - Optional: honey or maple syrup
- Instructions:
  1. Combine water, grated ginger, and lemon juice in a glass.
  2. Stir well and let it infuse for 10-15 minutes.
  3. Add honey or maple syrup if desired.
  4. Drink this refreshing infusion to support digestion and boost metabolism.

33. Fennel Seed Chewing

- Ingredients:
  - 1 teaspoon fennel seeds
- Instructions:
  1. Simply chew on a teaspoon of fennel seeds after meals to aid digestion, alleviate gas, and freshen breath.

34. Turmeric and Honey Digestive Paste

- Ingredients:
  - 1 teaspoon turmeric powder
  - 1 teaspoon raw honey
- Instructions:
  1. Mix turmeric powder and raw honey to form a paste.
  2. Consume a small amount after meals to soothe inflammation and promote healthy digestion.

35. Cinnamon and Apple Cider Vinegar Tonic

- Ingredients:
  - 1 cup warm water
  - 1 teaspoon apple cider vinegar
  - 1/2 teaspoon ground cinnamon
  - Optional: honey or maple syrup
- Instructions:
  1. Mix warm water, apple cider vinegar, and ground cinnamon in a glass.
  2. Sweeten with honey or maple syrup if desired.
  3. Drink this tonic daily to support gut health and regulate blood sugar levels.

36. Chamomile and Lavender Relaxation Tea

- Ingredients:
  - 1 chamomile tea bag
  - 1 teaspoon dried lavender flowers
  - 1 cup hot water
- Instructions:
  1. Steep chamomile tea bag and dried lavender flowers in hot water for 5-10 minutes.
  2. Remove the tea bag and strain out the lavender flowers.
  3. Drink this soothing tea before bedtime to promote relaxation and aid digestion.

37. Peppermint Oil Massage

- Ingredients:
  - 1-2 drops peppermint essential oil
  - 1 teaspoon carrier oil (such as coconut or olive oil)
- Instructions:
  1. Mix peppermint essential oil with a carrier oil.

2. Gently massage the oil blend onto the abdomen in a circular motion to relieve bloating and abdominal discomfort.

38. Dandelion Root Tea

- Ingredients:
  - 1 teaspoon dried dandelion root
  - 1 cup hot water
- Instructions:
  1. Steep dried dandelion root in hot water for 5-10 minutes.
  2. Strain and drink this herbal tea to support liver function and aid digestion.

39. Probiotic-Rich Foods

- Ingredients:
  - Fermented foods such as sauerkraut, kimchi, kefir, and yogurt
- Instructions:
  1. Incorporate probiotic-rich foods into your diet daily to promote a healthy balance of gut bacteria and improve digestion.

40. Warm Lemon-Ginger Water

- Ingredients:
  - 1 cup warm water
  - Juice of 1/2 lemon
  - 1 teaspoon grated ginger
  - Optional: honey or maple syrup
- Instructions:
  1. Mix warm water, lemon juice, and grated ginger in a glass.
  2. Add honey or maple syrup if desired.
  3. Drink this cleansing tonic in the morning to stimulate digestion and detoxify the body.

41. Mint and Coriander Infusion

- Ingredients:
  - Handful of fresh mint leaves
  - Handful of fresh coriander leaves
  - 1 cup hot water
- Instructions:
  1. Steep mint and coriander leaves in hot water for 5-10 minutes.
  2. Strain and drink this herbal infusion to soothe digestion and alleviate bloating.

42. Cumin and Lemon Water

- Ingredients:
  - 1 teaspoon cumin seeds
  - Juice of 1/2 lemon
  - 1 cup warm water
- Instructions:

1. Crush cumin seeds lightly and mix with lemon juice and warm water.
2. Drink this concoction before meals to stimulate digestion and reduce acidity.

43. Aloe Vera Juice

- Ingredients:
  - 1 tablespoon fresh aloe vera gel
  - 1 cup water or coconut water
- Instructions:
  1. Blend fresh aloe vera gel with water or coconut water.
  2. Drink this soothing juice to promote gut health and relieve inflammation.

44. Papaya Seed Salad Dressing

- Ingredients:
  - 1 tablespoon papaya seeds
  - 2 tablespoons olive oil
  - 1 tablespoon apple cider vinegar
  - Salt and pepper to taste
- Instructions:
  1. Crush papaya seeds and mix with olive oil, apple cider vinegar, salt, and pepper.
  2. Use this dressing on salads to aid digestion and support liver function.

45. Ginger and Cardamom Tea

- Ingredients:
  - 1 teaspoon grated ginger
  - 2-3 whole cardamom pods
  - 1 cup hot water
- Instructions:
  1. Steep grated ginger and cardamom pods in hot water for 5-10 minutes.
  2. Strain and enjoy this aromatic tea to alleviate indigestion and promote relaxation.

46. Pineapple and Kiwi Smoothie

- Ingredients:
  - 1/2 cup pineapple chunks
  - 1 ripe kiwi, peeled and diced
  - 1/2 banana, frozen
  - 1/2 cup coconut water or almond milk
- Instructions:
  1. Blend pineapple, kiwi, banana, and coconut water or almond milk until smooth.
  2. Drink this tropical smoothie to aid digestion and boost immunity.

47. Carrot and Beet Juice

- Ingredients:
  - 1 carrot, chopped
  - 1 small beet, peeled and diced

- 1/2 apple, chopped
- 1/2 inch piece of ginger
- Instructions:
    1. Juice carrot, beet, apple, and ginger together.
    2. Consume this nutrient-rich juice to cleanse the liver and improve digestion.

48. Turmeric and Coconut Milk Elixir

- Ingredients:
    - 1 teaspoon ground turmeric
    - 1 cup coconut milk
    - Pinch of black pepper
    - 1 teaspoon raw honey (optional)
- Instructions:
    1. Mix turmeric with coconut milk, black pepper, and honey (if using).
    2. Warm the mixture gently and drink to reduce inflammation and support digestive health.

49. Chia Seed Pudding

- Ingredients:
    - 2 tablespoons chia seeds
    - 1/2 cup coconut milk or almond milk
    - 1/2 teaspoon vanilla extract
    - Optional: sweetener of choice (such as maple syrup or stevia)
- Instructions:
    1. Mix chia seeds with coconut milk or almond milk, vanilla extract, and sweetener (if using).
    2. Let it sit in the refrigerator for at least 2 hours or overnight until thickened.
    3. Enjoy this nutritious pudding as a snack or dessert that supports digestive regularity.

50. Rosemary and Lemon Roasted Vegetables

- Ingredients:
    - Assorted vegetables (such as carrots, potatoes, and bell peppers)
    - 2 tablespoons olive oil
    - 1 tablespoon fresh rosemary leaves
    - Juice of 1/2 lemon
    - Salt and pepper to taste
- Instructions:
    1. Preheat oven to 400°F (200°C).
    2. Toss vegetables with olive oil, rosemary leaves, lemon juice, salt, and pepper.
    3. Roast in the oven until tender and caramelized.
    4. Enjoy these flavorful roasted vegetables to promote gut health and provide essential nutrients.

51. Chicory Root Coffee Substitute

- Ingredients:
    - 1 teaspoon roasted chicory root granules
    - 1 cup hot water
- Instructions:

1. Steep chicory root granules in hot water for 5-10 minutes.

2. Strain and enjoy this coffee-like beverage that supports digestion and liver function without caffeine.

52. Senna Leaf Tea for Constipation Relief

- Ingredients:
  - 1 teaspoon dried senna leaves
  - 1 cup hot water
- Instructions:

1. Steep dried senna leaves in hot water for 10-15 minutes.

2. Strain and drink this tea occasionally to relieve occasional constipation. Note: Consult a healthcare professional before using senna leaf as it can be potent.

53. Artichoke Leaf Extract for Bloating

- Ingredients:
  - Artichoke leaf extract supplement (follow package instructions)
- Instructions:

1. Take artichoke leaf extract supplement as directed to reduce bloating and support liver function.

54. Dill Seed Infusion

- Ingredients:
  - 1 teaspoon dill seeds
  - 1 cup hot water
- Instructions:

1. Steep dill seeds in hot water for 10-15 minutes.

2. Strain and drink this infusion to relieve gas and bloating.

55. Cabbage Juice for Ulcer Healing

- Ingredients:
  - 1/2 head of cabbage
  - 1 cup water
- Instructions:

1. Blend cabbage with water until smooth.

2. Drink this juice regularly to support ulcer healing and soothe digestive inflammation.

56. Marshmallow Root Tea

- Ingredients:
  - 1 teaspoon dried marshmallow root
  - 1 cup hot water
- Instructions:

1. Steep dried marshmallow root in hot water for 10-15 minutes.

2. Strain and drink this tea to soothe and protect the digestive tract.

57. Fenugreek Seed Infusion

- Ingredients:
  - 1 teaspoon fenugreek seeds
  - 1 cup hot water
- Instructions:
  1. Steep fenugreek seeds in hot water for 10-15 minutes.
  2. Strain and drink this infusion to aid digestion and reduce stomach discomfort.

58. Spirulina Smoothie

- Ingredients:
  - 1 teaspoon spirulina powder
  - 1 cup coconut water or almond milk
  - Handful of spinach leaves
  - 1/2 banana, frozen
- Instructions:
  1. Blend all ingredients until smooth.
  2. Enjoy this nutrient-rich smoothie to support gut health and boost energy levels.

59. Aloe Vera Gel for Acid Reflux

- Instructions:
  - Consume 1-2 tablespoons of pure aloe vera gel mixed with water to soothe acid reflux and promote healing of the esophagus.

60. Fiber-Rich Flaxseed Crackers

- Ingredients:
  - 1 cup ground flaxseeds
  - 1/2 cup water
  - Salt, herbs, and spices to taste
- Instructions:
  1. Mix ground flaxseeds with water and seasonings to form a dough.
  2. Roll out the dough thinly between two sheets of parchment paper.
  3. Cut into crackers and bake at a low temperature until crisp.
  4. Enjoy these fiber-rich crackers to support digestive regularity and maintain gut health.

61. Parsley Tea for Gas Relief

- Ingredients:
  - 1 tablespoon fresh parsley leaves
  - 1 cup hot water
- Instructions:
  1. Steep fresh parsley leaves in hot water for 5-10 minutes.
  2. Strain and drink this tea to relieve gas and bloating.

62. Cayenne Pepper Tonic

- Ingredients:
  - 1/4 teaspoon cayenne pepper

- Juice of 1 lemon
- 1 cup warm water
- - Instructions:
  1. Mix cayenne pepper and lemon juice in warm water.
  2. Drink this tonic to stimulate digestion and promote detoxification.

63. Dandelion Root Coffee

- Ingredients:
  - 1 tablespoon roasted dandelion root granules
  - 1 cup hot water
- Instructions:
  1. Steep roasted dandelion root granules in hot water for 5-10 minutes.
  2. Strain and enjoy this coffee alternative that supports liver health and aids digestion.

64. Turmeric and Black Pepper Tonic

- Ingredients:
  - 1/2 teaspoon turmeric powder
  - Pinch of black pepper
  - 1 tablespoon raw honey
  - 1 cup warm water
- Instructions:
  1. Mix turmeric powder, black pepper, and honey in warm water.
  2. Drink this tonic daily to reduce inflammation and support digestive health.

65. Sauerkraut Juice

- Ingredients:
  - 1/4 cup sauerkraut juice (from fermented sauerkraut)
- Instructions:
  1. Drink a small amount of sauerkraut juice daily to replenish beneficial gut bacteria and improve digestion.

66. Miso Soup

- Ingredients:
  - 1 tablespoon miso paste
  - 1 cup hot water
  - Optional: sliced green onions, tofu, seaweed
- Instructions:
  1. Dissolve miso paste in hot water.
  2. Add optional ingredients if desired.
  3. Enjoy this probiotic-rich soup to support gut health and aid digestion.

67. Apple Cider Vinegar and Honey Tonic

- Ingredients:
  - 1 tablespoon apple cider vinegar

- 1 tablespoon raw honey
- 1 cup warm water
- Instructions:
  1. Mix apple cider vinegar and honey in warm water.
  2. Drink this tonic before meals to improve digestion and balance stomach acid.

68. Cumin and Coriander Seed Tea

- Ingredients:
  - 1 teaspoon cumin seeds
  - 1 teaspoon coriander seeds
  - 1 cup hot water
- Instructions:
  1. Steep cumin seeds and coriander seeds in hot water for 5-10 minutes.
  2. Strain and drink this tea to ease digestive discomfort and reduce inflammation.

69. Pumpkin Seed Butter

- Ingredients:
  - 1 cup pumpkin seeds
  - 1-2 tablespoons olive oil
  - Pinch of salt
- Instructions:
  1. Blend pumpkin seeds, olive oil, and salt until smooth.
  2. Spread on toast or use as a dip for vegetables to support digestive health with its fiber and nutrient content.

70. Licorice Root Tea

- Ingredients:
  - 1 teaspoon dried licorice root
  - 1 cup hot water
- Instructions:
  1. Steep dried licorice root in hot water for 5-10 minutes.
  2. Strain and drink this tea to soothe digestive discomfort and support overall gut health.

71. Fennel and Anise Seed Tea

- Ingredients:
  - 1 teaspoon fennel seeds
  - 1 teaspoon anise seeds
  - 1 cup hot water
- Instructions:
  1. Steep fennel seeds and anise seeds in hot water for 5-10 minutes.
  2. Strain and drink this tea to relieve gas, bloating, and indigestion.

72. Peppermint and Lemon Balm Infusion

- Ingredients:

- Handful of fresh peppermint leaves
- Handful of fresh lemon balm leaves
- 1 cup hot water
- Instructions:
  1. Steep peppermint leaves and lemon balm leaves in hot water for 5-10 minutes.
  2. Strain and enjoy this aromatic infusion to calm the digestive system and reduce discomfort.

73. Soothing Banana and Coconut Smoothie

- Ingredients:
  - 1 ripe banana
  - 1/2 cup coconut milk
  - 1 tablespoon honey
  - Dash of cinnamon
- Instructions:
  1. Blend all ingredients until smooth.
  2. Drink this creamy smoothie to soothe inflammation and promote healthy digestion.

74. Cucumber and Mint Detox Water

- Ingredients:
  - 1/2 cucumber, sliced
  - Handful of fresh mint leaves
  - 1 lemon, sliced
  - 1 quart water
- Instructions:
  1. Combine cucumber slices, mint leaves, and lemon slices in a pitcher.
  2. Add water and let it infuse in the refrigerator for at least 2 hours.
  3. Strain and drink this refreshing detox water to flush out toxins and support digestive health.

75. Gentian Root Tincture

- Ingredients:
  - Gentian root tincture (follow package instructions)
- Instructions:
  1. Take gentian root tincture as directed to stimulate digestive juices and improve appetite.

76. Papaya Enzyme Supplement

- Ingredients:
  - Papaya enzyme supplement (follow package instructions)
- Instructions:
  1. Take papaya enzyme supplements with meals to aid digestion and reduce bloating.

77. Dandelion Greens Salad

- Ingredients:
  - Handful of fresh dandelion greens
  - Cherry tomatoes, sliced

- Cucumber, sliced
- Olive oil and lemon juice for dressing
- Instructions:
  1. Toss dandelion greens, cherry tomatoes, and cucumber slices together.
  2. Dress with olive oil and lemon juice.
  3. Enjoy this nutritious salad to support liver function and aid digestion.

78. Ginger and Garlic Broth

- Ingredients:
  - 2-inch piece of ginger, sliced
  - 3 cloves garlic, minced
  - 4 cups vegetable broth
- Instructions:
  1. Simmer ginger and garlic in vegetable broth for 15-20 minutes.
  2. Strain and drink this flavorful broth to improve digestion and boost immune function.

79. Psyllium Husk Fiber Supplement

- Ingredients:
  - Psyllium husk fiber supplement (follow package instructions)
- Instructions:
  1. Mix psyllium husk fiber supplement with water and consume as directed to promote regular bowel movements and relieve constipation.

80. Cilantro and Lime Quinoa Salad

- Ingredients:
  - 1 cup cooked quinoa
  - Handful of fresh cilantro, chopped
  - Juice of 1 lime
  - Salt and pepper to taste
- Instructions:
  1. Mix cooked quinoa with chopped cilantro and lime juice.
  2. Season with salt and pepper.
  3. Enjoy this refreshing salad to support digestion and provide essential nutrients.

Book 22: Dr. Sebi Mental Clarity

Enhancing Mental Focus and Clarity

Dr. Sebi's approach to enhancing mental focus and clarity revolves around nourishing the brain with specific nutrients, removing toxins that can cloud cognition, and promoting overall brain health through natural means. He believed that a clear mind begins with a clean body, and his dietary recommendations reflect this philosophy.

Central to Dr. Sebi's guidelines for mental clarity is the consumption of foods that are high in essential fatty acids, minerals, and antioxidants. These components are crucial for optimizing brain function and enhancing neurological health. For example, walnuts and hemp seeds are excellent sources of omega-3 fatty acids, which are vital for maintaining brain structure and function. Omega-3s are known to enhance the synaptic plasticity of neurons, improving memory and cognitive speed.

Dr. Sebi also emphasized the importance of alkaline-rich foods in the diet to reduce acidity in the body, which can adversely affect mental performance. Foods like avocados, cucumbers, and green leafy vegetables including kale and spinach are high in alkaline minerals and help maintain an optimal pH balance, facilitating better brain function.

Another key aspect of Dr. Sebi's dietary approach is the inclusion of natural herbs and supplements that support cognitive functions. Herbs such as ginkgo biloba, which has been used for centuries to enhance blood circulation to the brain, can significantly improve focus and memory. Gotu kola is another herb recommended by Dr. Sebi for its ability to enhance cognitive functions and reduce mental fatigue.

Dr. Sebi also stressed the importance of hydration for maintaining mental clarity. Drinking adequate amounts of spring water helps flush out toxins that can impede cognitive function and keeps the brain sufficiently hydrated to perform at its best. Dehydration is a common cause of brain fog and reduced cognitive performance, so maintaining hydration is critical.

Moreover, reducing intake of mucus-forming foods such as dairy and processed grains is also essential according to Dr. Sebi's teachings. He believed that excess mucus can lead to inflammation and congestion in the body, including the brain, which might affect mental clarity and cognitive functions.

Incorporating these dietary practices and natural herbs into everyday routines can help enhance mental focus and clarity, supporting brain health in a natural, holistic way according to Dr. Sebi's principles. This approach not only boosts cognitive functions but also contributes to overall health and well-being, demonstrating the interconnectedness of mental clarity and physical health.

Alkaline Foods that Boost Brain Health

Dr. Sebi emphasized the importance of alkaline foods for overall health, particularly for enhancing brain function and mental clarity. His approach focused on foods that support neurological health and improve cognitive functions by reducing acidity in the body and nourishing the brain with essential nutrients.

Alkaline foods high in essential fatty acids, antioxidants, and minerals are particularly beneficial for brain health. Avocados, for example, are a powerhouse of nutrients, including omega-3 fatty acids, which are crucial for maintaining brain structure and enhancing neural function. They also contain potassium, which helps deliver more oxygen to the brain, enhancing cognitive functions such as memory and concentration.

Leafy greens like kale, spinach, and arugula are loaded with vitamins A, C, K, and folate, along with minerals like magnesium and iron, all of which are important for brain health. These nutrients help reduce inflammation, a key factor that can affect cognitive performance and long-term brain health. The high levels of antioxidants found in these greens also help combat oxidative stress, which can damage brain cells.

Walnuts are another excellent source of omega-3 fatty acids and contain a high amount of alpha-linolenic acid (ALA), which boosts brain function. Regular consumption of walnuts has been linked to better memory and cognitive speed.

Alkaline grains like quinoa and amaranth are beneficial for brain health as well. They provide complex carbohydrates and B-vitamins that are vital for brain energy metabolism, ensuring the brain has a steady energy supply to function effectively.

Dr. Sebi also recommended consuming natural herbal teas such as gotu kola and ginkgo biloba, which support brain health by improving circulation and oxygen flow to the brain. This can significantly enhance memory, focus, and the overall cognitive process.

Including sea moss in the diet was another of Dr. Sebi's recommendations for boosting brain health. Sea moss is rich in iodine, a mineral essential for proper brain function and development. Its high mineral content supports neurological functions and overall brain health.

Herbs for Cognitive Function

Dr. Sebi emphasized the use of specific herbs to enhance cognitive function and promote mental clarity. These herbs are celebrated for their ability to increase blood circulation to the brain, improve neural connectivity, and reduce inflammation, all of which contribute to better mental performance and health.

One of the key herbs recommended by Dr. Sebi for cognitive enhancement is Ginkgo biloba. This ancient herb is renowned for its ability to improve blood flow to the brain and protect neurons. Ginkgo biloba is particularly beneficial in enhancing memory and cognitive speed, especially in the elderly or those suffering from cognitive decline.

Gotu kola is another herb highly valued by Dr. Sebi for its cognitive benefits. It is often used to enhance memory, increase attention span, and reduce anxiety. Gotu kola supports overall brain health by improving circulation and antioxidant capacity within the brain, which helps maintain cognitive function and mental agility.

Dr. Sebi also recommended the use of sage, which has a long history of use in traditional medicine for its cognitive-enhancing properties. Sage contains compounds that boost neurotransmitter levels in the brain, particularly acetylcholine, which is crucial for memory and learning processes.

Bacopa monnieri, or Brahmi, is a staple in Ayurvedic medicine, known for its ability to strengthen memory and intellect. Dr. Sebi appreciated its neuroprotective properties. Bacopa enhances brain function by promoting dendrite proliferation, thus improving neural signaling and ultimately enhancing mental performance and resilience.

Rhodiola rosea, often referred to as the golden root, is another herb known for its ability to reduce mental fatigue and improve concentration. Dr. Sebi noted its adaptogenic properties, which help the body resist physical, chemical, and environmental stress, thereby improving stamina and mental capacity under stress.

Daily Practices for Mental Wellness

Dr. Sebi advocated for incorporating daily practices that support mental wellness, emphasizing the importance of a holistic approach to health that includes the mind, body, and spirit. His recommendations centered around nurturing the brain through diet, reducing stress, and engaging in activities that promote mental clarity and emotional balance.

A key component of Dr. Sebi's approach was following an alkaline diet rich in natural, plant-based foods. He emphasized the importance of consuming foods that are high in essential nutrients for brain health, such as omega-3 fatty acids, antioxidants, and minerals. These include leafy greens, nuts, seeds, and fruits that not only nourish the brain but also help maintain the body's alkaline balance, which is crucial for optimal mental functioning.

Hydration was another vital practice stressed by Dr. Sebi, as it impacts brain function directly. He recommended drinking plenty of spring water throughout the day to ensure that the brain remains hydrated. Proper hydration helps in maintaining concentration and cognitive function while preventing mental fatigue.

Regular physical activity was also a cornerstone of Dr. Sebi's guidelines for mental wellness. Exercise increases blood flow to the brain, which can improve neural connections and enhance mood. Activities such as walking, yoga, or other forms of moderate exercise were encouraged not only for their physical benefits but also for their positive impact on mental health.

Dr. Sebi highlighted the importance of adequate rest and sleep for mental wellness. Sleep plays a critical role in brain health, as it is a time when the brain processes information, consolidates memory, and recovers from the day's activities. Ensuring a regular sleep schedule and creating a restful sleeping environment are essential for mental clarity and emotional resilience.

Stress reduction techniques such as meditation, deep breathing exercises, and spending time in nature were also recommended by Dr. Sebi. These practices help manage stress, which is crucial for maintaining mental clarity and preventing the mental fog associated with high stress levels.

Dr. Sebi encouraged engaging with community and maintaining healthy social interactions as part of daily life. Social engagement has been shown to improve mental health and provide emotional support, reducing feelings of isolation and stress.

Managing Stress for Mental Clarity

Dr. Sebi recognized that managing stress is crucial for maintaining mental clarity and overall well-being. He believed that high stress levels could cloud cognitive function and disrupt the body's natural balance, hindering one's ability to think clearly and maintain mental health.

To manage stress effectively, Dr. Sebi recommended several holistic practices designed to reduce stress naturally and foster a peaceful state of mind. Key among these was the practice of meditation. Meditation helps to calm the mind, reduce overthinking, and decrease anxiety. By focusing on the breath or a single point of concentration, meditation allows individuals to experience a state of deep relaxation and mental clarity.

Deep breathing exercises were also emphasized by Dr. Sebi as a simple yet powerful technique to manage stress. Deep breathing helps to oxygenate the blood, which increases energy levels and helps to relax the mind and body. Techniques such as the 4-7-8 breathing method, where you breathe in for four seconds, hold for seven, and exhale for eight, can be particularly effective in reducing acute stress and improving focus.

Physical activity is another essential component of Dr. Sebi's approach to stress management. Regular exercise, whether it's yoga, walking, or more vigorous activities, stimulates the production of endorphins, the body's natural painkillers and mood elevators. Exercise also helps to break the cycle of negative thoughts that often accompany high stress levels.

Dr. Sebi also pointed out the importance of connecting with nature as a way to reduce stress. Spending time outdoors, especially in green, natural environments, can significantly lower stress levels, improve mood, and enhance mental clarity. Activities like gardening, hiking, or simply walking in a park can provide substantial mental health benefits.

Lastly, Dr. Sebi stressed the importance of adequate rest and maintaining a regular sleep schedule. Sleep is crucial for cognitive function and emotional regulation, and lack of sleep can exacerbate stress and mental fog. Ensuring a restful environment free from distractions and sticking to a consistent bedtime routine can help improve the quality of sleep, thereby enhancing the ability to handle stress.

Nutritional Supplements for Brain Health

Dr. Sebi advocated for the use of specific nutritional supplements to support brain health and enhance mental clarity. He emphasized the importance of natural, plant-based supplements that align with the body's biological processes and promote optimal functioning of the brain. These supplements play a crucial role in nourishing the brain, improving cognitive functions, and maintaining overall neurological health.

One of the key supplements recommended by Dr. Sebi for brain health is sea moss. Rich in minerals and vitamins, sea moss provides an abundance of iodine, potassium, calcium, and natural silica. These elements are essential for maintaining neurological functions and supporting the production of thyroid hormones, which play a significant role in regulating brain and nervous system activity.

Bladderwrack is another supplement often used in conjunction with sea moss. Bladderwrack is a type of seaweed that is a natural source of iodine, an essential nutrient for brain health. It also contains fucoidan, a compound known for its anti-inflammatory and antioxidant properties, which can help protect brain cells from damage.

Dr. Sebi also recommended burdock root for its high concentration of antioxidants, such as quercetin and luteolin, which can protect the brain from oxidative stress and aid in maintaining healthy blood circulation to the brain. Improved circulation ensures that essential nutrients and oxygen are delivered to the brain, supporting cognitive functions and mental clarity.

Sarsaparilla is another beneficial supplement for brain health. It contains compounds that possess protective properties for brain cells and can help improve mental focus and reduce cognitive fatigue. Sarsaparilla's anti-inflammatory properties also contribute to its effectiveness in supporting brain health.

Additionally, Dr. Sebi suggested the inclusion of walnuts and hemp seeds in the diet, not as extracts but as whole foods that are naturally high in omega-3 fatty acids. Omega-3s are vital for brain health, promoting the structural integrity of neuronal membranes and enhancing neurotransmitter function, which is crucial for cognitive processing and mental clarity.

These natural supplements, when incorporated into a daily diet, can significantly contribute to improved brain function, enhanced mental focus, and overall brain health, reflecting Dr. Sebi's holistic approach to nourishing the body and mind.

Techniques for Improving Concentration

Dr. Sebi believed in the power of natural practices and dietary choices to enhance mental functions, including concentration. He emphasized several techniques that can help improve focus and mental clarity, aligning with his holistic approach to health.

Mindful Meditation: Dr. Sebi often stressed the importance of meditation as a tool for improving concentration. Regular meditation helps calm the mind, reduce mental clutter, and enhance the ability to focus. By sitting quietly, closing the eyes, and focusing solely on breathing or a specific mantra, meditation can significantly improve attention span over time.

Alkaline Diet: Consistent with his overarching philosophy, Dr. Sebi recommended an alkaline diet rich in fruits, vegetables, nuts, and seeds to support brain health. Foods high in essential nutrients like omega-3 fatty acids, antioxidants, and minerals contribute to improved neural functions and concentration. Avocados, blueberries, and walnuts are particularly beneficial for boosting cognitive performance.

Adequate Hydration: Dr. Sebi emphasized that staying hydrated is crucial for maintaining concentration. The brain is approximately 75% water, and even slight dehydration can lead to reduced cognitive function. Drinking plenty of spring water throughout the day helps keep the brain hydrated and functioning optimally.

Herbal Teas: Incorporating certain herbal teas into your routine can also aid concentration. Dr. Sebi suggested herbs like ginkgo biloba and gotu kola, which are known for their cognitive-enhancing properties. These herbs improve blood circulation to the brain, which can help enhance focus and mental clarity.

Physical Activity: Regular physical exercise is another technique recommended by Dr. Sebi to boost concentration. Exercise increases blood flow to the brain, which can help sharpen awareness and clear the mind. Activities such as walking, yoga, or more vigorous exercises not only improve physical health but also enhance cognitive functions.

Proper Rest: Dr. Sebi pointed out that sufficient rest is essential for good concentration. Sleep plays a critical role in brain function, including how neurons communicate with each other. Consistent, high-quality sleep each night allows the brain to recover from daily activities and improve overall mental focus.

Impact of Hydration on Cognitive Performance

Dr. Sebi emphasized the significant impact of hydration on cognitive performance, stressing that maintaining optimal hydration levels is crucial for overall brain health and mental clarity. Water is essential for numerous physiological processes, including the optimal functioning of the brain, which is composed of about 75% water.

Hydration affects the brain in various ways. It aids in the transport of nutrients to brain cells and the removal of toxins and waste products, which can impair cognitive function if allowed to accumulate. Adequate water intake helps to ensure that these processes remain efficient, thereby supporting brain health and enhancing mental faculties.

When the body is dehydrated, it can lead to reduced attention span, memory, and motor skills, as well as increased feelings of anxiety and fatigue. Dehydration slightly shrinks the brain tissue, creating a strain that can lead to a temporary decrease in cognitive functions. Dr. Sebi noted that even mild dehydration could impact brain function and mood, which is particularly crucial for those needing to perform mentally challenging tasks.

Dr. Sebi recommended drinking at least one gallon of spring water daily to maintain hydration and support cognitive functions. He pointed out that this amount could vary depending on individual needs, environmental conditions, and levels of physical activity, but the key is to consistently hydrate throughout the day.

Moreover, Dr. Sebi advocated for consuming high-water-content foods, such as cucumbers, melons, and leafy greens, which can further help maintain hydration. These foods also provide essential minerals and vitamins that support brain function and contribute to overall health.

In addition to promoting hydration, Dr. Sebi discouraged the consumption of dehydrating beverages such as those high in caffeine or sugar. These can lead to a temporary boost in alertness but ultimately result in greater dehydration and a subsequent decline in cognitive performance.

Book 23: Dr. Sebi Hormone Balance

Overview of Hormonal Imbalances

Dr. Sebi recognized hormonal imbalances as a significant factor affecting overall health and well-being, impacting everything from mood and energy levels to metabolism and reproductive health. Hormones, which are produced by glands in the endocrine system, act as messengers that tell other parts of the body how to function. When these hormones are out of balance, it can lead to a variety of health issues.

Hormonal imbalances occur when there is too much or too little of a hormone in the bloodstream. Because of their essential role in the body, even small hormonal imbalances can cause side effects throughout the body. Common symptoms of hormonal imbalances include fatigue, weight gain or loss, mood swings, and changes in sleep patterns. In women, symptoms might manifest as irregular menstrual cycles, symptoms of menopause, or problems with fertility. In men, hormonal imbalances can lead to reduced libido, erectile dysfunction, and changes in body hair growth.

According to Dr. Sebi, one of the primary causes of hormonal imbalances is a diet that contributes to acidity and toxicity in the body. Consuming foods that are highly processed, high in unhealthy fats, and loaded with sugars can disrupt hormonal functions. These types of diets can lead to an overload of toxins in the body, which may affect the glands and their ability to produce hormones properly.

Dr. Sebi advocated for a natural, plant-based diet rich in minerals and vitamins to help support the endocrine system and maintain hormonal balance. He emphasized the importance of consuming alkaline foods that help neutralize body acidity, reduce inflammation, and cleanse the body of toxins. Foods rich in essential fatty acids, such as nuts and seeds, were particularly emphasized because they are crucial for hormone production.

Natural Approaches to Balancing Hormones

Dr. Sebi advocated natural approaches to balancing hormones, focusing on diet, herbal supplements, and lifestyle adjustments to support the body's endocrine system and promote hormonal health. He emphasized the connection between diet and hormonal function, advocating for a plant-based, alkaline diet rich in nutrients essential for hormone production and regulation.

According to Dr. Sebi, consuming a diet that reduces acidity in the body is crucial for maintaining hormonal balance. Foods that are natural and unprocessed help to cleanse the body of toxins and support the health of the glands responsible for hormone production. Dr. Sebi recommended foods high in minerals, vitamins, and antioxidants, such as leafy greens, nuts, seeds, and sea vegetables. These foods are not only alkaline but also provide the necessary nutrients that aid in the optimal functioning of the endocrine system.

Herbal remedies played a significant role in Dr. Sebi's approach. He identified several herbs that are particularly effective in supporting hormonal balance. For instance, sarsaparilla is known for its plant steroids, which can mimic human hormonal activity and help balance hormone levels. Maca root is another powerful herb, celebrated for its ability to enhance energy, reduce stress, and regulate hormone production, particularly in relation to reproductive health.

Lifestyle changes are also integral to Dr. Sebi's method for achieving hormone balance. Regular physical activity, adequate hydration, and sufficient sleep are all essential for the endocrine system to function properly. Exercise, for instance, can help regulate hormones like insulin, cortisol, and sex hormones by improving insulin sensitivity, reducing stress, and increasing blood circulation.

Dr. Sebi also emphasized the importance of managing stress as a critical factor in balancing hormones. Chronic stress can lead to an overproduction of cortisol, which disrupts other hormone levels. Techniques such as meditation, deep breathing exercises, and spending time in nature can help manage stress and thus support hormonal health.

Diet and Lifestyle for Hormonal Health

Dr. Sebi's approach to maintaining hormonal health involves a holistic blend of diet and lifestyle choices designed to naturally balance the body's endocrine system. He believed that proper nutrition and a balanced lifestyle are fundamental to achieving and sustaining hormonal equilibrium, essential for overall health.

Central to Dr. Sebi's dietary recommendations for hormonal health is the consumption of a predominantly alkaline, plant-based diet. This diet focuses on reducing acidity in the body, which Dr. Sebi argued could disrupt hormonal balance. He recommended eating a variety of fresh fruits and vegetables, especially leafy greens, which are high in essential minerals and vitamins that support the endocrine system. Foods such as avocados, berries, nuts, and seeds are particularly beneficial because they provide healthy fats and proteins, crucial for hormone production and regulation.

Incorporating sea moss into the diet was also emphasized by Dr. Sebi for its rich mineral content, especially iodine, which is vital for thyroid health. The thyroid gland plays a critical role in regulating many bodily functions by releasing hormones that control metabolism. Sea moss, along with bladderwrack and burdock root, forms a mineral-rich trio that supports overall glandular health.

Dr. Sebi also pointed out the importance of eliminating processed and synthetic foods from the diet. These foods can contain harmful chemicals and preservatives that may mimic hormonal activity in the body, leading to imbalances. Instead, he advocated for natural, whole foods that support the body's detoxification processes and promote hormonal health.

Lifestyle adjustments are equally important in Dr. Sebi's protocol for hormonal balance. Regular physical activity is crucial as it helps regulate hormones like insulin and cortisol, enhances circulation, and improves stress management. Dr. Sebi recommended engaging in activities such as walking, yoga, or other forms of gentle exercise that stimulate the body without excessive strain.

Adequate rest and sleep are also vital for hormonal health. Sleep is a time when the body repairs itself, and the endocrine system regulates hormone levels. Ensuring a consistent, restful sleep schedule helps maintain this balance, supporting overall well-being.

Lastly, managing stress effectively is essential for maintaining hormonal balance. Chronic stress can lead to an overproduction of cortisol, which can disrupt other hormones. Dr. Sebi encouraged practices such as meditation, deep breathing exercises, and spending time in nature to help reduce stress levels and support endocrine health.

Specific Herbs for Hormone Regulation

Dr. Sebi emphasized the use of specific herbs to aid in hormone regulation, focusing on those that naturally support the endocrine system's health and balance. He identified several key herbs that have been traditionally used to support glandular function and help maintain hormonal equilibrium. These herbs not only aid in regulating hormone production but also assist in detoxifying and nourishing the body.

Sarsaparilla was one of Dr. Sebi's favorites for hormone regulation due to its rich content of plant sterols, which are known to mimic human hormones and can help normalize hormone levels naturally. Sarsaparilla is especially beneficial in regulating testosterone and estrogen levels, making it useful for both men and women dealing with hormonal imbalances.

Maca root is another powerful herb recommended by Dr. Sebi. It is an adaptogen, meaning it helps the body adapt to stress and balances hormones without containing hormones itself. Maca works by nourishing the pituitary and adrenal glands, which are critical regulators of many other glands in the body. It is particularly known for enhancing fertility and libido, balancing menstrual cycles, and providing relief from menopausal symptoms.

Nettle is highly regarded for its wide range of nutrients, including vitamins and minerals that support the endocrine system. Nettle acts as a natural detoxifier, which can help remove toxins that might be affecting hormonal balance. It is also beneficial for prostate health, making it a valuable herb for men's hormone regulation.

Red Raspberry Leaf is traditionally used for women's reproductive health. It is rich in nutrients and antioxidants and is particularly helpful in toning the uterus and regulating menstrual cycles. This herb also aids in easing menstrual cramps and managing premenstrual symptoms, contributing to overall hormonal balance.

Sea Moss, although not a herb in the traditional sense, was heavily promoted by Dr. Sebi for its mineral-rich profile that supports overall health, including thyroid function. The high iodine content in sea moss is essential for the proper function of the thyroid gland, which regulates metabolism, energy, and mood.

Incorporating these herbs into one's daily regimen can provide a natural way to support and regulate hormonal functions, aligning with Dr. Sebi's holistic approach to health that advocates for using natural botanical resources to heal and balance the body.

Case Studies on Hormonal Recovery

Dr. Sebi's approach to hormonal recovery is illustrated through various case studies that document the effectiveness of his methods in addressing and correcting hormonal imbalances naturally. These case studies highlight individual experiences of people who have followed Dr. Sebi's dietary and herbal recommendations, providing insight into the practical application and outcomes of his holistic approach.

One notable case involved a middle-aged woman suffering from severe symptoms of menopause, including hot flashes, night sweats, and mood swings. After adopting Dr. Sebi's alkaline diet and incorporating specific herbs like maca root and sarsaparilla, she reported a significant reduction in her symptoms within a few months. The dietary changes helped to naturally balance her hormone levels, reducing the intensity and frequency of her menopausal symptoms.

Another case involved a young man dealing with low testosterone levels and related issues such as fatigue, low libido, and difficulty gaining muscle mass. Under Dr. Sebi's guidance, he began using herbal supplements like sea moss and sarsaparilla, known for their rich mineral content and potential to support hormone production. Alongside a strict alkaline diet, he experienced noticeable improvements in his energy levels and overall well-being, with subsequent tests showing a marked increase in his testosterone levels.

A third case study features an individual with thyroid imbalances, specifically hypothyroidism, who struggled with weight gain, depression, and chronic fatigue. By incorporating sea moss, which is high in iodine, into her daily regimen and eliminating processed foods from her diet, she gradually saw improvements in her thyroid function. This holistic approach not only helped stabilize her thyroid hormones but also enhanced her metabolic rate and mood.

These case studies exemplify the core principles of Dr. Sebi's philosophy—that the body can heal itself when given the right natural tools and a conducive environment.

Effects of Stress on Hormone Levels

Dr. Sebi discussed the profound effects of stress on hormone levels, emphasizing how chronic stress can disrupt the body's hormonal balance, leading to various health issues. Stress triggers the release of cortisol, known as the stress hormone, from the adrenal glands. While cortisol is vital for helping the body cope with stressful situations, consistently high levels due to prolonged stress can be detrimental to health.

Elevated cortisol levels can suppress the normal production of reproductive hormones, leading to issues such as irregular menstrual cycles, decreased libido, and fertility problems. In men, chronic stress can reduce testosterone levels, which affects muscle mass, libido, and mood.

Stress also impacts the thyroid gland, which regulates metabolism, energy, and mood. High cortisol levels can inhibit thyroid hormone production, leading to symptoms like weight gain, fatigue, and depression. This condition, often referred to as thyroid dysfunction, can exacerbate other hormonal imbalances, creating a cycle of health complications.

Dr. Sebi advocated for managing stress as a crucial component of restoring and maintaining hormonal balance. He recommended practices such as deep breathing exercises, meditation, and spending time in nature to help reduce stress levels. These activities help decrease cortisol production, fostering a more balanced hormonal environment.

Furthermore, Dr. Sebi emphasized the importance of a natural, plant-based diet rich in nutrients that support the adrenal and thyroid glands and mitigate the effects of stress on the body. Foods high in vitamin C, B vitamins, and magnesium, for example, can help regulate cortisol levels and support overall hormonal health.

Foods That Naturally Boost Hormone Production

Dr. Sebi emphasized the importance of incorporating specific foods into the diet that naturally boost hormone production, supporting the body's endocrine system in maintaining balance and enhancing overall health. These foods are rich in essential nutrients that play critical roles in hormone synthesis and regulation.

Avocados are a staple in Dr. Sebi's dietary recommendations for hormone balance. Rich in healthy fats, particularly omega-3 and omega-6 fatty acids, avocados help in the production of prostaglandins, hormone-like substances that regulate many functions in the body, including hormonal balance and inflammatory responses.

Nuts and seeds, such as walnuts, almonds, flaxseeds, and hemp seeds, are also vital for hormone health. They are high in essential fatty acids and contain magnesium and zinc, minerals crucial for hormone production, including reproductive hormones like progesterone and testosterone.

Leafy greens, including kale, spinach, and arugula, are loaded with magnesium, a mineral that plays a pivotal role in hormone regulation. Magnesium helps improve insulin sensitivity and supports the production of steroid hormones such as progesterone, estrogen, and testosterone.

Sea moss is another powerful food recommended by Dr. Sebi for boosting hormone production. It is incredibly rich in iodine, which is essential for thyroid hormone synthesis. The thyroid regulates metabolism, energy, and mood, so maintaining its health with iodine-rich foods like sea moss is crucial.

Fruits rich in vitamin C, such as oranges, mangoes, and strawberries, help support adrenal gland function, which regulates cortisol production. Vitamin C is essential for adrenal gland health, helping to mitigate the effects of stress on the body and prevent excessive cortisol release, which can disrupt other hormone levels.

Legumes, particularly chickpeas and lentils, provide a good source of plant-based protein and are rich in fiber and minerals like iron. These nutrients are essential for maintaining balanced hormone levels and supporting the overall health of the reproductive system.

Incorporating these foods into a regular diet can help naturally boost hormone production and maintain hormonal balance, aligning with Dr. Sebi's holistic approach to healing and wellness. By nurturing the body with the right nutrients, one can support the endocrine system in functioning optimally, leading to improved health and vitality.

Managing Menopause Symptoms Naturally

Dr. Sebi's approach to managing menopause symptoms naturally involves a combination of dietary adjustments, herbal remedies, and lifestyle changes. By focusing on natural methods to balance hormones and support overall well-being, women can experience relief from menopausal symptoms such as hot flashes, night sweats, mood swings, and sleep disturbances.

Dietary Recommendations: Dr. Sebi advocated for an alkaline diet rich in plant-based foods that help maintain hormonal balance. Foods high in phytoestrogens, such as flaxseeds, are particularly beneficial during menopause. Phytoestrogens can mimic estrogen in the body, helping to mitigate the drop in estrogen levels that occurs during menopause and alleviate related symptoms. Other helpful foods include leafy greens, nuts, and seeds, all of which are high in vitamins and minerals that support the endocrine system and help stabilize mood and energy levels.

Herbal Remedies: Dr. Sebi recommended specific herbs that have been traditionally used to ease menopausal symptoms. For example, red clover is rich in isoflavones, a type of phytoestrogen that can help balance hormones and reduce hot flashes and night sweats. Black cohosh is another herb known for its effectiveness in reducing hot flashes and improving sleep patterns. Additionally, Dr. Sebi suggested herbs like maca root, which is known for its ability to enhance energy, reduce mood swings, and improve libido.

Hydration and Nutrition: Adequate hydration is crucial during menopause, as it helps regulate body temperature and reduce the frequency of hot flashes. Dr. Sebi emphasized the importance of drinking plenty of spring water and incorporating moisture-rich foods into the diet. He also highlighted the need for adequate calcium intake, from alkaline sources such as sesame seeds and amaranth, to support bone health as estrogen levels decline.

Lifestyle Changes: Regular physical activity is important to manage weight, improve mood, and enhance quality of sleep, all of which can be challenged during menopause. Dr. Sebi recommended gentle exercises such as yoga and walking, which also help reduce stress—a common trigger for menopausal symptoms. Adequate sleep is essential, and creating a calming bedtime routine can help improve sleep quality.

Stress Management: Since stress can exacerbate menopausal symptoms, Dr. Sebi advised practices such as meditation, deep breathing, and spending time in nature to help manage stress levels effectively. These practices not only improve mental and emotional health but also support overall hormonal balance.

Book 24: Dr. Sebi Longevity Insights

Principles for a Long and Healthy Life

Dr. Sebi emphasized a holistic approach to achieving a long and healthy life, focusing on natural methods to nurture the body and mind. At the heart of his teachings was the alkaline diet, which encourages eating plant-based, nutrient-rich foods that reduce acidity in the body. This diet includes leafy greens, fruits, nuts, and seeds that not only help maintain the body's alkalinity but also support detoxification processes.

In addition to dietary recommendations, Dr. Sebi promoted the use of specific herbs for their potent medicinal properties. Herbs such as burdock root, sarsaparilla, sea moss, and bladderwrack were frequently recommended. These herbs are believed to supply essential minerals and nutrients that support the functioning of vital organs and strengthen the immune system, components that are critical for long-term health.

Detoxification was a significant aspect of Dr. Sebi's approach to longevity. He taught that regularly cleansing the body of toxins is essential for preventing disease and maintaining overall health. This process involves not only following an alkaline diet to naturally cleanse the body but also using herbal teas and supplements that specifically aid in detoxification.

Dr. Sebi also emphasized the importance of hydration, advocating for the consumption of plenty of spring water to help flush toxins from the body and promote cell health. Proper hydration is crucial for all bodily functions and helps keep the skin healthy and organs functioning optimally.

Lifestyle modifications also play a critical role in Dr. Sebi's principles for a long life. Regular physical activity, sufficient rest, and stress management are all important factors. Activities like walking, yoga, and meditation can improve physical health while also reducing stress, which is often a precursor to many chronic diseases.

Anti-Aging Diet and Lifestyle Tips

Dr. Sebi's approach to anti-aging was deeply intertwined with his holistic view of health and wellness, emphasizing a natural diet and lifestyle changes that not only extend life but improve its quality. He believed that the key to slowing down the aging process lies in maintaining the body's alkalinity, reducing toxin intake, and enhancing nutrient absorption.

The foundation of Dr. Sebi's anti-aging strategy is an alkaline diet rich in plant-based, whole foods. He advocated for the consumption of fresh fruits and vegetables, nuts, seeds, and grains that alkalize the body, thereby reducing the cellular damage caused by excess acidity. These foods are high in essential vitamins and antioxidants that combat free radicals, molecules that contribute to tissue degradation and aging.

Dr. Sebi also emphasized the importance of herbal nutrition, recommending herbs such as burdock root, dandelion, and sea moss. These herbs are not only rich in vital minerals but also possess detoxifying properties that cleanse the blood and improve organ function, key factors in promoting longevity and reducing the signs of aging.

Hydration was another critical aspect of his anti-aging advice. Dr. Sebi advised drinking plenty of spring water throughout the day to support cellular health and detoxification. Proper hydration ensures that nutrients are efficiently delivered to cells and waste products are removed, which is crucial for maintaining skin elasticity and preventing premature aging.

Lifestyle modifications are equally important in Dr. Sebi's anti-aging regimen. He recommended regular physical activity, which can range from gentle exercises like walking and yoga to more vigorous activities, to improve circulation and vitality. Physical activity not only helps in maintaining muscle tone and joint flexibility but also supports cardiovascular health and enhances mood.

Adequate rest and stress management are also vital components of an anti-aging lifestyle. Dr. Sebi stressed the importance of quality sleep and relaxation techniques to allow the body to repair and regenerate. Techniques such as meditation, deep breathing exercises, and spending time in nature can help manage stress, which is known to accelerate the aging process.

Herbs Known to Enhance Longevity

Dr. Sebi advocated the use of specific herbs to enhance longevity, each selected for their unique health benefits and abilities to support vital organ functions, detoxify the body, and nourish at the cellular level. These herbs are central to his holistic approach, promoting health and vitality well into older age.

One of the key herbs in Dr. Sebi's longevity toolkit is sea moss, revered for its dense mineral content. Sea moss contains 92 of the 102 essential minerals the body needs, including iodine, calcium, potassium, and sulfur. Because of its nutrient-rich profile, sea moss supports thyroid function, improves metabolism, and promotes a healthy immune system, all of which are crucial for aging gracefully.

Burdock root is another herb favored by Dr. Sebi for its blood-purifying properties. It helps to cleanse the bloodstream of toxins, supports liver function, and aids kidney health. By promoting the elimination of toxins from the body, burdock root helps to alleviate issues that can accelerate aging, such as inflammation and oxidative stress.

Sarsaparilla is often recommended by Dr. Sebi for its ability to naturally mimic hormones in the body. This makes it particularly beneficial in balancing hormone levels as the body ages, supporting overall endocrine health and helping to mitigate age-related hormonal imbalances.

Dr. Sebi also valued dandelion for its wide array of nutrients, including antioxidants, which are vital for preventing cellular damage that leads to aging. Dandelion supports liver health, one of the most important organs for detoxification and metabolism, thereby helping to maintain youthfulness and vitality.

Nettle is included for its high content of vitamins and minerals, especially iron and vitamin C, which are essential for maintaining energy levels and protecting the body against age-related wear and tear. Nettle's anti-inflammatory properties also make it beneficial for maintaining joint health and mobility.

Incorporating these herbs into one's daily regimen, according to Dr. Sebi's recommendations, helps to address the root causes of aging at the cellular level, promoting longevity and improving overall quality of life as one ages. By embracing these natural herbal remedies, individuals can support their body's inherent healing abilities and thrive into their later years.

Daily Routines to Promote Health and Longevity

Dr. Sebi proposed specific daily routines designed to promote health and longevity, emphasizing natural, holistic practices that align with his principles of detoxification, nourishment, and balance. By incorporating these routines, individuals can foster a greater sense of well-being and enhance their lifespan through natural means.

Starting the Day

Dr. Sebi advocated beginning the day with a glass of spring water to hydrate and kickstart metabolism. Following this, he recommended consuming herbal teas such as elderberry or burdock root, which cleanse the blood and strengthen the immune system. This morning ritual sets a tone for a day focused on health and mindfulness.

Alkaline Breakfast

An alkaline diet was central to Dr. Sebi's philosophy. Breakfast might include a smoothie made with alkaline fruits, such as berries and apples, mixed with sea moss gel for its mineral-rich properties. This meal provides energy while maintaining the body's pH balance, which is crucial for optimal health.

Physical Activity

Regular physical exercise is essential in Dr. Sebi's routine. Gentle activities like walking, stretching, or yoga are recommended to improve circulation and mobility. These exercises help to oxygenate the blood and facilitate the removal of toxins, promoting better health and enhancing longevity.

Midday and Evening Meals

Meals should consist of plant-based, nutrient-dense foods including leafy greens, vegetables, and grains like quinoa or amaranth. Dr. Sebi emphasized the importance of including iodine-rich foods such as seaweed in the diet to support thyroid health, which is vital for metabolism and energy levels.

Herbal Supplements

Throughout the day, Dr. Sebi advised the use of natural supplements to support health and address any specific ailments or deficiencies. Supplements like sea moss, bladderwrack, and sarsaparilla contain essential minerals and nutrients that support overall health and help maintain the body's natural defenses.

Hydration

Drinking plenty of spring water throughout the day continues to be a staple in Dr. Sebi's daily routine. Adequate hydration is crucial for detoxification and maintaining cellular health, which are foundational for longevity.

Stress Management

To combat the effects of stress on the body, Dr. Sebi recommended practices such as meditation, deep breathing exercises, and spending time in nature. These activities reduce cortisol levels and promote a relaxed state of mind, which is necessary for health and longevity.

Restful Sleep

Concluding the day with a restful night's sleep is perhaps one of the most important aspects of Dr. Sebi's daily routine. Sleep is a time when the body heals and regenerates. Ensuring a peaceful sleep environment and aiming for 7-9 hours of sleep per night helps to support the body's natural repair processes.

Success Stories of Longevity with Dr. Sebi's Methods

Dr. Sebi's methods for promoting longevity have been embraced by many, with numerous individuals reporting significant improvements in health and vitality after adopting his dietary and lifestyle recommendations. These success stories highlight the transformative impact of Dr. Sebi's holistic approach to health and wellness.

One notable story comes from a woman in her late fifties who struggled with chronic fatigue and general ill-health for years. After switching to an alkaline diet based on Dr. Sebi's principles, which included eliminating processed foods and eating more raw and whole plant-based foods, she experienced a remarkable increase in energy and a reduction in health complaints. She attributed her renewed vigor and reduced signs of aging, such as better skin elasticity and fewer joint pains, directly to her new eating habits and the herbal supplements recommended by Dr. Sebi.

Another success story involves a man who suffered from high blood pressure and was at risk for heart disease. After following Dr. Sebi's regimen, which included daily consumption of herbal teas like hibiscus and green food supplements containing chlorella and spirulina, he saw a significant improvement in his blood pressure levels. His overall cardiovascular health improved, and he reported feeling more youthful and energetic than he had in decades.

A third individual, a middle-aged woman dealing with hormonal imbalances and weight issues, turned to Dr. Sebi's recommendations for help. By integrating sea moss into her diet for its rich mineral content and adopting an alkaline diet rich in fruits and vegetables, she not only lost weight but also stabilized her hormones. This change resulted in improved mental clarity and emotional stability, contributing to a better quality of life.

These stories, among many others, exemplify the potential of Dr. Sebi's methods to significantly enhance longevity and quality of life. Individuals who have followed his advice often speak of not just living longer but living better, with more energy, less disease, and greater overall vitality. This testimony to the power of natural, holistic approaches to health care continues to inspire many to explore Dr. Sebi's teachings and integrate them into their own lives for better health and longevity.

Nutritional Strategies for Aging Adults

Dr. Sebi's nutritional strategies for aging adults focus on maximizing the body's potential for health and vitality through natural, plant-based foods that enhance longevity. As adults age, their nutritional needs change, and Dr. Sebi's diet is designed to address these changes with specific foods and herbs that support healthy aging.

Central to his recommendations is the adoption of an alkaline diet, which minimizes acidic foods that can contribute to chronic diseases often seen in older adults, such as osteoporosis, arthritis, and heart disease. Instead, the diet emphasizes high nutrient-dense foods that reduce inflammation and oxidative stress, both of which are key factors in aging.

Leafy greens like kale, spinach, and chard are staples in this diet for their high mineral content, particularly calcium, magnesium, and potassium. These minerals are crucial for maintaining bone density and heart health. Dr. Sebi also encourages the consumption of nuts and seeds, such as almonds and sesame seeds, which are excellent sources of healthy fats and proteins that help maintain muscle mass and skin elasticity.

For hydration and detoxification, Dr. Sebi emphasizes the importance of drinking plenty of spring water and incorporating herbal teas. Herbs such as burdock root and dandelion are valued for their liver-supportive properties, helping to cleanse the body of toxins that can accumulate over years. These herbs also support kidney function, which can decline with age.

Fruits are another critical component of the diet, with a focus on those that are high in antioxidants and vitamins. Berries, pomegranates, and apples are recommended for their ability to fight free radicals, which contribute to the aging process. These fruits support immune function and promote skin health, helping to keep the skin supple and reducing the formation of wrinkles.

Dr. Sebi also recognizes the role of sea moss, a superfood rich in iodine and other minerals that support thyroid function, which often slows with age. Incorporating sea moss into the diet can help regulate metabolism and energy levels, keeping older adults more active and engaged.

Adapting to these nutritional strategies involves not only choosing the right foods but also preparing meals that are easy to digest and absorb, which becomes increasingly important as the digestive system ages. Cooking methods such as steaming and blending can make nutrients more accessible and help preserve the natural enzymes in foods.

Exercise and Its Role in Extending Lifespan

Dr. Sebi emphasized the importance of exercise as a vital component of a healthy lifestyle that extends lifespan and improves the quality of life. He believed that regular physical activity is crucial not only for maintaining physical health but also for enhancing mental and emotional well-being, all of which contribute to longevity.

Exercise plays a pivotal role in promoting cardiovascular health by strengthening the heart and improving blood circulation. This enhanced circulation ensures that oxygen and nutrients are efficiently distributed throughout the body, supporting all bodily functions, including those of vital organs and the immune system. Regular physical activity also helps to regulate blood pressure and reduce cholesterol levels, which are key factors in preventing heart disease and strokes.

Beyond cardiovascular health, exercise is instrumental in maintaining healthy bones and muscles. As people age, they naturally lose bone density and muscle mass. Engaging in weight-bearing exercises, such as walking, jogging, or yoga, helps to slow down this loss and can prevent osteoporosis and other related conditions. Strong muscles and bones reduce the risk of falls and fractures, which can severely impact the life quality of older adults.

Exercise also has significant benefits for metabolic health. It improves insulin sensitivity, which can help manage or prevent type 2 diabetes, a common age-related condition. Additionally, physical activity helps regulate hormone levels, including those of cortisol, the stress hormone, thereby enhancing stress management and reducing the negative impacts of stress on the body.

On the mental and emotional front, exercise releases endorphins, often known as feel-good hormones, which have mood-lifting properties. Regular exercise can combat depression and anxiety, promote better sleep, and enhance overall mental clarity. Dr. Sebi noted that maintaining a clear and active mind is as important as physical health in achieving a long and fulfilling life.

Dr. Sebi encouraged integrating exercise into daily routines, suggesting that even moderate activities can yield significant health benefits. He advocated for exercises that align with one's physical capabilities and preferences, ensuring consistency and enjoyment, which are key to making exercise a lifelong habit.

Mental and Emotional Aspects of Aging Well

Dr. Sebi's insights into longevity extended beyond physical health to include the mental and emotional aspects of aging well. He believed that maintaining mental sharpness and emotional balance is as crucial as physical health for a fulfilling and extended life.

Mental agility is essential for aging well. Dr. Sebi emphasized the importance of continually engaging the mind through activities such as reading, solving puzzles, learning new skills, or engaging in creative pursuits like painting or writing. These activities stimulate the brain, keeping it active and reducing the risk of cognitive decline associated with diseases like Alzheimer's and dementia.

Emotional health is equally important. Dr. Sebi understood that emotional disturbances could have profound effects on physical health, particularly as one ages. He recommended regular practices that promote emotional stability, such as meditation, deep breathing exercises, and spending time in nature. These practices help manage stress, reduce anxiety, and foster a state of calmness and clarity.

Dr. Sebi also highlighted the significance of social connections in maintaining emotional and mental health. Building and sustaining meaningful relationships with family, friends, and community can provide emotional support, reduce feelings of loneliness, and increase life satisfaction. Engaging in community activities or group hobbies can be particularly beneficial for older adults, providing both social interaction and mental stimulation.

Moreover, Dr. Sebi advised on the need to cultivate a positive outlook on life. He believed that a positive attitude helps to manage the inevitable changes and challenges that come with aging. Embracing aging with acceptance and optimism can lead to a healthier, more contented life.

Incorporating these mental and emotional health strategies into daily life, alongside physical health practices, is essential for aging gracefully. Dr. Sebi's holistic approach to longevity encompasses all aspects of health, offering a comprehensive blueprint for not just living longer but living well emotionally and mentally into older age.

Book 25: Dr. Sebi Skin Health

Skin Health and Alkaline Diet Connection

Dr. Sebi highlighted the profound connection between skin health and the alkaline diet, emphasizing that the skin's appearance and health are direct reflections of the body's internal health. According to Dr. Sebi, an alkaline diet can significantly improve skin health by reducing inflammation, removing toxins, and nourishing the skin at a cellular level.

The alkaline diet promotes eating foods that help maintain the body's natural pH balance, which is slightly alkaline. Dr. Sebi believed that many skin issues, such as acne, eczema, and psoriasis, are exacerbated by an acidic body environment created by consuming foods like meat, dairy, refined sugars, and processed foods. These foods can lead to inflammation and toxin accumulation, which manifest externally on the skin.

By adopting an alkaline diet rich in fruits, vegetables, nuts, and seeds, individuals can help their body detoxify and reduce inflammation. Foods such as cucumbers, spinach, avocados, and berries are particularly beneficial for skin health. These foods are high in vitamins, minerals, and antioxidants, which protect the skin from oxidative stress that can cause aging and skin damage.

Dr. Sebi also emphasized the importance of hydration for skin health. Drinking adequate amounts of spring water helps to keep the skin hydrated, elastic, and clear. It aids in flushing out toxins that can clog pores and lead to skin imperfections.

Furthermore, specific alkaline foods directly benefit the skin in particular ways:
- Avocados are rich in vitamins E and C, which are vital for healthy skin. Vitamin E acts as an antioxidant to protect the skin from oxidative damage, while vitamin C is crucial for the synthesis of collagen, which maintains the skin's elasticity and firmness.
- Almonds are another skin-friendly food, high in vitamin E and healthy fats that help nourish the skin and prevent dryness.
- Leafy greens such as kale and spinach are loaded with antioxidants and essential nutrients that support skin regeneration and protect against premature aging.

In addition to dietary recommendations, Dr. Sebi advised against the use of harsh chemical-based skincare products, which can disrupt the skin's natural pH and strip away essential oils. Instead, he recommended natural, minimalistic skincare routines that align with the body's natural processes and enhance the skin's health from the inside out.

Natural Skin Care Treatments and Remedies

Dr. Sebi's approach to skin health emphasized the use of natural skin care treatments and remedies, harnessing the power of botanicals and natural compounds to enhance skin vitality and address various skin conditions. His philosophy was rooted in the belief that skin health is a reflection of internal health, and therefore, treatments should focus on both external applications and internal adjustments.

Herbal Washes and Toners: Dr. Sebi recommended using natural herbal washes to cleanse the skin gently. Herbs like burdock root, which has blood-purifying properties, and chamomile, known for its soothing effects, can be brewed into teas and used as facial washes or toners. These herbal solutions help to remove impurities without stripping the skin of its natural oils.

Sea Moss Gel: Known for its high mineral content and soothing properties, sea moss gel was touted by Dr. Sebi as a superb skin hydrator and healer. Applied topically, it can help nourish the skin, reduce inflammation, and promote healing of skin conditions like eczema and psoriasis due to its rich iodine, calcium, and potassium content.

Aloe Vera: A staple in natural skin care, aloe vera was highly recommended by Dr. Sebi for its cooling and healing properties. It's effective in treating sunburns, reducing skin inflammation, and promoting collagen production. Aloe vera can be applied directly from the plant to the skin or used in its gel form for soothing irritated skin.

Clay Masks: Dr. Sebi often suggested using natural clays, such as bentonite clay, for detoxifying facial masks. These clays draw out toxins from the skin, helping to clear pores and reduce acne outbreaks. Mixing the clay with a bit of apple cider vinegar or pure water can enhance its detoxifying properties and leave the skin feeling refreshed and purified.

Dietary Recommendations for Skin Health: Alongside topical treatments, Dr. Sebi emphasized the importance of an alkaline diet rich in fruits, vegetables, nuts, and seeds to support skin health from the inside out. Foods high in antioxidants, such as berries and leafy greens, protect the skin from oxidative stress, while healthy fats from avocados and almonds keep the skin moisturized and supple.

Herbs for Skin Conditions

Dr. Sebi's insights into longevity extended beyond physical health to include the mental and emotional aspects of aging well. He believed that achieving a balanced state of mental and emotional health is essential for a long and fulfilling life. His approach integrated practices aimed at nurturing the mind and spirit, which are crucial for maintaining life quality as one ages.

Central to his philosophy was the belief that mental and emotional well-being directly influences physical health. Stress, anxiety, and negative emotions can have tangible effects on the body, leading to chronic inflammation, hormonal imbalances, and a weakened immune system. Therefore, managing these mental and emotional states is as important as maintaining physical health.

Dr. Sebi emphasized the importance of cultivating peace of mind through meditation and deep breathing exercises. These practices help reduce stress, clear the mind, and foster a state of calmness and clarity. Regular meditation can also enhance cognitive functions, such as memory and concentration, which are often affected by aging.

Connecting with nature was another crucial element in Dr. Sebi's approach to emotional health. Spending time outdoors, whether walking, gardening, or simply sitting in a natural setting, can significantly improve mood, reduce feelings of depression, and boost overall emotional well-being. The natural environment has a calming effect on the mind and can help rejuvenate the spirit.

Social interactions also play a key role in mental health as people age. Dr. Sebi encouraged maintaining strong relationships with family and friends, which can provide emotional support, reduce stress, and promote a sense of belonging and happiness. Social engagement has been shown to improve mental health and longevity, making it a vital aspect of aging well.

Lastly, Dr. Sebi believed in the power of lifelong learning and mental stimulation. Engaging in creative pursuits, learning new skills, and challenging the mind can help prevent cognitive decline and keep the brain active and engaged. Activities like reading, solving puzzles, or learning a new language can stimulate mental activity and contribute to a richer, more satisfying life in later years.

Dietary Adjustments for Healthy Skin

Dr. Sebi emphasized the importance of dietary adjustments for maintaining healthy skin, recognizing that what we consume has a direct impact on our skin's health and appearance. According to his teachings, a diet that supports skin health is rich in minerals, vitamins, and hydration, and it avoids foods that can cause inflammation and toxicity.

Central to Dr. Sebi's dietary recommendations for healthy skin is the focus on alkaline foods. He advocated for consuming a high amount of fresh fruits and vegetables that reduce acidity in the body and promote a more alkaline environment. Leafy greens like kale, spinach, and arugula are particularly beneficial as they are high in vitamins A, C, and E, which are crucial for skin repair and renewal. These greens also contain antioxidants that protect the skin from oxidative stress and premature aging.

Dr. Sebi also recommended including healthy fats in the diet, which are essential for maintaining skin hydration and elasticity. Foods such as avocados, nuts, and seeds are excellent sources of these healthy fats. They provide the body with essential fatty acids, which strengthen the skin's lipid barrier, helping to retain moisture and protect against environmental damage.

Hydration is another key element of Dr. Sebi's skin health diet. Drinking ample amounts of spring water throughout the day helps to flush out toxins that can clog pores and dull the skin. Proper hydration also ensures that nutrients are efficiently delivered to skin cells, aiding in their health and vitality.

To further support skin health, Dr. Sebi recommended specific herbs and supplements known for their skin benefits. Herbs like burdock root and dandelion are great for detoxifying the blood, while sea moss provides a rich source of minerals that are vital for collagen production and skin elasticity.

Additionally, Dr. Sebi advised against consuming mucus-forming foods such as dairy and processed wheat, as these can lead to inflammation and exacerbate skin conditions like acne, eczema, and psoriasis. Instead, he encouraged a diet that minimizes processed foods and emphasizes whole, natural ingredients.

Daily Skin Care Routines

Dr. Sebi's holistic approach to health emphasizes the interconnectedness of the body, mind, and environment. Just as he advocated for a balanced diet and lifestyle to promote overall well-being, his principles can also be applied to skin care. By understanding the body's natural healing mechanisms and respecting its innate balance, we can cultivate healthy, radiant skin from within.

Morning Rituals for Skin Wellness

As the sun rises, embark on a journey of self-care that honors your skin's natural rhythms. Begin by gently cleansing your skin with a nourishing, plant-based cleanser. Dr. Sebi often emphasized the importance of natural, organic ingredients in promoting optimal health, and the same principles apply to skin care. Choose products free from harsh chemicals and artificial fragrances, allowing your skin to breathe and thrive.

After cleansing, take a moment to tone your skin using a gentle, alcohol-free toner infused with botanical extracts. Dr. Sebi believed in the power of nature to heal and rejuvenate, and botanical ingredients such as aloe vera, rose water, and witch hazel can help restore balance to the skin's pH levels while soothing irritation and inflammation.

Nourishment and Protection Throughout the Day

As you go about your day, nourish and protect your skin with products that reflect Dr. Sebi's commitment to natural healing. Apply a lightweight, hydrating moisturizer infused with nutrient-rich botanicals to keep your skin soft, supple, and resilient. Look for ingredients such as jojoba oil, shea butter, and coconut oil, which mimic the skin's natural oils and provide long-lasting hydration without clogging pores.

Prioritize sun protection by applying a broad-spectrum sunscreen with an SPF of at least 30. Dr. Sebi understood the importance of protecting the body from environmental stressors, and shielding your skin from harmful UV rays is essential for maintaining its health and vitality. Reapply sunscreen throughout the day, especially if you spend extended periods outdoors, to safeguard against sun damage and premature aging.

Evening Rituals for Rejuvenation and Renewal

As the day comes to a close, indulge in a restorative evening ritual that nourishes your skin and promotes relaxation. Cleanse away the day's impurities with a gentle foaming cleanser or cleansing oil, massaging it into your skin with gentle, circular motions to dissolve makeup, dirt, and excess oil. Take your time and enjoy this moment of self-care, allowing the stresses of the day to melt away.

After cleansing, treat your skin to a luxurious serum or facial oil infused with potent botanical extracts and antioxidants. Dr. Sebi often spoke of the healing power of plants, and incorporating plant-based ingredients into your skincare routine can help replenish lost moisture, soothe irritation, and support the skin's natural renewal process.

Impact of Diet on Acne and Eczema

The skin reflects our internal health, and diet plays a pivotal role in determining its health and vitality. In his holistic approach to skincare, Dr. Sebi emphasized the importance of a balanced diet rich in nutrient-dense foods to promote clear, glowing skin free from issues.

Acne is a common skin condition that can be influenced by a variety of factors, including hormonal imbalances, inflammation, and dietary choices. Dr. Sebi believed that what we put into our bodies directly impacts our skin's health and appearance. Consuming processed foods, refined sugars, and dairy products, which are known to trigger inflammation and disrupt hormonal balance, can exacerbate acne symptoms. In contrast, adopting a diet rich in whole, plant-based foods such as fruits, vegetables, nuts, seeds, and legumes can help reduce inflammation, regulate hormones, and support overall skin health.

Eczema is a chronic inflammatory skin condition characterized by red, itchy patches that can be triggered by a variety of factors, including allergens, irritants, and stress. While eczema is often treated with topical medications, Dr. Sebi believed in addressing the root cause of the condition through dietary and lifestyle changes. He advocated for an alkaline-rich diet centered around plant-based foods, which can help reduce inflammation and support the body's natural healing processes. Additionally, he recommended eliminating potential trigger foods such as dairy, gluten, and processed foods, which can exacerbate eczema symptoms in some individuals.

The link between diet and skin health is undeniable. By adopting a diet rich in whole, nutrient-dense foods and eliminating inflammatory triggers, we can support our skin's natural ability to heal and thrive. Dr. Sebi's holistic approach to skincare emphasizes the importance of nourishing the body from within to achieve clear, radiant skin that reflects optimal health and vitality.

Natural Moisturizers and Their Benefits

In the quest for healthy, radiant skin, the utilization of natural moisturizers can prove immensely advantageous. Dr. Sebi advocated for the incorporation of ingredients sourced from nature, as they often contain potent nutrients and antioxidants that nourish the skin from within.

Shea butter, derived from the nuts of the shea tree, stands out as a prime example. Rich in vitamins A, E, and F, as well as essential fatty acids, shea butter serves as a luxurious moisturizer that deeply hydrates the skin, leaving it soft, smooth, and supple. Its anti-inflammatory properties make it especially suitable for soothing dry, irritated skin conditions like eczema and psoriasis.

Another versatile option is coconut oil, which is readily absorbed by the skin, providing instant hydration without a greasy residue. With its abundance of lauric acid and medium-chain fatty acids, coconut oil possesses antimicrobial and anti-inflammatory properties, safeguarding the skin against infections and alleviating inflammation. It proves particularly beneficial for dry, sensitive skin and can serve as a natural remedy for dermatitis and acne.

Jojoba oil, closely mirroring the skin's natural sebum, emerges as an excellent moisturizer suitable for all skin types, including oily and acne-prone skin. This lightweight oil penetrates deeply, delivering essential nutrients and forming a protective barrier that seals in moisture. Its capacity to regulate sebum production makes it effective in maintaining the skin's oil levels and preventing breakouts.

Aloe vera gel, renowned for its soothing and healing attributes, has been a staple ingredient in skincare products for centuries. Packed with vitamins, minerals, and antioxidants, aloe vera gel hydrates the skin, diminishes inflammation, and fosters cell regeneration. It proves particularly valuable for sunburned or irritated skin, providing immediate relief and expediting the healing process.

Lastly, avocado oil emerges as a rich and nourishing option. Laden with vitamins, minerals, and essential fatty acids, avocado oil deeply moisturizes the skin, leaving it soft and supple. Its high content of oleic acid, in particular, makes it beneficial for dry, mature skin, helping to replenish lost moisture and improve skin elasticity.

So, natural moisturizers offer a wealth of benefits for skin health and vitality, providing hydration, nourishment, and protection while harnessing the power of nature's bounty. By incorporating these ingredients into your skincare routine, you can nurture your skin and achieve a radiant complexion aligned with Dr. Sebi's holistic approach to wellness.

Protecting Skin from Environmental Damage

In today's world, our skin is constantly exposed to environmental stressors that can take a toll on its health and appearance. From UV radiation and pollution to harsh weather conditions, these factors can contribute to premature aging, pigmentation, and other skin issues. Dr. Sebi emphasized the importance of protecting the skin from such damage through a combination of lifestyle choices and skincare practices.

One of the most significant sources of environmental damage to the skin is UV radiation from the sun. Prolonged exposure to UV rays can lead to sunburn, premature aging, and an increased risk of skin cancer. Dr. Sebi advocated for the regular use of sunscreen with a high SPF to protect the skin from UV damage. Additionally, he recommended seeking shade during peak sun hours and wearing protective clothing, such as hats and sunglasses, to minimize exposure.

Pollution, cigarette smoke, and other environmental toxins can generate free radicals in the skin, leading to oxidative stress and cellular damage. Antioxidants play a crucial role in neutralizing these free radicals and protecting the skin from their harmful effects. Dr. Sebi promoted the consumption of antioxidant-rich foods, such as fruits, vegetables, and green tea, to support the body's natural defense mechanisms. Additionally, he recommended using skincare products formulated with antioxidants, such as vitamin C and E, to bolster the skin's resilience against environmental damage.

Maintaining proper hydration is essential for supporting the skin's natural barrier function, which acts as a shield against environmental aggressors. Dr. Sebi advised drinking an adequate amount of water each day to keep the skin hydrated from within. Additionally, he recommended using moisturizers and emollients to replenish lost moisture and strengthen the skin's protective barrier. Ingredients like hyaluronic acid, ceramides, and fatty acids can help restore the skin's natural balance and resilience to environmental stressors.

Conclusion

Dr. Sebi's core treatment philosophy revolves around pairing an alkaline diet with anti-inflammatory agents. He advocated for the incorporation of minimally inflammatory, organic, and plant-based elements to address prevalent modern-day ailments such as diabetes, CKD, and heart conditions. His suggested remedies aim not only to enhance overall well-being and bolster immunity but also to combat illnesses, fostering a life of longevity and vitality. However, before embarking on any new dietary regimen, it's essential to undergo a thorough medical examination conducted by a licensed health professional and take into consideration any preexisting medical conditions. While Dr. Sebi provided nutritional and herbal recommendations for general health maintenance, it's imperative to seek medical clearance before attempting these treatments for serious illnesses.

Made in the USA
Columbia, SC
08 September 2024

42011839R00117